Starting Your Ow

COFFEE AND TEA SHOP

EMMA MILLS AND MICHELLE ROSENBERG

Starting Your Own

COFFEE AND TEA SHOP

EMMA MILLS AND MICHELLE ROSENBERG

crimson

This edition first published in Great Britain 2010 by
Crimson Publishing, a division of Crimson Business Ltd
Westminster House
Kew Road
Richmond
Surrey
TW9 2ND

A catalogue record for this book is available from the British Library.

ISBN 978 1 85458 477 9

Printed and bound by TJ International, Padstow

Acknowledgements

With many thanks to all the coffee and tea shops for being so generous with their stories and offers of a fresh cup:

Raymond at Royal Teas
Tim at Redroaster Coffee House
Shelagh at Lantana
Simon at Leoni
Nevina at Costa
Samantha at Bettys Café Tea Rooms
Sahar and Henry at Coffee Republic

Thanks also to Beth Bishop, for being a brilliant and very patient editor, and to Sally Rawlings and all the team at Crimson and to Sara Rizk and Matt Thomas for their help and insight into businesses, great and small.

Emma: Thanks and love to my parents and to Richard, for their support, encouragement and humour and also to Tom at Cosy Coffee Shops.

Michelle: As always, to Mum, Dad, Jamie, Jeremy and my gorgeous Lola and Maddie.

Contents

Introduction

It's estimated that 70 million cups of coffee are made on a daily basis in the UK, and that the average Briton drinks four cups of tea a day. The quality of coffee available has never been better, and our knowledge about the varieties of tea around has come on in leaps and bounds since the days of PG Tips and chimpanzees in dresses. Meanwhile, research group Allegra Strategies estimates that Britain's coffee and tea culture generates an annual turnover of £2.5bn.

How many times have you sat down in a coffee shop, taken a look at the décor, the menu, the waiting staff, sampled the coffee and the obligatory piece of cake on offer and thought: 'I could do better than this'?

Next question. How many people do you know who have begrudgingly eaten the aforementioned slice of decidedly average confection and have actually put their money where their mouth is and researched the idea of setting up on their own properly? It won't be surprising if your answer is not too many.

It's the massive leap that's so hard to do – moving from a dream to reality. And that's what this book's about. So many people imagine setting up on their own – but how many actually do it? The fact that you are reading this book at all is a good sign. It's a start. The aim of this book is to inspire you to turn your dream into reality: a successful coffee or tea shop. However, it will also give you a reality check: you aren't going to have your dream handed to you on a plate. That would be having your cake and eating it too.

This is no job for the fainthearted. You will need guts, self-belief, determination, and the ability to work around the clock without flagging. A good apple pie recipe wouldn't go amiss either. You will need to give up your social life, if not permanently then at least for the first year. Your family may have to take a back seat, unless they intend to help you out in the running of your new venture. And if you have a young family, make sure you can balance the two and you won't feel guilty sending the kids to your mother-in-law yet again because your tills are on the blink.

Put simply, starting a coffee or tea shop, or indeed any new business in the service industry, will be one of the most exhausting and gruelling experiences of your life. If you aren't prepared for that right now, it might be easy to remain a passive observer, and enjoy your latte from the other side of the counter. It's hard, it's very very hard, and nothing short of hard work will make your coffee or tea shop a success. You have to know that before you start.

Warning over, the rewards can be incredible.

Well-established brands, as well as proud independent establishments, have shared their experiences in this book and it's clear to see how much they love what they do. You will find the individual stories of these successful and dedicated coffee or tea shop owners on pages 5–15, and there are tips and anecdotes throughout the entire book. Sahar Hashemi, founder of Coffee Republic, describes how she adored working with her brother and educating a market about the joys of a good cup of coffee; June Wood, Bettys' Harrogate Branch Manager, describes the joy and fulfilment in keeping to the traditions set down by the tea shop's founder over 80 years ago. Raymond Voce reveals his coffee shop is more of a way of life and passion for creating a community than a job; Shelagh Ryan describes her determination to bring the Australian coffee shop experience to London.

This book will take you through the process of starting your own coffee or tea shop step by step. Whether you are a coffee aficionado determined to go it alone, a tea lover desperate to share your knowledge with the world, or you have seen a potentially profitable gap in the market near you, this book will help you achieve this. Although you will undoubtedly come across hurdles, the country's most successful coffee and tea shop entrepreneurs and businesspeople were once in the same boat. With their advice, and the guidance in this book, you should be able to avoid some of the more challenging areas, making your own business journey a whole lot smoother.

The book starts by reminding you just how carefully you have to think through your idea, before you even spend a single penny. Everything from the type of coffee or tea shop you want to run, the quality of drink you want to serve, the location you should choose, what décor will work and what furniture you need, to the intricate legalities of running a business, managing PR, and employing staff, to any future plans you have for the business. The book will also guide you through the concept of identity, highlighting the importance of decisions such as name, branding and reputation.

There's also help with every aspect of turning your idea into a reality. Not sure what kind of business structure you need to trade under? Read Chapter 2.3

(*Registering your business*) to find out. If you have never written a press release or dealt with the media before, pay close attention to Part 6 on launch and ongoing marketing. It's crucial too that you study Chapter 2.4 (*Getting Legal*) so you aren't caught out by the laws and regulations that govern the beverage industry.

We also have information on the food side of things – should you serve sarnies, or stay with cakes? Cookies or pies? Sweet or savoury? These are just some of the things you will need to have considered, and there are numerous possibilities which require thinking about. Check out Part 4 (*Menu planning*).

This book doesn't just focus on the steps involved in launching your coffee or tea shop. There's also plenty of advice on getting through your first few months of trading. Equally, if you intend to run not just one, but a chain of shops, there is a section on business development (see Part 8). Perhaps you want to turn your concept into a franchise. You may even want to sell it on, and start something from fresh. While you may not be considering the future of your coffee or tea shop that far in advance, it's helpful to know what may lie ahead.

We've aimed to give you a solid framework as well as food for thought. Whether you decide to launch your coffee shop this year, or in five years time, we wish you every success and would love to hear your stories.

Good luck – and make mine a mocha with extra whipped cream.

Case studies

FROM THE EXPERTS

These experts have been there and done it, and turned their coffee or tea shops into a sensation. Costa and Coffee Republic are two of the UK's most successful chains, yet they started off with just one shop and independents can learn valuable lessons from them. Bettys is a national institution and fosters traditional ideals, along with savvy business sense.

IN MY EXPERIENCE

These coffee and tea shops are independent and proud of it. Located around the UK, from Brighton to Yorkshire, they are the best people to turn to for real advice on opening a coffee shop. Whether they've been running for one year or 10, they've all been there!

FROM THE EXPERTS:

Sergio and Bruno Costa, Costa (now owned by Whitbread)

Location: 866 stores in the UK and over 300 overseas

Start year: 1971

Brothers Sergio and Bruno Costa sailed to England in the late 1960s looking for an opportunity to make their fortune. When they saw how unsophisticated the UK coffee market was, they returned home to Italy to learn their craft in the coffee roasting houses of Milan. On their return to the UK, Sergio and Bruno bought a three-storey building in London, not far from the Houses of Parliament and the present Costa Roastery in Lambeth. It was here that they set up their new business in 1971.

The Costa coffee saga started with a Petroncini Italian drum roaster and Probat coffee silos. The coffee beans were winched to the top floor of the building, where they were also stored. The coffee was roasted on the middle floor, and the ground floor was given over to packaging and shipping. At first, the Costa brothers were wholesalers and roasters, supplying top quality restaurants and speciality shops. But by 1978, they had opened their first store on Vauxhall Bridge Road. The shop, which is still there today, was run by their wives Elida and Yolanda and quickly proved successful. So the Costa brothers expanded their coffee shop business, involving their friends and family by getting them franchises and licences. All the coffee-making equipment came from Italy, from coffee machines to grinders as well as grilling machines and dishwashers. This personal ownership and painstaking attention to detail drove the business from strength to strength.

By 1990, Bruno had decided to sell his share to Sergio, for a cool £5m. A mere five years later, Sergio sold on the business to Whitbread for £45m. Whitbread, which had spotted the growing popularity of coffee shops in the USA, wanted to make its mark in the UK and saw Costa as the perfect vehicle. The company took the Costa coffee business from its 41 shops to a huge international expansion programme. Costa's first and, incidentally biggest, international store opened in Dubai in 1999. Its 1000th store was opened in Moscow in 2008. At present, Costa has around 866 stores in the UK and over 300 overseas in 25 markets, from Bahrain to Bulgaria, Serbia to Saudia Arabia and Poland to Pakistan.

But the ethos of the business has not changed. 'Although we are a market leader, at heart we remain a small Italian family business and are as passionate about the welcoming environment we offer our customers as we are about making great coffee. The interaction between the bean and our people is what differentiates us,' says John Derkach, Managing Director at Costa.

It's no wonder then that even though there are only three master Italian Roasters in the whole of the UK, all three are employed by Costa.

FROM THE EXPERTS:
Sahar and Bobby Hashemi, Coffee Republic

Location: Nearly 200 bars in the UK

Start year: 1995

Brother and sister team Sahar and Bobby Hashemi were behind the original trend for the UK high-street coffee chain. The Hashemis turned Coffee Republic into a well known and respected high-street brand, before selling it in 2001. In mid 2009, the company went into administration, a result of the 2008/2009 recession. This, however, does not take away from the achievements of the Hashemis, as they set out in the 1990s to start a coffee business from scratch.

The defining moment for the entrepreneurs was the death of their beloved father in 1993. Sahar, a former lawyer, had recently returned from New York and was lamenting London's lack of espresso bars providing proper cappuccinos and muffins. Bobby, until now a successful investment banker in New York, suddenly remembered that a prospectus of a US chain of coffee bars had recently crossed his desk so he knew that a market existed for them. In a Eureka moment, he literally woke up and smelt the coffee.

Sahar spent a day on the Circle Line, getting off at each of the 27 stops to investigate the coffee on offer. Although it was being sold in large quantities everywhere she looked, both the quality and presentation were poor and coffee itself seemed to be an after thought in comparison to the other food and beverages on offer. Sahar realised there was a huge demand for proper coffee, and from that day onwards, Sahar was dedicated to creating an authentic coffee-drinking experience, complete with baristas, delicious snacks and warm, welcoming ambience.

The Hashemis did their research meticulously, speaking to suppliers, coffee machine manufacturers, looking up shop fitters in the *Yellow Pages*, sourcing potential sites and even embarking on a free coffee-making course. 'When we started, I was naïve, it all had a certain mystery to it and my attitude was "life is an adventure"', Sahar recalls. 'It is much easier and nicer being two people. You have to be very lucky to have a good partner. I was lucky with Bobby.' Bobby and Sahar were turned down by 22 high-street banks but they kept on going until they secured a £100,000 loan from NatWest backed by the Department of Trade and Industry's Small Firms Loan Guarantee Scheme.

The huge, established competitors in the coffee industry never intimidated the pair. 'Maybe it's just an attitude of mind', Sahar says. 'I just got on with my own idea and my own vision. I think it would be very daunting if one did say, "oh, I'm up against the big boys", because you would never do anything. So I just focus on what I can focus on. Starbucks were strong competitors with more might than us – so what happened was what would in any market environment.'

The Hashemis knew they wanted the company name to encapsulate the entire coffee-drinking experience, and after several false starts, they settled on 'Coffee Republic'. However, their first attempt at having the logo professionally designed was a disaster and cost them their full-allotted budget of £400. Although the problem was rectified, it meant they then couldn't afford Coffee Republic branded cups. They ended up roping in friends to stick branded stickers on them instead.

When it came to product, Sahar viewed her suppliers as partners and looked to them to demonstrate a similar sense of entrepreneurialism. She knew exactly what type of coffee blend she wanted and her first supplier, from the London-based branch of an Italian roastery, shared her passion. The resulting concoction subsequently won numerous awards including the Best Cappuccino in London (*Independent on Sunday*) and Best Espresso in London (*Guardian*). They moved on to sourcing the right food, from pastries and muffins to croissants and bagels, all to support their vision of providing the perfect coffee experience. Hiring the right calibre of staff was a challenge in itself. Their first employees included two members poached from sandwich bar, Pret a Manger.

The Hashemis gave themselves a year to establish the brand and opened their first outlet in London's South Molton Street in November 1995. It broke even in nine months. In 1997 with turnover reaching £30m, the business floated on the stock market. Sahar and Bobby retained 27% of the company. At that point, they had six stores – the Coffee Republic model had steamed ahead, proving highly successful. By 1998, Coffee Republic had expanded to 20 stores and by the following year, they had hired a managing director, with Bobby as chief executive officer and Sahar as marketing director. Sahar estimates that at its peak, Coffee Republic had 110 outlets, 35 full-time office staff, and around 1,500 part-time staff. Before the company went into administration they had almost 200 outlets in the UK, concessions in the likes of Cineworld Cinemas and WH Smith and bars in places as diverse as Bulgaria, Kuwait, Malta and Turkey.

Sahar eventually stepped down from Coffee Republic in 2001. It's her one lasting regret. 'Looking back, it was a mistake to leave at that stage,' she says. 'The problem is when you bring in managers. Things change, people take on egos and you lose touch with the core of the business.' In recognition of her business flair, Sahar has been named a 'Pioneer to the life of the nation' by the Queen, one of the 100 Most Influential Women in Britain 2003 by the *Daily Mail* and one of the 20 most powerful women in Britain by the *Independent on Sunday*.

FROM THE EXPERTS:

Frederick Belmont, Bettys Café Tea Rooms

Location: Yorkshire

Start year: 1919

At the turn of the century a young Swiss confectioner, Fritz Butzer, left his native Alps and travelled to England. Inspired by the dream of building his own business, Fritz originally planned to head towards the resorts of the south coast. But, unable to speak a word of English and confused by the bustle of a busy London station, he boarded the wrong train and several hours later, found himself in the depths of Yorkshire.

Fortunately the countryside reminded him of his native Switzerland – so much so, that he decided to stay. In 1919 he opened his first Café Tea Rooms in the fashionable spa town of Harrogate. 'I formed a private company with a capital of £5,000 to found a first-class confiserie and café,' he wrote to his sister Ida, who was living in Switzerland. 'My own share is one-quarter. A property was bought for £7,000. A mortgage was arranged and then came the equipping.'

Fritz describes himself as the only shareholder who understood the business; thus the weight of the organisation fell upon his shoulders. He was determined to establish his business in style. 'Opening day was 17 July 1919. And now came a time of "either/or", "sink or swim". Here I now had a shop exquisitely fitted out, the showcases in precious wood, mirrors and glass on the walls, the café furnished in grey, with muted pink panels with old-silver borders, with old-silver electric candleholders in the centres.'

The costs of running the tea room were high and the staff very new. The first day's takings amounted to a mere £30. However, not much later, just one week after opening, the takings had jumped to £220, making this small business an immediate success. Fritz quickly changed his name into the very English 'Frederick Belmont', and set about running the show. He was in charge of everything, from supervising the production rooms to buying the actual products. The combination of Swiss confectionery and Yorkshire warmth and hospitality in such an elegant setting proved irresistible. Bettys was instantly popular and was soon able to boast 'Royal and Distinguished Patronage' on its letterhead.

Encouraged by Bettys' early success, Frederick dreamed of opening other tea rooms in Yorkshire, including in one of his favourite cities – York. The site, when he eventually acquired it, cost him £25,750. Bettys hired the interior designers and shop fitters of the cruise liner

Queen Mary to fit out the rooms in spectacular fashion with walnut pillars and panelling, etched glass and exquisite marquetry. The York Bettys Café Tea Rooms opened on 1 June 1937, 18 years after the opening of that first tea room in Harrogate.

However, Frederick quickly regretted opening another tea room, as it doubled his responsibility – and stress levels. He did not think that the new business would survive, but he persevered. And despite his reservations, Frederick made a success of his new venture, and a purpose-built bakery was built in 1922, with a tea room in Bradford following in 1927. 'It is really gratifying to have accomplished my ambitions.' Eighty years on and Bettys is still a family business, owned by Frederick Belmont's descendants. Despite countless requests Bettys has firmly refused to open branches outside Yorkshire. 'Our commitment to keeping small and special means that we can keep a watchful eye on every detail,' says Bettys' Harrogate Branch Manager, June Wood. 'And make sure every visit to our tea rooms is a memorable one.'

Bettys is committed to buying locally and working with local farmers and suppliers. According to Executive Chef David Parker. 'It's quality first and then it's local. Buying from suppliers on our doorstep helps cut down food miles and lets us work in partnership with farmers so we can guarantee we're buying the best.' Martin Dellar, Purchasing Manager for Bettys couldn't agree more: 'With such a rich food and farming heritage on our doorstep, it makes sense to buy from Yorkshire.'

Bettys now has six café tea rooms, all in Yorkshire, but after nearly 90 years the identity of 'Betty' still remains a family mystery, although over the years many explanations have been offered. Frederick may have named his tea rooms after the late Queen Mother, Elizabeth Bowes Lyon, who was born at the turn of the century, or perhaps a former manageress of the Harrogate Spa, Betty Lupton, 'Queen of the Harrogate Wells.' 'There's also a sentimental tale of young Betty, a doctor's daughter, who died of tuberculosis and whose father's practice on Cambridge Crescent later became the first Bettys Café Tea Rooms,' explains June. The favourite story, however, is the one which tells of a small girl interrupting the very first board meeting when the issue of what to call the tea rooms was being discussed. The girl's name, of course, was Betty.

IN MY EXPERIENCE:

Shelagh Ryan, Lantana

Type: Café and coffee shop

Location: Fitzrovia, London

Start year: 2007

'Lantana is a beautiful, flowering plant introduced into Australia from South America and has taken hold and thrived because it is so hardy. It has become a "weed of national significance". We hope that Lantana the café will also thrive on foreign soil.'

In May 2007 Shelagh Ryan travelled to London from Australia to open a café with her sister and brother-in-law. 'I was inspired by all the fantastic cafés in Australia, particularly in Melbourne, where I've been living for the last eight years. Good food and coffee in independently run cafés is something you expect and take for granted there.'

Shelagh worked in a café/deli for a year to learn about the London market. 'I did a lot of foot research to learn about the food and coffee offerings here and to locate the areas where we thought there was a strong customer base for our café concept,' she says. Aided by several small-business books, family and friends, she put a business plan together, funded with private investment from the four original founders. 'I developed selection criteria for the type of area I thought would be right for our café; a mix of workers and residents, professionals and large numbers of Antipodeans.' There were a few parts of London which met the criteria and then it was just a question of their finding an affordable site.

It wasn't all fun menu planning though, as Shelagh says: 'I don't think I really appreciated how many aspects there were to running a small business; from doing wages, dealing with pest control and council permits to finding out how to fix broken refrigerators. Sadly it's not just about making nice coffee and creating menus.'

Shelagh sourced the decorations, furniture and crockery from eBay and salvage shops. She and the team used an architect with experience in café fit-outs to design the layout. At Lantana, there is as much emphasis on the quality of the coffee as there is on the quality of the food. 'Often places do one or the other well, but not both. I was also keen for my personality to come through. I hate going into bland, homogeneous café chains.'

Shelagh was 'amazed' by their customers' enthusiastic reception. 'People said it was the best breakfast and coffee they had ever had. It made all the hard work seem worthwhile. Making a good coffee is not an accident; it requires skill, knowledge, good quality coffee beans and equipment, and most importantly, love.'

IN MY EXPERIENCE:

Simon Robertson, Leoni

Type: Coffee shop

Location: Malton, North Yorkshire

Start year: 1996

For Simon Robertson, founder of independent coffee shop, Leoni, the essence of espresso and café culture is escapism for a few moments in the day.

Simon set up Leoni in November 1996. Since then, he has been the UK Barista Champion three times, and has represented the UK in the World Barista Championships. He retired ranked eighth in the world. Leoni won best coffee shop in 2006/2007.

A business enterprise organisation helped Simon with his business plan. 'I had, however, invested my life savings,' he says. 'I had, because of four years travel, no real career prospects and there was hell of a lot of pride at stake. It was because of these factors, experience or not, that I became business minded very quickly!' Funding initially for Leoni was comparatively little. 'My coffee shop is quite small,' explains Simon. 'The shop fit worked with the ergonomics of the building and therefore only required some superficial alteration.'

Simon was determined to re-create a genuine café culture. 'My market research involved standing opposite what would become my shop, counting how many potential customers walked past. Establishing potential customer type was based on nothing more scientific than appearance. Of course for the benefit of the bank and the business plan I documented this as "Socio Economic Grouping".' The building Simon discovered was very original, 'old fashioned' and had exactly the right atmosphere and character. All Simon had to do was apply for a 'change of use' before converting it to a coffee house and he continued to make improvements until he felt the café was running up to speed.

Simon found the local environmental health authority helpful when he designed the kitchen and working area. Somewhat more challenging was choosing the right coffee machines. 'Just about every machine distributor will claim their machine is ideal for your business. This not as bad as it seems because on the whole the coffee industry is a very ethical one, there are very few "cowboys".' (Most coffee suppliers will offer barista training.)

His loyal customers are a testament to Simon's choice of coffee; he calls the shots on what's served, based on quality, consistency and most importantly, whether he likes it. The biggest mistake Simon made was over predicting the profit margins on his business plan, putting down 80% when it was closer to 65%. 'That 15% loss of GP would have meant disaster had I not made one other big mistake and that was turnover; the turnover actually proved to be 40% more than predicted in the first year.'

IN MY EXPERIENCE:

Raymond Voce, Royal Teas

Type: Vegetarian café and coffee shop
Location: Greenwich, London
Start year: 2000

Raymond, a former teacher and Virgin flight attendant, took over Royal Teas in 2000 and set about creating a community-led venue. With the business already established for nearly 20 years, at least he didn't have to worry about choosing a new name. 'Royal Teas already had its name when I took it over. If it had been a terrible dive then I would have changed it and started afresh but although it wasn't financially successful it still had a charm and was a name already in the psyche of the local community.'

Royal Teas employed professionals for the electrics in the 1840 listed building, but flew solo for the fundamental design. 'I am lucky that I know a lot of artists, designers and tradesmen and so all previous favours were called in,' says Raymond. Also, being familiar with the industry through magazines and visiting new eateries, Raymond felt confident in what he wanted to achieve.

Forecasting what people are going to eat was a challenge though. 'If only,' says Ray. 'I supplement our bulk food orders with daily visits to our local supermarket. It is near impossible to second guess what the public will order.' Food notwithstanding, the basis of a true coffee shop is the quality of its beverages. 'We have taken advice from our supplier as to what coffee to serve. The most popular coffees are the medium ones. We rent our machine from our coffee supplier and they showed us how to work it. One also learns from staff members. Presently we have someone that can do coffee art. If I was starting out I would go and work for a while in a coffee shop before embarking on starting my own.

'Someone yesterday described the café as a favourite old jumper,' says Ray. 'We have created a warm sociable environment that people want to come and spend their down time in. We listen, have a laugh and offer good quality food and drink to enjoy.' While he cites 'life experience' as the best to have when contemplating setting up your own coffee shop/café, 'be prepared to never again have a day off sick,' he advises.

Royal Teas didn't organise any special event when it opened. 'We just opened our doors and started trading. We were lucky that word spread fast and so there was no need to shout "here we are". If I was to do a launch I would open for a couple of weeks to make sure everything was running as it should before embarking on any advertising campaign/launch party.' Ray believes Royal Teas works because it is an independent café. 'We focus on giving a very personal service to our customers. Chains also have their place but in my opinion lack the warmth and charm our lovely café has.'

IN MY EXPERIENCE:

Tim and Caroline Hume, Redroaster Coffee House

Type: Coffee house
Location: Brighton, Sussex
Start year: 2000

The Redroaster Coffee Company was formed in Brighton in 2000 as a successor to 'The Coffee Company', which was founded in 1994. The original inspiration was the rapid development in the USA and Canada of espresso-based gourmet drinks service during the late 1980s and early 1990s and the phenomenal growth of Starbucks. Two of the original owners, Roger Hume and Robin Mann had an oil exploration business based in Calgary, Alberta, Canada. It took a true family effort to get Redroaster going, with Roger's two brothers, Jon and Tim, getting involved in the design and location of the first café and later the Redroaster Coffee House.

Tim became head of operations when the café was opened in The Lanes tourist area in August 1994. He began roasting coffee at home and formed a business partnership with locally based friends involved in the international entertainment industry, who provided the finance for the setting up of Redroaster Coffee Company. All funding came from partners within or was generated by the business. A business plan was prepared and a registered company formed without a single penny being borrowed from outside sources. The name evolved from the colour of the company's roaster. A friend with a local graphic design business designed the logo at a very economical rate. They chose their suppliers by quality, availability and lastly, by price. When it came to buying coffee-making equipment, they researched, took advice, talked to other users and salesmen and read reviews.

Redroaster Coffee House opened in September 2000. As expertise developed, Redroaster Coffee House became a supplier itself to local cafés, restaurants, hotels and other businesses. During 2007 Tim and his wife Caroline bought out their partners and became sole owners of the business. A separate purpose-built roastery was opened during 2008 to cater for growing demand. That same year, Redroaster Coffee House won the award of second runner up as 'UK Independent Coffee Shop of the Year' at Allegra Strategies European Coffee Symposium.

Tim says: "We have evolved our own way of doing things that is a bit more indigenous than the chains which are either American, pseudo-American, pseudo-Italian or both. We're a coffee *house*. Roasting coffee on the premises sets you apart in the UK.'

> “The mere chink of cups and saucers tunes the mind to happy repose.”
>
> George Gissing, The Private Papers of Henry Ryecroft

> “Performance art can be produced in a coffee house setting.”
>
> Jack Bowman

1

Opening up

1.1 Are you cut out for it?

You've got as far as deciding you are going to run a coffee or tea shop but there is a lot to think about and think through before you even start putting a business plan together or suggesting the idea to friends and family. It's vital you make sure you have what it takes and that you are fully aware of the trials and tribulations of running your own business. You will also need to think about how this new challenge will affect your family and personal life, making sure it doesn't take over everything else, as well as ensuring you have a strong support network for when the going gets tough.

In this chapter we'll cover:

- Who is suited to running a coffee shop
- The experience you need
- Business partners
- Support networks

IS RUNNING A COFFEE OR TEA SHOP RIGHT FOR YOU?

Running a coffee shop, much like running any business, can only bring you real success if you want it badly enough. But is there a 'type' of person that is more suited to it? And are you doing it for the right reasons?

You don't have to be a junior version of Richard Branson or Anita Roddick to succeed. Just because you didn't start selling sweets in the school playground at the age of seven or turn over your first million by the age of 21 doesn't mean you can't do it. Not all successful business men and women are built the same way. And research shows that your nationality, ethnicity, sex, age, education, class, experience or wealth shouldn't stop you or mean you can't fulfil your ambition.

In theory, there is no one, from any background and any walk of life, who can't successfully start and run their own business. So be assured, whatever your concerns and anxieties: you can do it. But remember that 'doing it' is the key point here and marks the difference between those who can do it and those who do do it. People who manage to start their own business are the ones who stop talking about their dreams and plans and actually make them happen.

WHAT MOTIVATES YOU?

So what motivates people to do something as challenging as starting a coffee or tea shop from scratch? It's a hard slog, and a career choice which comes with anti-social working hours. That first million isn't going to appear in the first year. If ever.

Perhaps surprisingly then, money is often not the main motivator for setting up on your own. For most people, it's the opportunity to call the shots and be their own boss. It's the idea or desire to live a life that's more fulfilling, whether that be working closer to their family, in an environment they are more comfortable with. It might be the passionate belief that they can do 'it' better than anyone else out there. It's about having a greater work–life balance or simply the challenge of earning their own income.

Influence of the economic climate

The economic downturn in 2008 and 2009 saw a radical shift in career choices. Many people, faced with redundancy, are choosing to rethink their path in life and embark on a new adventure. For some, it's teaching. For others, it's swapping the 'suits and boots' to make a go of a coffee or tea shop.

And research shows that recession is a great time to make the change, to start a new business. Over 200 more new business banking relationships started in the first quarter of 2009, compared with the same time of year in 2008, according to the British Bankers' Association (BBA). Business Link, a government-funded programme based in London, also reports that it has had a 25% increase in people enquiring about starting a new business.

Recession, and its aftermath, affect both businesses and consumers. Businesses have to work hard to retain their custom, and consumers have to become more discerning about what they spend their money on. Yet, this is exactly why your business could thrive and grow in a recession as consumers look for affordable luxuries to spend their hard earned pennies on. Jim Surguy, senior partner of Harvest Consulting, illustrates this with the example of a well-known ice cream brand, which was started in a recession and is now a global phenomenon. 'In the last recession in the early 1990s one of the things that was successful was Häagen-Dazs ice cream. It was luxurious in its sector, but it wasn't hugely expensive and so was an affordable treat'. So if you can provide quality and service, at a good price, there is real potential for success in a recession.

A period of recession is also a good time to launch something new as you can take advantage of sales and deals. Rent and property prices, for instance, are often lower, and premises in good locations are much more common – just look around your local town centre. You might also be able to acquire some good value furniture, equipment and produce at low prices from companies that are closing down, or offering recession busting deals. Lastly, if you have the courage and commitment to start a business in a recession, you may find yourself in an enviable position when the economy finally rights itself. That said it won't be a walk in the park, so you need to make sure you are cut out to go the distance.

PERSONALITY

What sort of person do *you* have to be to open a coffee or tea shop? Anyone running a successful business will tell you that it's all about passion. If you don't love what you do, it's hard to get out of bed in the morning to do it – and if it's your own business on the line then there is no else to do it for you. So you do have to be inspired by and excited about coffee and tea – as you will be making it, serving it, smelling it, talking about it, reading about it and buying it every single day for at least the first year.

IN MY EXPERIENCE:
Simon Robertson, Leoni

If there is a stereotype for running a coffee shop then the same stereotype would be suitable for any business. In any business a total belief in the product is essential; in the case of the coffee shop that belief is actually more to do with passion and appreciation. If your passion is coffee and you have the motivation then in my opinion you would be suited to running a coffee shop.

Enthusiasm and motivation aren't all it takes of course, as proved by the number of businesses which fail within the first year. But if you are really determined to do it, you can't be put off by statistics. Becoming your own boss and setting up a business is not only one of the most rewarding, exciting and fulfilling things you can do in life, but it's also one of the most stressful, testing and demanding experiences.

It would be naïve to think you will be writing that novel you always meant to in your spare time behind the till. This will be you, just you, running your own business and being totally responsible for your own livelihood and your own pay cheque. The buck stops with you.

TIP

It's often said getting married and moving house are the two most stressful events most people take on in life but you could quite easily argue starting a business tops that list.

You can't go to HR (human resources) for advice when one of your staff steals from you; nor can you call IT when the till breaks. You can't lie to your boss about being sick and then take the day off to go to the seaside. You will need to be able to fix the fridge, understand tax, calm down irate customers, know the workings of your espresso machine intimately and be willing to unblock toilets – all in the space of an hour.

For at least the first two to three years, you can expect to put the holidays on hold and to work longer and harder than you are now. You can also expect to make sacrifices with family and friends who, no matter how much you explain, won't understand why you have turned into a bore who ruins dinner parties and nights out with obsessive rants on the price of milk or stories of the customer from hell. You will need to be tough to cope with feeling isolated from your usual support networks, and will need to find the time to create new ones. The hours can be long and holidays may only happen if you can afford them and trust your full-time staff to open up, close, go to the bank for you, not mess up your supplier relationships and get up in the middle of the night if your alarm rings.

Raymond Voce at Royal Teas candidly admits he's not in the business solely for the money. 'It is a lifestyle,' he says.

ANALYSING YOUR SKILLS

While passion, ambition and determination are compulsory assets for any entrepreneur, there are certain skill sets you should have in order to make it. Be honest with yourself. Make an honest assessment of your skills and think about what you are good at and where you may need to think about getting in some help. In short, make sure you have:

- A basic understanding of accounting
- An ability or inclination to sell
- An interest in/knowledge of coffee and tea
- Decisiveness
- Leadership
- Plenty of initiative
- Social and people skills
- A firm understanding of the customer experience
- Patience

PRIOR EXPERIENCE – DOES IT MATTER?

A big question that often comes up is 'Do I need to have worked in a coffee or tea shop before?' Well, the answer is yes and no. You simply can't dive into running a business without some prior experience – and this goes for any business. A venture such as a coffee or tea shop is incredibly hard work and you need to know beforehand all the aspects of the job that you will be expected to do. It does help if you have done some waitressing previously, or worked in a local bar for instance.

You should also have some idea of how demanding the service industry is. Just because someone drinks a lot of coffee doesn't mean they have the necessary knowledge of how to sell it. Be careful you don't fall into this trap. For instance, when you bought that latte last week were you really thinking about what shifts the person serving you was on that week, how much they earned, what percentage of the coffee shop's income that was, how much the mark-up on the menu was, when the next delivery was due or who lets the cleaners in and out?

Of course it's fantastic if you have been able to spend some time getting to know how a coffee or tea shop business works. But realistically, if you are coming to this as a second career, or a life change, then chances are you haven't had much time to be getting work experience in your local establishment.

IN MY EXPERIENCE:

Shelagh Ryan, Lantana

I've always believed (for what it's worth) that if you are an intelligent person prepared to work hard and are passionate about what you are doing you can try your hand at anything.

Gaining the relevant experience

Even though most people know they should get some experience, they often aren't sure where to fit it in or even how to go about getting it. If you are working full-time it's unrealistic to expect you to get a job in a café during the evenings, especially if you have got family commitments. Likewise, once you have stopped working and have sacrificed the security of a salary, getting a job in a coffee or tea shop for the sake of picking up some experience can use up valuable planning time. You need to think carefully about the option that is best for you.

TIP

Why not ask the owner of your local coffee or tea shop if you can shadow them for a day to get a real feel for the business? At the very worst, you will just get a refusal.

It makes sense to do some work in the type of coffee or tea shop you are planning to open, or observe it from an inside point of view. Talk to owners who run similar operations to the one you are planning. As long as they are in a completely different area and your business won't open in competition to theirs, you may find them willing to let you gain a little experience.

Or you could take a leaf out of Sahar Hashemi's book; the co-founder of Coffee Republic spent a day on the Circle Line, getting off at each of the 27 stops to investigate what type of coffee was on offer. Either way it's important to make sure you have spent some time considering the business from more than just a customer's point of view.

Business partnerships

One way to ensure you have all the experience you need is to go into business with someone who has the skills you are lacking. Perhaps you love coffee and have a real commitment to customer service, but find accounting and managing the funds a terrible prospect – sharing the business with someone who has a good head for numbers and the bottom line is a great way to pool resources and allow you both to utilise the things you do well.

You may already have someone in mind that you want to run the business with – these ideas are often cooked up with two people creating a vision of how they 'could do better' over a coffee. Or you may feel that you would like to share the experience with someone – but how do you decide and whom do you choose? Aside from having the skills you don't have and vice versa, look for a partner with whom you have a natural business chemistry; someone who can enthuse you and whom you can inspire. Good partnerships combine characters who together can create a greater sum total than their individual efforts and that's what you should aspire to build.

FROM THE EXPERTS:
Sahar Hashemi, Coffee Republic

It is much easier and nicer being two people. You have to be very lucky to have a good partner. I was lucky with (brother) Bobby.

Going into business with partners, friends or family

Coffee and tea shops are a popular type of business to go into with family or even friends. After years of living separate working lives, couples often view opening up their own shop as a way of spending more time together. Likewise, who better to trust sharing such an enormous financial and emotional challenge than with your family or trusted friends? It's easy to see why, idealistically at least, it appeals. When you consider how much of our waking lives we spend earning money to enjoy in comparatively small spaces of time with the people that mean most to us, combining the two to get the best of both worlds is a compelling argument. What's more, it can work brilliantly. The attributes for a healthy relationship – trust, honesty, the ability to listen, understanding, the unity of or tolerance of shared or different interests – translate well into business.

If you do plan to go down this route, first of all, aside from your personal relationships, make sure there is a business case for working together. Ideally your skill sets should complement each other so the coffee or tea shop benefits from supporting two people: if it's unlikely you would otherwise recruit this person then think again. If your decision to work together does make business sense, there is no reason you shouldn't continue: just be aware of the consequences. If the business doesn't work out then relationships could turn sour and the trauma of losing a business could be doubled by also losing an otherwise lifelong friend or partner. Is it worth it? Ultimately it's your call, but be wary of rushing into something you could regret and agree early on how you will communicate inevitable frustrations with each other to keep the relationship healthy. If your business partner is more of an associate than a friend, you need to be clear in your mind that you trust and like this person. It's likely you will be working intensively with them for a number of years so you will clearly need to get on.

TIP

Don't be tempted to go into business with someone simply because they've got the financial backing you haven't, or because they've got the great contacts you need. If a partnership doesn't have a natural foundation it won't work. You can still use these people as a part of your support and business network without actually being their business partner. Read more about support networks on page 28.

IN MY EXPERIENCE:

Simon Robertson, Leoni

I work with a product that I am passionate about; it involves pride and self-belief. The coffee I serve is my coffee. I created it. Having a partner who had the same thoughts would, for me, undoubtedly, create war. Apart from that I am a Yorkshire-man, and too stubborn to work with anybody.

Setting the boundaries

You will need to balance reward, responsibility and risk. Make sure you're clear what your goals are for the business on a shared and personal level, what you want in the short, medium and long-term, be clear what your respective roles are and ensure you are each staking the same degree of risk. Be clear about what you each expect an average day to entail, and how you would deal with problems. And, simple as it sounds, make sure you are happy and comfortable, and have established clear lines of communication to enable it to stay that way.

As with all partnerships, expect the unexpected and be professional about it. Two out of three marriages end in divorce but that shouldn't dissuade you from entering into a commitment with someone. However, it is advisable to get a legally binding shareholder agreement that will cover what happens to the business and shares if any combination of unthinkable outcomes occur including, as morbid as it might seem, the death of either partner. Type 'shareholder agreement' into Google and you will find plenty of companies willing to do this for you for as little as £50. You can also have your solicitor draw something up.

IN MY EXPERIENCE:

Shelagh Ryan, Lantana

I've gone into business with my sister and her husband and we are very close and honest with each other. For me I think it is easier doing business with family than it would be with friends. We know each other's strengths and weaknesses and have a strong underlying trust in each other.

Support networks

Probably the most important support network you will need is your family and friends, regardless of whether or not they are directly involved. New businesses require a tremendous amount of time and nurturing to develop and become successful; time that is taken from elsewhere, often from the family. No matter how hard you attempt to make sure it doesn't, starting and running a business will impact on your family, so it's essential you prepare them for what's ahead. Unless you are starting a 'family' business where all members are participants, someone will inevitably feel left out, or neglected.

Starting up . . . with a family

To make sure your family doesn't suffer due to your own ambitions, before you pursue your dream business, sit down with them and discuss the following:

- Will the business venture take away from quality time spent with family members? If so, how much is acceptable to all involved?
- Do you have small children and if so are you going to feel comfortable spending time away from them? Who will pick up the slack when you can't look after them?
- Will the new business be initially funded or supported using family monies? If so, will this put a financial strain on the family and create new tensions?
- Do all family members agree this is a potentially successful business idea?
- Do all family members realise that most new businesses do not succeed?
- If the business is not showing signs of becoming successful, what operational time period will the family tolerate before the business is considered a failure and should be sold or closed down?
- Who is going to be the main breadwinner while your new venture gets underway?
- Is there a set budget you can agree as a family to commit to spending on your coffee or tea shop?

- Can you afford it – financially and emotionally?
- If the new business fails, what is the alternative plan for income?

Some of the questions listed above may not have obvious answers until the business has started up and operated for some period of time. Since circumstances may vary regularly with a new business, it might be a sensible idea to review this list with your family every six months to see what situations may have changed. Your family needs to be in total support of your new business idea, or somewhere and at some point, somebody will suffer. Consider whether your 'big idea' is worth the possibility of distancing yourself from your loved ones. Business owners with complete family support stand a much greater chance of success. Talk to your family and trust in their opinion.

Other entrepreneurs' experience of support

The reason we asked successful business people in the coffee and tea shop world to contribute to this book is that there is simply no better place to get advice than from those that have, as the saying goes, 'been there and done it'. Like all relationships you will find that with support networks you get out what you put in. Networking comes naturally to some people; it fills others with dread. If you are the first sort of person, you are probably already aware of the value of getting out and meeting others. In business you can't know too many people or have enough 'friends' to call on to get you out of a mess. If you are the second type of person, you are going to have to be brave and bite the bullet. Get yourself to a business networking event, have a glass of wine and simply chat to people about what you are doing.

TIP

Events such as Startups Live (which you can find more details about at www.startupslive.co.uk) will give you the opportunity to meet hundreds of other budding entrepreneurs and new business owners, some of whom will know the answers to the questions you are struggling to find answers to. The likelihood is it won't be half as scary as you imagine. Remember, most people have been, or still are, in the same boat as you.

Networking is a great way of picking up recommendations. Most people recommend people they use – whether good or bad – so don't swallow their advice blindly, but knowing an accountant or lawyer who is experienced in your sector or knowledgeable of the area is a far more valuable lead than your standard Google search.

Other ways of networking

Trade associations are another vital source of business support. Often they provide workshops and events that are great for expanding your product knowledge and doing some research; and the social aspect of these events will allow you to 'talk shop' with other coffee and tea shop owners. Simon Robertson from Leoni also recommends being involved in competitions, which can prove very useful in networking and forging friendships within the industry.

Don't confine your networking to physical events, however. Social networking is growing beyond the fun and games of Facebook and MySpace into a serious business tool and with websites such as LinkedIn, Smarta.com, BT Tradespace and Startups.co.uk you can interact with other entrepreneurs and business advisers. Of course, while it lacks the face-to-face personal touch it can be far less daunting.

Official groups

Business bodies and lobby groups can also provide a wealth of information, support and training for small businesses and coffee shops. There are a range of small business groups and ones dedicated to the hospitality industry as well as specific coffee and tea organisations.

General small business groups

- The Federation of Small Businesses (FSB)– www.fsb.org.uk
- The Forum of Private Business (FPB)– www.fpb.org
- The British Chambers of Commerce (BCC)– www.britishchambers.org.uk
- Business Link:– www.businesslink.gov.uk
- Regional Development Agencies– www.englandsrdas.com

All of the above are recognised lobby and small business groups that aim to represent, champion and advise small businesses in all industry sectors.

Industry-specific organisations

- **British Hospitality Association (BHA)** – the national trade association for hotels, restaurants and caterers (www.bha.org.uk).

- **British Coffee Association** – a representative voice for all aspects of the UK coffee industry; also a fantastic source of information on all things coffee related (www.britishcoffeeassociation.org).
- **UK Tea Council** – an independent non-profit making body dedicated to promoting tea and its unique story for the benefit of those who produce, sell and enjoy tea (www.tea.co.uk).
- **European Tea Council** – brings together a range of member groups dedicated to tea throughout Europe (www.etc-online.org).
- **Beverage Service Association** – dedicated to encouraging the growth of the UK out-of-home beverage market, raising the quality of beverages produced and the standard of service provided (www.beverageserviceassociation.com).
- **Tea Guild** – a members-only organisation that represents and encourages outlets that are dedicated to brewing and serving tea to high standards; part of the Tea Council (www.tea.co.uk/teaguild).
- **Speciality Coffee Association of Europe** – lobbies to promote quality coffee worldwide, and its members network, inform and share views on the latest developments in speciality coffee (www.scae.com).
- **British Sandwich Association** – promotes excellence and innovation; is a source of information for the industry and provides a collective voice for all those involved in making, distributing and retailing sandwiches (www.sandwich.org.uk).

Miscellaneous websites

There is also a range of great websites where coffee and tea experts, professionals and enthusiasts share information and news about the beverage industry. Check out:

- www.talkaboutcoffee.com
- www.realcoffee.co.uk
- www.stashtea.com
- www.learn-about-tea.com

You might also find it useful to subscribe to some trade magazines that write directly for anyone involved in the beverage, hospitality or coffee and tea industry. Have a look at:

- *Boughton's Coffee House* magazine: www.coffee-house.org.uk
- *Café Magazine*: www.cafémagazine.co.uk
- *Caterer Magazine*: www.catererandhotelkeeper.com

BUSINESS MENTORING

Finally, think about having a mentor. Several organisations provide matching services, for example, the Prince's Trust. You can, of course, find an experienced mentor who has done exactly what you wanted to do, and done it well. There is nothing to be lost in simply asking if you can turn to them once every month for advice. Don't be scared to approach someone you don't know. Many entrepreneurs feel a responsibility to encourage and help others and are usually willing to help. If they are not it's almost certainly because they are simply too busy (either running their own business(es) or possibly helping someone else). If that's the case, ask someone else. You will soon get used to moving on quickly and without a grudge when met with the word 'no'! There is a whole section on the startups.co.uk website on how to find, approach and deal with a business mentor. The website will also point you in the right direction to getting a mentor on board for your own business.

Things to remember:

- Know what you are getting into before you start.
- If you aren't fully committed to seeing your plan through before you start, it could be a costly exercise.
- If you don't have enough experience, get some before you plan your own start up.
- If you can't do it alone, think carefully about the type of person you would want as a partner.
- Talk it through with friends and family. They may still offer support even if they are not convinced by the idea.

1.2

Is now a good time to start up?

Let's face it. You would have to be on Mars to have not heard of, or more likely, experienced first hand the economic downturn. It's tough out there and most people will think you are being a bit rash to think about starting a new business. With small businesses closing at an alarming rate, you certainly have to be confident your idea can work and survive. Therefore on the one hand, it's more important than ever to research your market. When big chains such as Starbucks are announcing job cuts of over 1,000 and the closure of 600 cafés, you need to be savvy. On the other hand, this may make you more determined to start your own independent coffee shop that won't make the same mistakes as the 'big boys'.

In this chapter we'll cover:

- The financial climate
- Independents vs chains
- The future of coffee and tea shops

THE FINANCIAL CLIMATE

It's certainly a tougher climate in which to raise funds now for a business than it was just a few years ago. This, of course, also impacts on what people have to spend, and leisure activities such as eating out suddenly become less affordable for a lot of people. It's no surprise that newspapers and magazines are bursting with features on how 'staying in is the new going out'. That said, in research conducted in April 2009 by Allegra Strategies with 130 senior coffee executives and key suppliers, 83% of interviewees said that coffee consumers' expectations have risen as a result of the economic downturn, which creates a real opening for independent coffee and tea shops whose focus is on quality and standards. Essentially, there is never a bad time to start a good business, so don't let market conditions put you off: just make sure you plan even more carefully to get your offering spot on.

INDEPENDENTS VS CHAINS

The gap between independents and chains is a distinctive one; like two opposing political parties, both sides are equally passionate and will argue their case. You only have to visit websites such as I Hate Starbucks and Delocator, a list of independent coffee shops, to gauge how high passions are running in the independent camp.

IN MY EXPERIENCE:

Simon Robertson, Leoni

The chains have, and depend on, a brand-driven lifestyle concept that is made fashionable. The origins of espresso have a very different ethos and are based on deep-rooted culture and are dependent on the quality of the product and the atmosphere of the place it is served rather than brand, and is very much more a 'way of life' than a 'lifestyle'.

This book is focused on helping you set up as an independent, giving you ideas on how to compete with the chains and how to make your offering different from them. Many independents, for example, claim their establishments genuinely foster a sense of community, something they say chains are sorely lacking in.

Many believe that the quality of coffee in the chains suffers as a result of their autocracy. Independents turn up their noses at the so-called designer style coffees (half-caff, de-caff, soya mocha latte) so beloved of the chains.

Chains can be soulless, characterless, expensive, lacking in a unique quality that sets them apart, and impersonal both in style and service. You can offer personality, character, innovation, quality, great prices and a genuinely friendly service. And with consumers more likely to think carefully about where they spend their money in a tempestuous climate, you could well find that supporting local businesses and appreciating quality, service and cost comes high on most people's lists.

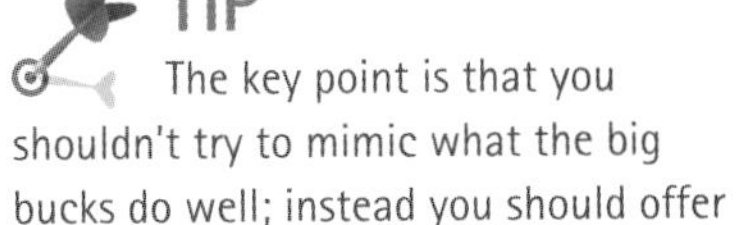

TIP

The key point is that you shouldn't try to mimic what the big bucks do well; instead you should offer everything that they don't – which does include a lot.

THE FUTURE OF COFFEE AND TEA SHOPS

According to the British Coffee Association, the UK consumes over 68 million cups of coffee a day, and Allegra Strategies Research found that a quarter of UK adults or 11m people visit coffee and tea shops at least once a week. In the tea industry, a growing interest in unique and more diverse ranges of tea means the green tea industry is expected to grow by 61% by 2011, and the herbal tea industry by 31%, according to Euromonitor International.

So the demand is most definitely there, and the industry is responding: the number of coffee and tea shops in the UK increased by 5% between May 2008 and May 2009. In a climate where many industries are showing a slump in growth, this is encouraging news. The beverage market is still forecast to grow strongly over the next five years and is likely to be made up of an equal mixture of independents and branded coffee and tea shops. In fact, *The Independent* recently reported that 20% of all independents started within the past couple of years. So the chains aren't killing off all the competition yet. Equally, if it's true that 'staying in is the new going out', customers are more likely to flock to you for a good cup of coffee and dessert, rather than splurge on a three-course dinner at a pricey restaurant. And you are more likely to find friends meeting for a cuppa and a cake, than for lunch.

As the UK coffee and tea drinking market also becomes more astute, consumers are waking up and smelling the coffee; in short, they are getting pickier about the quality, provenance and taste of their beverage. What you need to do is to appeal to the more discerning coffee drinker; the consumer who knows and cares about the quality of their bean, who is interested in who your suppliers are and how local they are, and whether you stock coffee and tea that is organic, fair-trade and from a sustainable source.

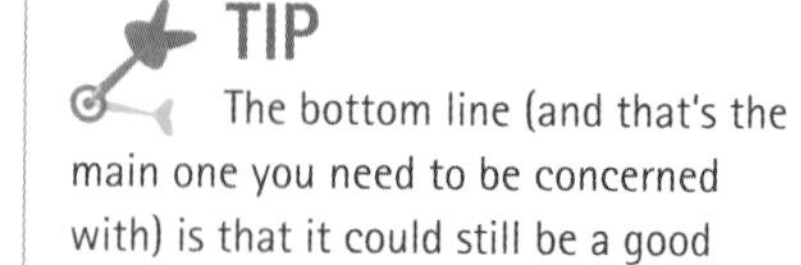

TIP

The bottom line (and that's the main one you need to be concerned with) is that it could still be a good time to open a coffee or tea shop.

How the big boys are doing

Costa has expanded by 150 outlets since 2007; close competitor Starbucks boosted its stable by 101 stores to end with 650 while the third largest brand, Caffé Nero, has grown by 68 venues to total 360. However, it's not all roses with franchises. Starbucks announced the closure of around 616 US stores with the loss of 12,000 workers in 2008, blaming poor sales and the downturn in the economy.

INDEPENDENT POWER

Benefits

The benefits of being a chain are obvious: you have great buying power; access to some of the best suppliers worldwide; a solid recognisable brand that people defer to if they are unsure; the ability to buy in serious bulk and cut down costs significantly; the money for advertising, sponsorship and promotion which grows your brand and your ability to dominate the market; and crucially the big bucks to buy up top locations both in terms of footfall and proximity to town centres, as well as scoring the big deals with shopping centres, airports, book stores and department stores.

But it's not all plain sailing for the chains, the three main brands generally being seen as Starbucks, Caffé Nero and Costa. An independent has several benefits the chains can only dream of.

- **It's your place** – you don't have to answer to anyone (apart from your accountant!) in terms of branding, type of coffee machine, choice of coffee beans, menu and opening hours.
- **It's your show** – which means the customer gets to know YOU. You can put your personality, your unique stamp and your passion into everything including décor, produce and service.
- **Freedom** – you can make your own decisions, and aren't tied down by the bureaucratic red tape of big organisations which means any new initiative or decision requires endless meetings and sign-offs. You can change things quickly and react to dips and flows in trade as you need to. If you get into work one day and it's unexpected boiling sunshine outside, you can decide to offer a promotional free ice tea with any sandwich at lunchtime and you don't have to check with anyone.
- **Quality control** – in the beginning, if you want to, you can make every cup of coffee you serve, therefore being sure that what you are providing is top notch. With fewer staff you can also ensure service is both professional and personal.
- **Feel-good factor** – you can support local businesses and tradesmen easily, and openly. In a time when sustainable practices and support for local trade are becoming paramount, you can do this as standard, without having to make a promotional song and dance about it.
- **Connection** – most people who start a business do so because they have a passion for their product. As an independent you never lose that connection to the dream and the vision and you will always be around coffee, tea and your customers, not stuck in the office headquarters in long meetings about profit margins, marketing budgets and global franchising!

TIP

According to the consumer watchdog, *Which?*, you are more likely to get a good cup of coffee at a decent price in an independent coffee shop than one of the big chains.

Location advantage

With so many of the chains choosing to locate in the big cities, one of the main advantages independents have is success in more rural areas, where you can play on the local, individual and classic themes. You are also likely to get the regular and consistent support of locals here, much more so than in big cities. However, while cities are a Mecca for the bigger brands, it does mean the independent can stand out in a world of bland mediocrity; and you can't deny the benefit of passing trade and tourists. Location is actually the most important thing when it comes to considering your coffee shop, with 63% of people saying they choose where to have their daily cuppa based on location, according to research group Allegra Strategies. There is more on location in Part 5, *Setting up shop* (see pages 200-202).

The taste of independence

Tom Hiskey runs the non-profit Cosy Coffee Shops blog (www.cosycoffeeshops.co.uk). He explains what he loves about independent coffee shops:

'I have nothing (much) against chains. But independent coffee houses are just . . . better! By and large, they offer great value. And not only are the drinks cheaper, they are usually finer quality (Starbucks customers: ever noticed you are drinking little more than flavoured milk?).

'As a nation, we're in the early stages of our coffee appreciation. But things are changing. And as our collective taste buds start to discern the notes of Arabica blends, more and more of us will fall in love with the skills of a proper barista, who, more often than not, would not be seen dead in a Starbucks or a Costa. The UK is making great strides, with good showings at the World Barista Championships, including a winner in 2007. And, to those of you who do not consider yourselves connoisseurs of the black stuff, at places like Leoni (Malton), Fernandez & Wells and Monmouth Coffee Company (London), believe me, you will really be able to tell the difference! I'm not a connoisseur, but the coffees I had there were smashing (and there are many more brilliant places across the country).

'Value and quality are big draws of the good independents. But the thing that will ensure my return is their charm. There is a place in York called Coffee Culture; the coffee's not great, but the rickety old building has been decked out something lovely, and the owners are as friendly as they come. It's unique and full of atmosphere, and one of the finest examples of why I'm passionate about independent coffee shops. So can independents succeed while Starbucks branches close? I believe they can. Chains are convenient but they do not garner loyalty and are overpriced. When our pennies are stretched, we're more likely to head for the revitalising, friendly atmosphere of a unique independent coffee shop.'

Allegra Strategies also notes that independents have a larger slice of the market than the chains, with a combined 38% share against Starbucks and Costa, who have only 24% each. But the research also shows that only 12% of consumers picked an independent as their establishment of choice. Are you up to the challenge of changing their minds and re-educating them that biggest isn't always best?

THE INDEPENDENT BRAND

While chains have the benefit of solid, and often global, branding, it's not to say that you can't create your own brand. Bettys Café Tea Rooms in Yorkshire is a renowned brand, synonymous with heritage and tradition, yet it remains exclusively in Yorkshire and has never opened a branch outside the county, despite numerous requests. The success of the tea shop is down to an insistence on staying true to the traditions of the original café, ensuring that the name 'Bettys' continues to represent the legacy of quality it has become so famous for.

TIP

While Bettys has had just short of 100 years to build up its brand, branding is something anyone can do, even with just one coffee or tea shop: all you need is a rigorous commitment to the standards you have set yourself and a key focal point to be remembered by.

Simon Robertson's coffee shop Leoni is all about quality and excellent coffee, and he has proved this by winning countless barista competitions. The Yumchaa tea shop in London has stayed true to its commitment to serving and selling only the best quality loose-leaf tea, and made a name for itself with its 'No Teabagging' policy and running a 'Free your Tea!' campaign. The Redroaster Coffee House in Brighton has maintained its unique market position by importing its own beans direct from the growers, roasting the coffee on site and selling it to customers and local restaurants and cafés. Far from refusing to share its excellent coffee with the competition, Redroaster has chosen to be remembered for its commitment to quality, over its need to beat the competition. The fact that a Starbucks has been operating on the same street for over a year with no dent in Redroaster's business is testament to how independents can offer a real alternative to the big chains.

If they can do it, so can you. Yes, as an independent coffee and tea shop owner, you will not have the financial clout and marketing genius of the chains, but you will offer the customer something very important: choice. And besides, everyone loves the underdog, so why not give them a run for their money? For more information on branding see Part 6 on marketing (page 256).

Things to remember:

- A tough financial climate is a challenge, but it can work positively for you, especially as consumers want to get more for their money, or some well-priced luxury.
- The coffee and tea industry is growing fast, despite the economic downturn, so if you pitch your coffee or tea shop right there is no reason why you can't be a part of that growth.
- As an independent you only have to answer to yourself and have the freedom to evolve your business as you want.
- Make sure you develop a strong and distinctive identity, as this is what will set you apart.

1.3 Your idea: is it any good?

You might already know what type of coffee or tea shop you want to open. Indeed, when you first stumbled on the idea of getting into the business, you were almost certainly thinking of running a certain type of establishment. Now is the time to analyse this idea thoroughly, and hone it down into a definite, tangible concept. In this chapter, we cover every aspect of your idea – from the concept, to your customer base and where you will be located. By the end of it, you should have a firm idea and be ready to write your business plan with the knowledge you have gained.

In this chapter we'll cover:

- Your big idea – unique selling points (USPs)
- The strength of your idea
- Identifying your customers
- Testing your concept
- Choosing a location
- Buying an existing business

YOUR BIG IDEA

What type of establishment do you imagine your coffee or tea shop to be? It may be as simple as wanting to run the type of coffee or tea shop you have always enjoyed drinking in – you may have been mentally taking notes for years as you visited other establishments. It may be that you have a passion for fresh leaf tea and want to specialise in top quality teas from around the world. Or it may represent an opportunity to spend your working day embracing a hobby, such as entertaining people, playing host or indulging in a passion for great brews and pastries. The more opportunistic and entrepreneurial among you will have spotted a trend or gap in the market for a certain type of coffee or tea shop. That said, you may simply be attracted by the lifestyle of running a coffee or tea shop, and with a serious lack of cafés serving great tea and coffee in your area, you are wanting to open one. But how do you decide what kind of place you want to open?

> **TIP**
> The kind of establishment you want will shape everything else you do from this point on so it's crucial you have a clear vision to follow from the outset.

Firstly, think about what it was about running a coffee shop that suddenly inspired you. When you imagined running a tea shop what image came to mind first? The way it looked, what you were doing, how much money you had, the smell of the coffee, the sound of customers talking, or something else more abstract? Don't over-think it or read too much into it at this stage, just go with your gut instinct.

Secondly, ask yourself some important questions:

- What kind of atmosphere do you want to create?
- What three words would you like people to use to describe your coffee or tea shop?
- What will you provide that will make them return?
- What colours will you associate with your coffee shop?
- What would be a perfect day in your coffee or tea shop?
- What one thing will they remember from your coffee shop?
- What does an average customer look like, dress like and what do they order?
- What will be your signature drink?
- What do customers see through your windows that entices them in?
- What does the competition fail to provide that you can?

At this stage these are just general questions so don't agonise over the answers, or worry about the 'how' for the moment – have fun with them, and be bold. Write down everything that comes to mind and then look at what you have written down: a theme will have started to emerge. It might be clear that relaxed friendly service is what you value the most, or that superior quality coffee in trendy surroundings is your passion. You might have focused less on drinks and food and more on a buzzy vibe and funky décor, or you may have imagined something homely and cosy with log fires and big sofas.

Whatever you have come up with is clearly what motivates you and it's crucial you don't lose sight of this vision; so spend some time with the idea, share it with friends and family and see what their reactions are. Do remember to hear their suggestions or comments.

TYPES OF DRINK AND FOOD

For most coffee shop owners, the types of beverage they intend to serve when dreaming up ideas for a new venture forms the basis of their concept. The whole business revolves around the type and origin of the coffee or tea on offer. For others, the idea stems more from the concept of the coffee or tea shop – a new approach to service, an entertaining accompaniment to the coffee or tea drinking experience, an unforgettable style of décor. If your big idea revolves more around the physical coffee shop than the coffee itself, you need to give special consideration to your menu choices from a very early stage as they won't come as naturally to you.

We will cover coffee and tea in greater detail in Part 3 and food in greater detail in Part 4. For the moment, make a list of every drink and snack you are considering, and then assess what on the list fits in with the concept of your coffee or tea shop.

- Is there enough selection?
- Ask your family and friends what they think.
- Would they like more variety or a simpler choice?
- What would they like to see alongside the various coffees and teas?
- What is their ideal coffee accompaniment?
- What can you offer that hasn't been done before?
- Visit other coffee shops at different times of the day: see what they are offering and what you would buy, and what their customers are buying.

The size of your coffee or tea and food menu is also crucial. Will you and your staff be able to commit to making the perfect coffee concoction for 15 different varieties? How will you cope if there is a large queue and 10 different orders? Freshly made-to-order sandwiches might sound like a nice idea, but the reality of making them during a busy lunch rush hour is completely different.

The important thing to remember here is that your drink and food offering should match with the identity you want to create. Do you aim to be an Italian coffee expert or a provider of good, honest loose leaf tea? Are you providing quick and healthy snacks for office workers, or homemade cakes for families and pensioners? See pages 138-140 for more on choosing the type of coffee, and pages 185–190 for ideas about matching food to your clientele.

FROM THE EXPERTS:
June Woods, Bettys Café Tea Rooms

Bettys is proud to be a self-sufficient business. All of its cakes, breads and chocolates – more than 300 specialities a day – are made at its craft bakery in Harrogate. It's a place where craftspeople rather than machines take centre stage.

WHAT CAN YOU OFFER?

TIP

Whatever you decide to offer, and you can start simply with just great coffee or tea and good service, it will form part of your identity and be something you are renowned for, so choose wisely and think carefully about it.

Of course you will offer tea, coffee and something to eat – whether it's the odd biscuit or a full scale lunch menu – but what else can you offer, and how can this tie in with your theme? What will make you unique? Here are some ideas for the different offerings you might consider:

- Crockery painting/arts and crafts (great for children's parties)
- An attached art gallery, promoting local artists
- Specialising in French cakes/patisserie
- Gourmet deli

- Florist
- Gift/tourist shop
- Retail items (either bags of coffee and tea, branded cups and mugs, or something else – the coffee chain Tchibo changes its goods every week)
- A bookshop
- Internet café
- Juice/shake bar
- Sandwich bar
- Chocolatier
- Outside catering business
- Speciality tea rooms
- Children's soft play area – great for grown ups!
- Selling antiques
- Making and selling wedding cakes
- French bistro
- Vegetarian food
- International themes – Italian, Cuban, Indian, Chinese, Dutch, etc

Remember these are just suggestions, you can offer whatever you want to, and the possibilities are endless! The key thing is that you have the freedom to offer a range of things that chains can't, and it is partly here that your unique selling point (USP) will lie.

IN MY EXPERIENCE:

Tim Hume, Redroaster Coffee House

For many indefinable reasons we have a genuine place in the local community, the main one being we are not a chain, so we have a closer, genuine relationship with our customers, many of whom are real supporters. Also, because we roast coffee on the premises the nature of the coffee house is different from the identikit chain outlets. Also, our coffee is better than theirs.

THE USP

Once you are clear on the kind of atmosphere you want to create – and it might well include some of the things we mentioned in the previous section – and the food and drink you are likely to serve, you need to start to identify your USPs, as these are the things that will ultimately define how your place is different from the competition and will slowly build its identity and brand. Write down some prompts that will help you keep the vision in mind – perhaps five words that describe your coffee or tea shop, some of the furniture you might want, the drinks you want to serve and the other things you want to offer.

TIP

Keep referring to your prompts, and think your idea through. And amend it if necessary – this is your vision, but it's also got to be a business, so it's likely to evolve as you learn more.

Suggestions for USPs

When drawing up your USPs, consider the following points to differentiate your offering:

- Superior customer service
- No frills
- A more niche or premium selection of coffee or tea
- Budget offering
- Child-friendly/family atmosphere
- Trendy/city slicker ambience
- Faster or quicker coffee experience
- Luxury coffee experience
- Exceptional food
- Combination of food and entertainment – pottery/florist/deli etc
- Retail focus – a deli, cake counter or coffee and tea goods (cups, mugs, teapots)
- Ethically sourced or environmentally friendly
- Focus on particular culture
- Focus on the arts, literary stuff or music

There are sure to be many USPs to differentiate your business. Don't try to add them for the sake of it, but ensure your business is clearly defined from what's already out there and that you have a firm idea of what makes your offering special.

IN MY EXPERIENCE:

Simon Robertson, Leoni

On table 3 a customer, an old gentleman, was drinking his coffee. As I walked past he gently grabbed my arm and said that he thought the coffee was very good. 'Thank you' I said. 'In fact,' continued the gentleman, 'it's the best coffee I have had since I was last in Italy.' Something about the way he said this provoked my question which was 'When were you last in Italy?' He replied 'I was stationed there during the war'. It was this conversation that to me is more significant and is more a statement on the success of my business than the money in the till. By getting the coffee right, the brief moment the gentleman spent in my shop evoked memories and took this man's thoughts back to wartime Italy. If more people purporting to sell good coffee understood this point then they would make sure the coffee they served was served to a better standard.

YOUR CUSTOMERS

TIP

Write down your three main USPs here, and keep referring back to them.

Picking the drinks you will serve, the food you will offer and the ambience you will provide is only half the challenge. Next you will need to explore exactly what your offering to a specific market will be, and most crucially who your market is. Without doing this you won't be able to properly plot the viability of your business in a business plan.

It's not enough to say you want to start an authentic Italian coffee house. Will you be catering for high-end customers or casual shoppers wanting a quick, cheap cuppa? Will you have a coffee bar, counter or table service – or a combination of all three? Is the emphasis on quality with a price tag to match; healthy, organic food for the ethically or eco-minded; or cheap and cheerful coffee for the masses?

Visit coffee and tea shops that are similar to the ones you want to open; think about what they offer and how they generate custom – why would you go in there? What kinds of people are in there and what are the general proportion doing and drinking in there? Who do they go with – are people alone, with family, friends, business associates or their partners?

Think about the reasons people visit coffee shops and why would they come to yours. Some people go to a coffee or tea shop for peace and quiet, some to work, some to read, some to meet friends, and some to escape bad weather or wait for the next bus. People might want to be in and out of the place quickly – perhaps 75% of the coffee in your coffee or tea shop will be takeaways. Or will your coffee or tea shop have a relaxed, gentle feeling – so that people would be in there for several hours, J K Rowling style, working on their next novel on a battered laptop balanced on their knee and a cup of hot chocolate to accompany them?

IN MY EXPERIENCE:
Shelagh Ryan, Lantana

Try to find a market where there are customers who have a need which is not being met by the current providers. Our customers are people who care about the quality of the food and coffee they eat and drink, and want an alternative to chain stores.

Proving there is a customer base

Unfortunately there are plenty of great sounding 'ideas' that simply aren't viable. Banks will expect to see evidence of an existing customer base and so should you if you are using your own money or, quite simply, you want the business to have a chance of working. To assess if your coffee or tea shop will succeed as a business, you will need to prove there are enough people in the area you are based who want to have a drink and snack out for the price you are serving it for. For some coffee or tea shops and cafés that are reliant on tourism, or affected by seasonal peaks and troughs, this can be a complicated process and will involve looking at visitor levels as well as regional populations; calculating varying incomes against monthly and annual overheads.

TIP

Don't fall for the mistake of convincing yourself that just because you love the idea, others will too. Too many people skip the process believing 'if you build it, they will come'. If the market's not there or customers can't afford your prices or if there is a longstanding popular place two doors down, they won't be coming.

Doing your groundwork

Before you can explore whether your customers exist in sufficient numbers you need to establish exactly who you are looking for. You can use standard demographic data on consumers to find this out.

Social grade	Social status	Occupation	Annual earnings estimate
A	Upper middle class	Higher managerial, administrative or professional	£50,000+
B	Middle class	Intermediate managerial, administrative or professional	£35,000–£50,000
C1	Lower middle class	Supervisory or clerical, junior managerial, administrative or professional	£25,000–£35,000
C2	Skilled working class	Skilled manual workers	£15,000–£25,000
D	Working class	Semi and unskilled manual workers	£7,000–£15,000
E	Those at lowest level of subsistence	State pensioners or widows (no other earner), casual or lowest grade workers	£5,000–£7,000

You essentially want to know what the profile of your target customer is: are they male or female? How old are they? What's their disposable income? What brands do they consume? How much would they spend with you and how frequently?

Use the table above to make an initial profile of your average customer – it might seem a bit staid and not in keeping with the bohemian ambience you are hoping to create – but if you don't do this you won't know if there is a business opportunity there, and you risk losing a lot of money.

Once you have established the socio-economic bracket your customers fall into, consider some of the things mentioned above:

- Why they might visit a coffee shop, and when?
- Will they come in once a week, or daily?
- Are they mainly tourists or locals?

- What do they spend their money on?
- What sort of values do they have?
- What things matter to them?
- Even consider what political party they might vote for, what newspapers they read etc.

Researching the customer market

Now you need to know if the people you want to come to your coffee or tea shop actually exist. Not only must they exist, they must exist where you can find and afford premises. One of the best places to start is by getting hold of a copy of your area's latest census, either online at www.ons.gov.uk/census or from your local library. Even better, get hold of censuses for several areas you could feasibly operate in so that you can make direct comparisons. Even if you are stuck on one location, having statistics proving its suitability can make a compelling case to the bank. A census will give you all sorts of information such as the population of the area; percentage of home ownership; percentage of people economically active (employed); the percentage of those retired. The good thing about a census is that it uses the same questions for all areas so it's easy to compare the results of one region to another. In addition, several websites provide regional demographic information, such as www.upmystreet.com.

IN MY EXPERIENCE:

Tim Hume, Redroaster Coffee House

The best thing would be to test your idea out by talking to people whose opinions you value. Don't talk to small business people as they are a doom-laden bunch. Independent traders with exciting businesses of their own are an exception and people in speciality coffee are generally an open bunch who will talk and offer advice all day.

Consult coffee and tea shop statistics released by the British Hospitality Association and similar groups to identify trends in the type of coffee or tea shop you are looking to start and look for breakdowns by region. Business Link and the British Library can also give you access to market reports and data that would cost you thousands of pounds to buy copies of.

Useful market research contacts

- British Coffee Association: www.britishcoffeeassociation.org
- British Sandwich Association: www.sandwich.org.uk
- British Hospitality Association: www.bha.org.uk
- Business Link: www.businesslink.gov.uk
- The British Library: www.bl.uk

Getting these results will put you in a much more informed position; ensure you take the time to analyse the information properly. Do some simple sums, working out how many people in the area fall into your ideal customer bracket, how likely they are to spend and how much they are likely to spend. Consider the other information you have found out, such as tourist numbers, passing traffic and seasonal issues, so you start to have an overall picture of the customer base for your coffee or tea shop and how it might change over the year. All of this will be vital for your business plan, which we cover in Chapter 2, but is also vital in helping you to understand whether you have enough customers in the area to support the kind of business you want to run.

DIY surveys versus research companies

It's essential to carry out your own research with the public as well. Take to the streets and carry out surveys and questionnaires which explore anything that can prove your case that a market for your coffee shop exists. Ask respondents how often they would buy a cup of coffee or treat themselves to a piece of cake with friends per month in a venue of your type and price, and how far they would be willing to come for food served with your USP. You shouldn't ask personal questions such as people's income or age; instead ask them to choose from ranges that will fit with the demographic research you have unearthed and have identified as your target customer. The more people you interview within these ranges, the more powerful your research will be.

DIY market research

Here are some questions to ask members of the public in your chosen location:

- How often do you buy a cup of coffee – hardly ever, once or twice a month, once or twice a week, more than twice a week?
- What's your coffee beverage of choice?
- How old are you – under 18, 18–24, 25–34, 35–50, 50+?
- What's your wage bracket – under £15,000, £15,000–£20,000, £20,000–£30,000, £30,000–£50,000, £50,000–£100,000, £100,000+?
- Do you usually visit a coffee or tea shop for relaxation, socialising, work, convenience, other?
- Would you welcome a coffee or tea shop here?
- What do you think a reasonable cost for a coffee/muffin is for a coffee shop/café in this area?
- What would you like to see in a coffee or tea shop that you haven't seen before?

There are professional research companies that you can hire to carry out feasibility studies. For most of you their services will be out of your price range and be wary of companies who claim to do this for comparatively low rates as it's likely they'll merely accumulate information already in the public domain – something you could do for yourself.

TIP

Know your market. Simply taking the time to get to know your area can be extremely helpful.

Well-carried-out professional research can prove worth the investment, however, especially if you are seeking substantial finance. If you pursue this route, be clear exactly what you are looking to achieve and perhaps even research what investors want first and find out how you can meet their expectations. However, be careful of how much you spend. While some investors will be impressed by

TIP

Try the Research Buyers Guide (www.rbg.org.uk) when looking for reputable sources for market research. The website has a fully searchable directory of market research providers.

professional research, others will question your business acumen if you have spent a considerable slice of your start-up capital just to prove a market exists.

Coffee in our hearts

'We've fallen in love with the whole scene, with arranging to meet "for coffee", with the frisson of delight we get on discovering that the prime-position sofa space in our absolute fave coffee outlet is gloriously unoccupied. We've fallen in love with solitary lattes, 20 minutes alone in a caff, with a coffee and a book, interludes that have gained an almost spiritual quality in our (caffeine-frazzled) brains. We've fallen in love with coffee as a vice; people tell us to give it up, and we drink more.'

Polly Vernon, Journalist, *Guardian*

THE COMPETITION

Considering the competition is of course the next step. You might have a large number of potential customers, according to your research, but if their needs are already being catered to, then are they really potential customers?

Competition tends to come in two forms:

- Directly from other coffee or tea shops in your area
- Indirectly from other ways customers can spend the money they would otherwise spend with you.

Direct competition

The chains

Chains are often seen as your biggest competition, so you should spend some time researching what's about in your area, and how you can compete with them for customers, or, crucially, offer something different. Spend some time in the chains, looking at who's in there, go back often over the course of week and see if there are numerous regulars or just people popping in on a one off. Also make sure you take notice of some of the following:

- What food and drink do they offer? And what are their bestsellers?
- How fresh is everything, including their coffee and tea?
- Is the food homemade or delivered every morning from somewhere else?
- How long is the wait for a coffee?
- How many people take away, and how many eat in? If they eat in, how long do they sit there?
- What is the décor like, how new does it look?
- What are their opening hours, and what are their busiest times?
- And most important – how many of your ideal, average target market do you see in the coffee or tea shop on a daily basis? What are they buying?

While doing this bear in mind the kind of coffee or tea shop, customers, food and drink you have envisaged so you can see if this is being offered anywhere else. It's also vital to think about how you can either appeal to a different market, or offer something more special than that which the chains are offering.

TIP

It's important to acknowledge that the chains do have a certain power – money, marketing budget and branding – so trying to compete at their level won't work; you have to offer something that they don't.

FROM THE EXPERTS:
Sahar Hashemi, Coffee Republic

I just got on with my own idea and my own vision. I think it would be very daunting if one did say 'Oh, I'm up against the big boys' because you would never do anything. So I just focus on what I can focus on. Starbucks were strong competitors with more might than us – so what happened was what would in any market environment.

Independents

While having a chain up the road from your coffee shop presents a challenge of some sort, it is likely the coffee or tea shop you want to run will offer all the things they can't: personality, quality, character, service, and individuality. But if your big competition is not a chain, but another independent, how should you approach this? The key is to research, research, research. Just as with the chains above, visit the independent and consider how much of what you would like to offer they already do. Ask yourself the key questions above, and be honest with your answers. However, there is some good news: although another independent could mean you have to think carefully about whether this is viable as a business, a successful café or coffee or tea shop in an area could also suggest there is room for another, especially if customers are frustrated at not being able to get a table in the only good place in the area.

Bringing it all together

Crucially, you should cross-reference the number of competitors in your area, and their USPs, with your demographic data to establish if there is room for another business. It could be that on reflection you identify a new USP that would give you a better chance of securing market share, and that's perfectly healthy. Competitors should also provide a way of benchmarking your proposition and pricing. Visit them, take in the experience, where possible speak to customers to get a feel for their reputation and try to identify as many places as possible where you can score an advantage.

> **TIP**
>
> If you are feeling especially brave, go and speak to the owners. Be honest and say you are thinking of starting a coffee or tea shop in the area, and ask them for tips and advice. You will find many are surprisingly helpful and even with the ones that aren't, you won't be any worse off, and you will know more about the kind of people you are up against.

Indirect competition

While you research the chains and other coffee shops and ensure there is space for you as well, it's harder to predict how something such as a recession will affect you. As we've suggested earlier, you may find that when the economy is tough, people may prefer to pop out for a coffee rather than a full meal at a restaurant; so in a perverse way, tough economic times could work in your favour.

The key point is to ensure that what you offer has a pulling power that will last the distance, and this can only be achieved by both researching and analysing the competition beforehand, and then being adaptable to change once you are open.

FROM THE EXPERTS:
Henry Rungan, Coffee Republic

Coffee is a kind of addiction. If you have the flair and passion in doing your job, and manage to prepare the way the people like their coffee then that customer will be a loyal one and will not go anywhere else and your business is safe no matter how many competitors you have.

HOW TO TEST YOUR CONCEPT

Take every opportunity you can to test your concept. It's likely you will still be tweaking it a year into opening, but by then you will have all the overheads, time constraints and running responsibilities to deal with, so take every chance you get while researching and starting-up to test, test and then test again. To test if people like what you have to offer, give some away in exchange for honest feedback – and that doesn't mean to friends and family whose opinion is always biased no matter how much they insist they are being truthful. For any concept testing you do, make sure you record the results. It's all good for tweaking your model and also compelling evidence to use in your business plan and when pitching for finance or even for PR (public relations).

CHOOSING THE RIGHT LOCATION

IN MY EXPERIENCE:
Tim Hume, Redroaster Coffee House

Right location? The three basics are: footfall, footfall and footfall.

Location, as everyone says, is paramount. And it could play a key part in the type of coffee or tea shop you have, how you deal with the competition and what sort of prices you can set, so make sure you think about this very carefully from the beginning. Choosing a location isn't just about picking an area to set up your coffee or tea shop in. You need to consider everything from whether you will be located on a high street or in a shopping centre, right down to the side of the road you are positioned on.

By now you should have proved that there is a significant volume of customers in the town, city or village you are looking to open your shop in, but that's only half the battle. Unfortunately, even a great coffee bar with fantastic food at a great price won't guarantee sufficient visitors unless you find a location that makes it convenient to get people through the doors.

The local council might be able to provide local footfall figures, detailing walk-through populations by street. Market research companies will also sell you this, but it is something you can usually measure yourself. If you do so, be careful to take samples at different times of the day taking into account traditional periods of influential activity such as rush hours, lunch times, after pub closing, etc.

TIP

It's worth speaking to your local council or regional development agency to see if there are any incentives, grants or tax breaks for opening in a certain area – or even relocating to a different city. It might not be what you had planned, but free rent and a support grant could make all the difference to your business's survival.

While circumstances such as where you currently live or that a certain location may have been the inspiration for your coffee or tea shop in the first place, may mean you know where you want to set up, it's important to consider the pros and cons of different locations so that you are prepared for what's ahead.

Rural areas, suburbs and small towns

With so many of the chains choosing to locate in the big cities, one of the main advantages of independents is success in more rural areas, including suburbs, villages and towns. Scenic locations, a solid tourist trade, loyal regulars and access to high quality local produce means independent local coffee shops, such as Royal Teas and Bettys have thrived. They also have a certain exclusive feel to them, and aren't inundated with passing traffic so the people who tend to visit them know what they are expecting.

IN MY EXPERIENCE:

Raymond Voce, Royal Teas

We at Royal Teas rely primarily on the local community for custom. Repeat trade is fundamental to our existence. Although after a very lovely write up in *The Times* recently we were inundated with 'outsiders'. We were almost a destination café for a while. Is it bad if you are tucked away? I think not. People like to think they have discovered you. You need to be good if you want them to return though.

It's also important to consider what kind of offerings you might have that would fit with the area you are in – quiet, local areas are popular for quite traditional tea shops, for instance, where the busy, aggressive nature of some trendy coffee shops doesn't sit so well. However, upmarket rural or seaside locations, often known as Chelsea-on-Sea, for instance, equally need to rise to meet the weekender trade from London.

There are challenges though, as Raymond Voce points out – you have to be that good so people return, as you can't depend on passing traffic to make up for your mistakes with previous customers. And if this is the case for your location then a commitment to consistently excellent service and really good coffee or tea is paramount.

Urban areas

Often seen as the more challenging place to be, especially as it's a common domain for most big chains, an urban location can, however, reap all sorts of rewards. We've already covered for instance, how having a chain in the same area doesn't necessarily provide just competition, but can actually serve to highlight everything that is independent, unique and special about what you have to offer.

There are a number of other benefits too. Certain areas, or boroughs in big cities, have their own personalities, which your coffee or tea shop might not only fit in with but be able to assert its identity through. In London, for instance, if you are wanting to run something with a boutique, upmarket theme, you would fit in perfectly in some of the richer celebrity haunts, such as Chelsea and Primrose Hill; or if you are going with a more relaxed, wholesome vibe, you might look at some of the more bohemian areas such as Stoke Newington and Camberwell. Equally, as Shelagh Ryan at Lantana explains, having a theme that appeals to a certain demographic living in the city - Aussie, European, Russian, Caribbean, etc - provides a loyal trade, and with the added bonus of numerous tourists passing your door regularly, an urban location can provide the combination of regular and new business that you need to survive.

Of course it's often more expensive to find property in a busy urban location, and your customers will be surrounded by other options, so the pressure to stand out is pretty high. And you will certainly have to put some legwork into PR and getting a name for yourself.

Specific location issues

It makes sense to think about the more specific factors concerning location: what's near you, how it might or might not fit into your vision - certain locations attract different kinds of people and will you be offering what they need?

For instance:

- Are you near a school, will parents come in for a coffee around 2.45pm while waiting to pick up their kids - will you be able to manage the rush and will there be enough seats for them?
- Are you near the beach - can you provide a relaxed ambience, with a laid back dress code so bare feet and bikinis aren't frowned upon? Will you mind people traipsing sand through your coffee shop?
- Are you near a university, can you offer free refills and use of the internet? Do you want traditionally frugal students to be your main customers?
- Are you near a hospital - do some of your customers need a supportive, quiet environment to escape to and can you realistically provide this if you are planning live music and laid back service?
- Are you near a park - are you happy for your clientele to bring dogs, or is there somewhere safe for them outside? And will you have enough space to fit buggies and prams in your coffee or tea shop?
- Are you near a large building site - can you create a space where builders feel able to come in for a quick cuppa, in dirty, paint covered overalls? Equally, will this be noisy and distracting for customers? What happens when the building work is finished?

- Are you near a train station – do your customers need quick, efficient service, and an easily visible clock? Are you prepared for the fact that at least half your custom won't be from the local area and things such as bad weather and bank holidays, which reduce the train service, could affect your business?
- Are you near a big commercial complex – will you be catering for business people, their clients and secretaries? Do they need table service and a professional, efficient atmosphere? Will you have to provide free WiFi and power points as standard to ensure you are up to the competition?

BUYING AN EXISTING BUSINESS

You don't have to start from scratch and coffee bars are one of the most popular businesses to buy. There are many reasons to buy instead of setting up. As well as premises, you will be acquiring a ready-made proposition and customer base. It'll certainly take less time than starting up yourself and if you buy a healthy, profitable business it'll almost certainly be cheaper too as it's more likely to survive than a new business. The challenge is finding a business to buy that is 'healthy and profitable' and doesn't just have the potential to be, or worse still, has no chance of fulfilling its potential. What you won't ever see is a sales blurb telling you this. It'll be up to you to distinguish what's worth buying and what's not and it's a notorious minefield. Again, resources such as the British Coffee Association are useful, as are the websites www.businessesforsale.com and www.rightbiz.co.uk, which at last check had over 300 and 222 tea and coffee shops for sale, respectively.

Do your research

Make sure you speak to people. Ideally, you will want to speak to the sellers. If you are buying directly, this won't be a problem but be wary of sellers who are reluctant to divulge too much information or open up the books; you can be sure there is a reason why. Be careful too if you are buying through an agency that is reluctant for you to speak to the seller directly. A good seller will be open about their reasons for selling, although it's fair to assume someone will be more forthcoming about wanting to retire or move away than dwindling sales, but you should be able to see this from their books.

Speaking to the owners will also help you establish if it's worth paying for 'goodwill', where you pay a premium in exchange for existing client contacts and customer information and the reputation the place has built up within the community. Speak to customers (if the sellers are happy for you to do this, it's a good sign); customers visiting competitors (ask them why they are not shopping at the place you are looking to buy and what would make them change their mind); and chat to suppliers to establish how relationships have been left and to suss out any bad debts. Make sure you speak to staff as well. If you take over, you will be expected to honour their contracts under the Transfer of Undertakings (TUPE) regulations, but just as importantly, they will know the business better than you will. Keeping them on board, at least until you have found your feet, is likely to make sense and be good for continuity.

TIP

Get an accountant involved. They'll be able to check the books for anything of concern or unscrupulous and will also advise you on the most tax efficient way to structure the purchase.

Once you have made a purchase, it's likely you will still want to stamp your authority on the business. Certainly you will need to be just as clear in your offering as if you were starting from fresh. The rest of this book is about starting a coffee or tea shop from scratch, but all the principles are just as relevant to the first-time entrepreneur who's acquired a business as they are to someone starting out on their own.

Things to remember:

- Identify a USP from the very beginning and keep true to it.
- Carry out thorough research of the market and your potential customers.
- Know your competition inside out, and be clear about how you can go up against them.
- Be rigorous about your location and how your business will fit in.
- Don't rule out the possibility of buying and adding to an existing business.

1.4 Deciding your identity

Creating your business identity should be one of the most enjoyable and exciting challenges when starting your coffee shop. It's probably something you have already given a great amount of thought to – this is a good start as it will form a major chunk of your start-up planning. The key thing is to make sure you take the time to develop a brand that you are excited by and an identity that ties in with what you want to offer. Your brand and identity will form the basis of everything you do, including logos, how you market yourself, and how you stand out from the competition, so it's a very important process.

In this chapter we'll cover:

- Establishing your identity
- Logos and themes
- Coffee or tea shop internal design
- Business names
- Branding

WHAT IS YOUR IDENTITY?

No doubt you had a vision when you first embarked on this journey, of standing in the middle of a buzzing room watching your baristas serving a lengthy queue of passionate coffee drinkers who can't get enough of your accompanying home-made confections. It will be that image that forms the basis of your coffee shop's identity and makes it different from everyone else.

Your identity isn't just about the type of coffee or tea you serve (although to real aficionados, it will play a big part), it's about creating a location, environment and overall experience that pulls in customers and encourages them to spend again. And again. And again.

FROM THE EXPERTS:
June Woods, Bettys Café Tea Rooms

For over 80 years we have remained true to the principles of our founder, Frederick Belmont, that everything should be 'fresh and dainty' and that if we want things just right, we have to do them ourselves. Bettys has retained its unique combination of Yorkshire hospitality and Swiss attention to detail.

Your core values

Keep going back to those unique selling points (USPs, pages 45-46): other than the quality of coffee or tea it serves, what is your coffee or tea shop? What will it look and feel like? If it's upmarket premium coffee you are serving to a customer with a high disposable income, then the identity – from logo to location, price to coffee cup arrangements – should reflect that. In turn, if you serve ethically sourced food and drinks, you will want that to be a part of all that you do. Many businesses talk about core values that reflect their business's identity as a reminder to themselves and staff. It can certainly pay to constantly revisit your values to ask: is this what we're about? Are we sticking to our USPs? Are we doing what we set out to do?

Food for thought

'Many independent coffee shops criticise the big branded chains precisely because they feel they are responsible for creating a lifestyle brand of coffee drinking at the expense of quality, ethical and environmental considerations and fair pricings. It is understandable that people might want to be part of this based on the fact that it is clearly popular and therefore must be profitable. This approach to business can overlook certain key factors; the most important factor being overlooked is the product itself. This business plan is based more on 'good profit selling a product' than 'selling good product with profit'.'

Simon Robertson, Leoni

Choosing a name

This can actually be more difficult than it seems. Owning a place with your name above the door may have been part of your dream from day one or the name could have been core to the vision. If not, you might agonise over it, then kick yourself for wasting time over something that will eventually seem so obvious. Think of your favourite coffee bar, and in almost every instance, the name is the very last consideration and least important factor in your conscious decision for liking it. Sahar and Bobby Hashemi knew they wanted the company name to encapsulate the entire coffee experience; after several attempts, including Java Express, they finally decided on Coffee Republic.

Business names are how we all identify and refer to those establishments, and it's often what we remember most. And while some names bear little significance to anything, the smartest names undoubtedly form part of the branding and identity that pulls us in. That said, it's essentially what you offer, for what price and how good your coffee service is, that will determine whether people like your establishment or not.

A good name will:

- Draw attention and attract people through the door
- Communicate a clear message about your coffee shop's identity
- Lend itself well to PR (public relations) and set you aside from the competition

A poor one will hinder all of the above. These are the basic principles you should work on when planning a name.

IN MY EXPERIENCE:

Raymond Voce, Royal Teas

If I was to start from scratch, the name would need to symbolise what the café was all about. No mean feat. Previously, I have helped in naming a few new enterprises and nothing beats making a shortlist and getting a variety of people to comment. Their comments can be quite revealing, seeing things from quite a different perspective than yours.

Regional names can work if you don't have aspirations of expanding or relocating. Locals might consider they are supporting a town's trade if you carry its name. If you are serving dishes in an area renowned for its produce, it also makes sense to take advantage of that reputation.

Legal rules

If you decide to incorporate your business you need to make sure you pick a name nobody else has. If you run your business as a sole trader this is not as much of an issue but you still need to be aware of the legal implications of choosing an offensive moniker, or one with certain banned words. Read Chapter 2.3 (*Registering your business*, page 101) for more on the legal aspects of choosing a name.

Some ideas for names

Coffee/tea-specific

Something to do with coffee or tea is always a good idea and can work well:

- The Bean Counter
- Coffee Express
- Time for Tea
- Tea for You/Tea for Two
- The Teapot
- Flat White

- Mocha
- The Coffee Spoon
- Earl Grey

Straightforward

Perhaps you want to be clear about what you are, or name it after yourself, your location or a local landmark, or make a play on words, e.g.

- Central Perk
- The River Coffee Shop
- Parkside Tea Rooms
- Carla's Coffee
- Preston Café

Abstract and quirky

The name doesn't even have to have anything to do with coffee or tea, but can be something that conjures up an image you feel represents your café, such as Leoni and Lantana, or uses a few words from a famous quote, or is named after a character or book, e.g. Starbucks.

- Pearl
- Flavour
- Sweet Offering
- Repose
- Sweet as Love
- Amour

Making it web-friendly

You will also need to think about web presence when considering the suitability of a name. It's so easy and cheap to get a website to publicise your business nowadays that you would be wise to consider it as essential. When thinking about names that will work on the internet, think 'search'. Nine-tenths of visitors to all websites arrive at them via a search engine (e.g. Google). Some names work well for a coffee or tea shop, but will have a different impact on a search. Regional names will allow locals to find your website when they search with location included. However, it can also work against you. If you are called Camberwell Cappuccino, you are sure to appear in a 'Camberwell + Cappuccino' search but will you get lost among all the other results? Here, a unique name could work to ensure you appear, get seen and people can also find you when they type in your name. If you like the idea of 'Cambridge Cappuccino' or similar – why not blend it – Cambuccino – no one else will have that!

> **TIP**
> Possibly the best and most fun way to come up with your business name is around a table with friends, and several bottles of wine!

Artistic theme and logos

Think through the identity and atmosphere of your coffee or tea shop before you commit time or funds to a logo or an artistic theme. Your logo is one way people will remember you and it's certainly how many of your customers will form their first impression. Images and colours are powerful methods of communicating messages and you want to think carefully about the logo that should emblazon your shopfront, signage, coffee or tea cups, napkins, bills, receipts, advertising, PR, company brochures and uniforms. Don't waste money on a brand research group. It's often just a case of finding a logo which simply and clearly radiates your business identity. Play around with words, colours, shapes, images and pictures; invite friends to submit their own ideas, especially if they are naturally creative; share a selection of the results with people around you; and have a relaxed meeting with friends and family to get an honest discussion of what works and what doesn't.

If you commission a designer to help you, then the fuller the brief you can write about what your coffee or tea shop is all about and who your customers are, the better for the results you will see.

> **TIP**
> Give a designer a 'look book' of logos you like and don't like.

A logo created by a freelance designer or small design company might give you the independent edginess that makes you stand out. You may have no option but to pursue this route, mostly because of cost implications.

IN MY EXPERIENCE:

Shelagh Ryan, Lantana

We tried to develop the branding and logo to be consistent with our concept –individual, quirky, simple, quality.

Another option is to ask local design colleges or students to submit entries, offering them a prize or a free coffee for a week once you are open; plus they may be grateful to get the experience and kudos of designing a genuine logo. A number of websites feature budding, freelance or small design companies, where you can pitch such competitions or request enquiries (www.logosauce.com is probably the best). Just post your brief (remember to be as detailed as possible), set a deadline, then wait for 'bidders' to upload their best efforts and contact the ones you like.

TIP

Having a number of designs to choose from certainly helps you decide what works well, so even if you decide to give the project to one person or company ask them to give you at least a couple of options and colour schemes. You are likely to favour one and then ask to see several variations of that until you are happy.

Logos should work well in a number of sizes; whether it applies to you or not, think postage stamp and billboard. They should work well online as well as offline, and on a larger scale if you are planning a future coffee or tea shop chain.

Making artistic themes work

Remember: there is no such thing as good or bad taste. Not everyone will share your personal idea of fantastic design. This isn't your house you are choosing a theme for, it's your coffee or tea shop. While it might be 'yours', its success will be dependent on others wanting to eat there, so remember, niches are niches for a reason. Instead, design for the broadest possible range of people you are looking to serve.

Do your research: get out and look at how your competition style their identity and visit other coffee and tea shops to see what they get right. Also force yourself to study a successful coffee or tea shop whose identity doesn't particularly appeal to you and consider what it is that makes it work for its customers. As a rule though, create a detailed brief, get a number of designs to choose from and go with what works best for your customers, not you.

Shop design

We'll cover design in more detail in *Décor and Furniture* (page 215) but it is important you have an idea of what you want for your coffee or tea shop during the planning stage. Everything from the colour of your walls to the style of furniture you pick to whether you decide to feature local art will have an effect on the overall mood and ambience of your coffee or tea shop, and form a big chunk of its identity.

TIP

Think about the kind of noise level you want in your coffee shop as this will heavily influence your design. Carpets and soft furnishings absorb sound, giving a more quiet and relaxed atmosphere. However, they are harder to keep clean. Bare tables and chairs create more of a buzzy atmosphere, which might be what you are after.

Give careful consideration to the little details that can also add to your identity and brand, for example:

- How bright should your coffee shop be? Do you want softer and darker lighting for a more romantic feel or bright lights for a lively atmosphere?
- What will your food and coffee be served on and in? Traditional white mugs, oversized cappuccino bowls, unusually shaped cups or branded china?
- Will your baristas wear a uniform? Will this include your own branding?
- How much will you charge? We've focused on price strategy in planning, but it's not just about breaking even. Your price says a lot about your identity too. Are you cheap and cheerful or posh with a price tag?

BRANDING

Branding differs from identity as it focuses more on what people think of your business and what it stands for. Whether you like it or not, people will form opinions of your coffee or tea shop from the minute it opens: on what it looks like, the quality and range of coffee it serves, the attitude and turnout of you and your staff. They will assign it, consciously or not, among the other brands they are exposed to.

TIP

The things you wrote down about your shop will be a useful reference document to refer back to when making buying decisions and will help form marketing decisions and, eventually, a fuller branding strategy.

Branding for you, as a start-up coffee or tea shop owner, shouldn't be a massive pre-occupation but as it's closely aligned to identity, and your overall sales story, it's a very worthwhile exercise to refer back for guidance to that original USP and the list of words you would like others to describe you with.

Thinking ahead

How much you care about branding is likely to be dependent on how much you intend to grow your business. If your sole ambition is to open one site and make a nice living from it, you probably don't need to think too much about building a brand, as simply maintaining your reputation in your local community should suffice. However, if your intentions are to one day establish a chain, branding needs to be at the forefront of your thinking. Either way, returning customers will be crucial so you should be considering how people think about your business, and that means more than just the physical site. It's the way you treat customers and how you communicate in your advertising or marketing.

FROM THE EXPERTS:
Bettys Café Tea Rooms

By doing things ourselves, we can ensure that everything is of the highest quality – so we keep everything in-house, from design, to marketing and PR. All of our wrapping, labels, boxes and literature is designed in-house to complement the products within. Our smart, traditional uniforms and the décor of our branches is, again, all designed to reflect the quality of our brand.

Things to remember:

- Remember that identity must go hand-in-hand with every aspect of your planning, from décor to coffee price.
- The name should ultimately represent the ethos and USPs you came up with at the beginning of this process.
- Keep your branding as consistent as possible.
- Don't agonise over your coffee shop's name but do give it careful consideration.

CHECKLIST

☑
☐
☐
☐
☐

> “Drink your tea slowly and reverently, as if it is the axis on which the world revolves – slowly, evenly, without rushing toward the future.”
>
> Thich Nat Hahn

> “I have measured out my life with coffee spoons.”
>
> T.S. Eliot

2

Realities and legalities

2.1 Creating your business plan

We've put business plans first in this part of the book because it's essential that you perfect your business plan *before* you start pitching for investment and looking for premises. Your business plan needs to outline how your coffee or tea shop is going to be financially viable, how you plan to grow it, and include an accurate assessment of what you will need to spend to get it off the ground, with extra budget built in for 'just in case' contingencies.

In this chapter we'll cover:

- Writing your business plan
- Setting prices and budgeting
- Revenue forecasts
- Financial sheets

YOUR BUSINESS PLAN

Why you should have one

Don't panic and don't be put off by the thought of writing a business plan. It's not difficult and the actual process of writing the business plan for your coffee or tea shop should further feed your enthusiasm for your venture. Why? Because by the end of the process you should feel you are able to transcend from idea to an actual establishment. What's more, you need to have a document for others, especially the banks, to believe in you too.

Before you start putting a plan together, try to get hold of some examples from the internet or even ask your bank what kind of document it expects to see. You could even ask your own favourite coffee or tea shop if you could look at theirs. Don't worry too much about the design and layout of a business plan at this stage. Much like CVs, people often obsess unnecessarily about the supposed best format, structure, length and layout when what's far more important is that the document contains all the necessary information and is easy to understand.

TIP

A good business plan will give you something to constantly refer back to when making tough decisions and strategy calls; it should be a working document you update as the business progresses.

What to include in your business plan

Start by identifying and gathering the basic information you will need. Ask yourself the following questions: How are you going to develop your business? What timescales are you looking at? Who is going to be involved, and in what capacity? How are you intending to manage the money?

A standard business plan should outline the following:

- Who you are and why you are going into business
- What your coffee or tea shop will do
- Why you believe you have got the skills and expertise to run a coffee or tea shop; your qualifications and experience
- Who your customers will be
- Why people will drink in your coffee or tea shop

- Evidence that the market exists and its potential
- Evidence of why your business will survive when others haven't
- Analysis of the competition
- Details of any other directors or key management roles
- How you will fund the setting up of the business
- How you will repay any money you borrow
- What your ongoing costs and overheads will be
- Sales and revenue forecasts for the first 12 months of business
- Details of suppliers and contracts
- Your goals for the first 12 months and then beyond

Your business plan should present a watertight argument of why and how your coffee shop will work. If it doesn't, then you should be asking yourself why and if it's still such a great idea.

Keep the plan simple and don't write reams – an overly long and wordy plan will irritate more than it impresses, and investors will be far more concerned with being able to access concise key information than they will with your writing skills or the quality of the paper. Where appropriate use bullet points and break up the text as bite-size chunks of information are far easier to absorb. Don't leave anything out, but keep it brief; people can always contact you if they need to know more.

> **TIP**
> Use your business plan to prove to yourself that your venture can survive and prosper, not just as a tool for accessing finance.

Getting started

However unique your business idea, there will be companies elsewhere doing something similar and undertaking some market research on these will help you understand your target market a little better. Companies have been classified into various categories by the UK government under the Standard Industrial Classification (SIC) system. Start by identifying your particular class and identifying your SIC code. This will then help you search for data on your competitors and other industry participants. Then, seek some data from sources such as Cobweb (www.cobwebinfo.com), which produces various business profiles. This will enable you to obtain an external perspective on the characteristics of similar shops and cafés, chains and independents.

IN MY EXPERIENCE:

Tim Hume, Redroaster Coffee House

In the real world there is a lot of instinct involved in evaluating the market. Obviously there has to be a considerable volume of potential customers available but you will never know if you have the right concept until you do it.

Assessing demand levels

One of the most difficult things to predict is the level of demand for your products or services. The general rule is to use conservative estimates on likely demand and to use proxies where data are hard to come by. One should also use proxies to help even when the idea is innovative or unique, rather than plucking figures from the air, or claiming there are no comparative figures available.

Sales projections

Sales grow slowly at first, but then shoot up boldly with huge growth rates, as soon as 'something' happens. Have projections that are conservative so you can defend them. When in doubt, be less optimistic. Be honest and don't exaggerate revenues and underplay overheads in order to make the plan work. Bank managers will have seen thousands of applications in their time and will see straight through it, and, of course, you will be kidding yourself and invalidating your business plan as a useful document. If anything, veer on the side of caution.

TIP

Bobby and Sahar Hashemi were turned down by 22 high street banks before they secured a £100,000 loan that was backed by the DTI Small Firms Loan Guarantee Scheme.

Many entrepreneurs have said, with the benefit of hindsight, when planning a business you should halve the income you anticipate and double the expenses you expect to pay – any discrepancy in your favour will be a bonus. Others insist they would never have secured the funding they needed without a few white lies and that whatever you ask for, the bank will give you 20% less. Ultimately it's your call, but remember: your business plan should plot your progress and adjusting it for any purpose limits how much it can help you.

TIP

Your business plan should plot your progress so be realistic about anticipated levels of profit – you need to strike a balance between what you know you can achieve and what will sway investors in your favour.

What to avoid: Cash not profits

How often have you heard small business owners saying they simply haven't got time to plan? The reality is, probably all too often – many businesses draw up a business plan only when they need it for a specific reason, such as to raise finance. But the busier you are, the more you need to plan.

Most people think in terms of profits instead of cash. When you imagine a new business, you think of what it would cost to make the product, what you could sell it for, and what the profit per unit might be. We are trained to think of business as sales minus costs and expenses, which equal profits. Unfortunately, we don't spend the profits in a business. We spend cash. So understanding 'cashflow' is critical. If you have only one table in your business plan, make it the cashflow table (see page 338).

TIP

If you are taking over a pre-existing coffee or tea business or franchise, you will have the benefit of a financial history with which to approach any bank for further funding should you require it.

Inflating your ideas

Don't overestimate the importance of the idea. You don't need a great idea to start a business; you need time, money, perseverance, and common sense. Few successful businesses are based entirely on new ideas. A new idea is harder to sell than an existing one, because people don't understand a new idea and they are often unsure if it will work. Plans don't sell new business ideas to investors, people do. Investors invest in people, not ideas. The plan, though necessary, is only a way to present information.

Leave out the vague and the meaningless business phrases (such as 'being the best') because they are simply hype. Remember that the objective of a plan is to secure results, and for results, you need tracking and follow up. You need specific dates, management responsibilities, budgets and milestones. Then you can follow up. No matter how well thought out or brilliantly presented, your business plan means nothing unless it produces results.

Using your business plan

Tailor your plan to its real business purpose. Business plans can be different things: they are often just sales documents to sell an idea for a new business, but they can also be detailed action plans, financial plans, marketing plans, and even personnel plans. They can be used to start a business, or just run a business better. In all these different varieties of business plan, the plan matches your specific situation. For example, if you are developing a plan for internal use only, not for sending out to banks or investors, you may not need to include all the background details that you already know. Description of the management team is very important for investors, whereas financial history is most important for banks.

DIFFERENT TYPES OF BUSINESS PLAN

Start-up plan

The most standard business plan is a **start-up plan**, which defines the steps involved in setting up and running a new business. It covers standard topics including the company, product or service, market, forecasts, strategy, implementation milestones, management team, and financial analysis. The financial analysis includes projected sales, profit and loss sheets, balance sheets and cashflow forecasts. The plan starts with an executive summary (a summary of the highlights of your business plan) and ends with appendices showing monthly projections for the first year.

Feasibility plan

A feasibility plan is a very simple start-up plan that includes a summary, mission statement, keys to success, basic market analysis, and preliminary analysis of costs, pricing, and probable expenses. This kind of plan is good for deciding whether or not to proceed with a plan, to tell if there is a business worth pursuing.

Internal plans

Internal plans are not intended for outside investors, banks, or other third parties. They might not include a detailed description of the company or the management team. They may or may not include detailed financial projections that become forecasts and budgets. They may cover main points as bullet points in slides (such as PowerPoint slides) rather than detailed paragraphs.

Operations plan

An operations plan is usually an internal plan, and it might also be called an internal plan or an annual plan. It would normally be more detailed on specific implementation milestones, dates, deadlines, and responsibilities of teams and managers.

Strategic plan

A strategic plan is usually also an internal plan, but it focuses more on high-level options and setting main priorities than on detailed dates and specific responsibilities. Like most internal plans, it wouldn't include descriptions of the company or the management team. It might also leave out some of the detailed financial projections. It might be more in the form of bullet points and slides than paragraph text.

Growth and expansion plans

A growth plan or expansion plan, or new product plan, will sometimes focus on a specific area of business, or a subset of the business. These plans may or may not be internal plans, depending on whether they are being linked to loan applications or new investment. For example, an expansion plan requiring new investment would include a full company description and background information on the management team, as much as a start-up plan for investors. Loan applications will require this much detail as well. However, an internal plan used to set the steps for growth or expansion funded internally might skip these descriptions. It might not include detailed financial projections for the whole company, but it should at least include detailed forecasts of sales and expenses for the company.

BUDGETING FOR THE YEAR

Predicting figures for the first year of your business when you are just off the starting blocks might seem a little premature, but when you are working out your costs, it's essential that you plan for the first 12 months – not just your start-up costs but overheads too. To make this more manageable, break these down into one month, six months and then first-year budgets. This will help you to plan your business finances, assessing areas such as how much money you have and how much revenue you need to generate your target profit. Budgeting will also be a good measure of whether your business plan is along the right path, or whether it needs adjusting.

TIP

As well as estimating sales figures, it's essential to work out and keep track of how much you are spending, in order to build up a full picture of your budget.

Setting your prices

Before you can plan anything – make any forecasts, plot any projections or arrive at a principal sum you will need to borrow to start your coffee or tea shop – you need to think about how much money you can make from the food and beverages you intend to serve. We'll cover pricing strategies compared with the chains in more detail in Part 3 (*The beverage essentials*, page 178), but it's good to have a clear idea of how your pricing will work during the planning stages, so you can see whether your idea is viable at all.

IN MY EXPERIENCE:

Simon Robertson, Leoni

Pricing for Leoni was initially based on average market prices and even when the business was established and the quality of the product was recognised, we kept them there; the difference was that Leoni had become the busiest café in town.

Working it out: basic profit margins

For your coffee or tea shop to succeed as a business, which is exactly what it is, you will need to know at all points what any coffee, tea, panini or fairtrade dark chocolate bar you sell costs you to buy and how much you make when you sell it. If you can't do this you cease to be running a business, whose aim, remember, over and above all the work–life balance benefits it brings you, is to make money. It's that profit that will pay your salaries, mortgage and holidays, and what the bank manager or an investor needs to be confident about if they are to lend you money.

You will also need to consider the price of milk in your drinks, as this will be a big cost, and milk is often more expensive than the coffee or tea. Spend time researching local suppliers, in the same way you did for your choice of tea and coffee, to ensure you get a good deal, and buy it in bulk where possible. Of course you will have to stagger your deliveries to ensure fresh milk.

The simple way to work out your costs

1. Cost of 1 kilo bag of roasted coffee beans
2. This will make around 130 espressos (7g measures)
3. Multiply 140 by the amount you wish to sell your espressos for; subtract the cost of the bag of coffee and you have your profit.
4. From here you can then subtract the other operating costs you will have worked out in your business plan, and establish roughly where your prices need to be.

For example:

1. 1 kilo bag of coffee = £15
2. 140 espressos @ £1.50 a cup = £210
3. Profit = £195
4. Cost per cup = 11p

For a cappuccino or latte you will need roughly 160ml of milk, and you might pay £2 for four litres, which means your milk cost per cup is around 8p. This means a cappuccino will cost you 11p + 8p = 19p. If you sell a cappuccino for £1.80, you will make £1.61 profit. Sounds great? But that's just the start.

Simple sums like the one shown in the box above can seem quite positive at the outset, *but* remember that is the sum before you take into account property and staff costs, etc. Obviously there are many other factors to consider, and this is what your business plan and further sums are for – see below for working out your break-even point, which will give you more of an idea about the kinds of pricing you need to consider to make the business viable.

> **TIP**
> The average profit margin for coffee or tea shops is 60%–85%, with coffee and tea providing the highest margins (some at 90%). Food is less profitable as it is perishable, usually delivering a return of 40%–50%.

Ultimately pricing your drinks is something that you must continue to think about and keep in mind throughout the initial and set-up stages. Continually refer back to and adjust your numbers to establish if the pricing you are working from, and the purchasing, property, staffing and stock decisions you are making, leave you with a profit that makes sense rather than a loss.

Working it out: break-even point

Once you have established profit margins and worked out a possible price for your coffees or teas, you need to link this to all your other operating costs. This is the time to sit down with a calculator and play with the figures, and to be realistic. It is vital that once you have worked out how many cups of coffee you need to sell to at least break even, you decide that this is realistic and achievable. Having to sell 2,000 cups of coffee a day to break even isn't feasible and it means you will need to adjust your operating costs for instance, or buy cheaper stock.

To calculate your break-even point, start by working out your fixed monthly operating costs (those expenses that your business will incur on an ongoing basis; essentially what you will need to pay out each month). These costs may include:

- Your salary
- Staff/barista salaries
- Rent or mortgage payments
- Telecommunications
- Utilities

- Stock
- Storage
- Distribution
- Promotion
- Loan payments
- Office supplies
- Maintenance
- Professional services (i.e. accountancy fees)

Let's say this figure is £4,500. If you then buy £700 worth of goods per month - coffee, tea, milk, food etc - you need to make £5,200 per month to break even. If you sell each cappuccino for £1.80 (see box above) you need to sell 2,889 cappuccinos a month, or more tangibly, 96 cappuccinos a day. However, if you do the same sums, but sell one cappuccino at £2.20, you will only need to sell 78 drinks a day. It's easier, but can you really raise your prices - is the market there? See pages 47-53 for more information on researching your customer base.

TIP

Just cutting stock costs won't balance your budget that easily. For instance, a medium-sized coffee shop might use around 30 kg of coffee a week. If it gets its coffee £1 per kg cheaper, it will only save about £1,500 per year, which isn't enough to make a difference between losing or making money.

Of course taken together, it isn't this simple, as you may not be open for seven days a week, and are also likely to incur other costs, and sell less and more, depending on things such as the weather, days of the week, financial climate. But it's a rough way to start understanding the kind of figures you will be looking at. An accountant can help you put this together in a more detailed way for your bank if necessary. There are some formulas such as the one below that can be used to demonstrate this:

Break-even point (£) = Fixed costs ÷ gross margin percentage.

This level of information should give you a much more powerful overview of not just how viable your business is, but what funding is required and when. It also enables you to pre-empt when you may need assistance with cashflow or credit.

We're tried to help you see the bigger picture in order for your business to be long-lasting and commercially viable. Also, having this at your fingertips won't just impress investors and the banks but should also give you a much firmer grasp on your buying decisions when it comes to finding and fitting out premises. But first go back to the start of this section and make sure it's all safely listed in your business plan.

Working it out: expenses

For a full budget and to see how viable your business is you will need to balance revenue forecasts against costs. We'll come to forecasting later but it's just as crucial to work out and keep track of how much you are spending, not just the sales you hope to get through the till. Without expenses, any forecasts or even sales prove very little as regards how profitable your coffee or tea shop can be. The good news is that it's far easier to work out reliable costings than revenues, especially if you veer on the side of caution. Begin by looking at all your initial start-up costs. All the costs of getting your coffee or tea shop up and running go into the start-up expenses category. These expenses may include:

- Business registration fees
- Initial supplies
- Rent deposits
- Down payment on property
- Down payments on equipment
- Shopfitting costs
- Utility set-up fees

This is just a sample list and you probably won't have trouble adding to it once you start listing your costs. Then add to this your list of operating costs.

Once you have completed your own lists you should have a fairly good idea, even if they are rough figures, of what revenues and/or funding you are going to need to support your coffee shop business over a month, six month and yearly basis. These figures should go into a financial budget plan towards the end of your business plan, which also takes into account how much money you can realistically make.

MAKING REVENUE FORECASTS

Sales forecasting isn't easy and therefore this is where many business plans fall apart. It's usually either because the owner manager is overly optimistic or the plan only succeeds in proving the business isn't viable because the number of sales needed to generate a profit means coffee or tea beverages need to be priced at an unrealistic amount for people to pay. The difficulty here is that you don't have any previous sales history to guide you. But this is also where hopefully your market research can help with examples of average turnover per square foot/metre for similar coffee or tea shops in similar locations and of a similar size. Also, consider how many people there are within certain distances and what percentage of their disposable income you can reasonably hope to secure. Are the locals in the right income bracket to be visiting your coffee or tea shop on a regular basis?

The simplest forecast starts by working out what you hope to be making within six months.

- Work this out per drink served per day – so you have a gross daily sales figure and multiply that by the number of open days in a month.
- Next look to scale proportionately from month one, where you are unlikely to have as many customers, upwards to month six. You can then extrapolate that scale over 12 months for an annual sales forecast.
- In addition to that one forecast, carry out the process three times with a pessimistic, optimistic and realistic outlook.
- Next try to put a real-time calendar next to your 'month one', 'month two', etc., taking into account the peaks and troughs in trade you anticipate and is also suggested from your research. Many coffee or tea shops see huge variations between the seasons, if not month by month, whether it's a lull during the summer holiday months or a boom in tourist numbers.

This level of information should give you a much more powerful overview of not just how viable your business is, but what funding is required and when. It also enables you to pre-empt when you may need assistance with cashflow or credit. Having this at your fingertips will not only impress investors and the banks but should also give you a much firmer grasp on your buying decisions when it comes to actually sourcing stock, for example.

➡ COMPILING A FINANCIAL SHEET

Once you have worked out your financial outgoings (both initial start-up and ongoing costs) you can put the two together to produce a clearer analysis of the viability of your coffee or tea shop on paper and when it's likely to break even. Begin by compiling month-by-month expenses and sales forecasts. In the same way you accounted for peaks and troughs in sales, look at months where you expect expenses to be higher than others. Again, ensure you prepare three income/outgoings projections: pessimistic, optimistic, realistic.

Also try to account for the fact that the price you can purchase ingredients for will hopefully decrease as your sales levels increase because you will be buying in bulk. However, that might be a calculation you want to reserve for your optimistic forecast unless you have already got such an agreement in place from suppliers. While your calculation will inevitably alter from month to month (something you will need to be wary of when managing cashflow) the point where your sales equal your expenses is where you actually break even and anything above that is profit.

Things to remember:

- Don't just write your business plan for your investors; use it as your main guide for the direction of the business.
- Include all the necessary detail, but don't overload it. A good plan is thorough but succinct.
- Be realistic with your sales forecasts. It's better to underestimate than overestimate.
- Prepare three different trading forecasts – pessimistic, optimistic and realistic.

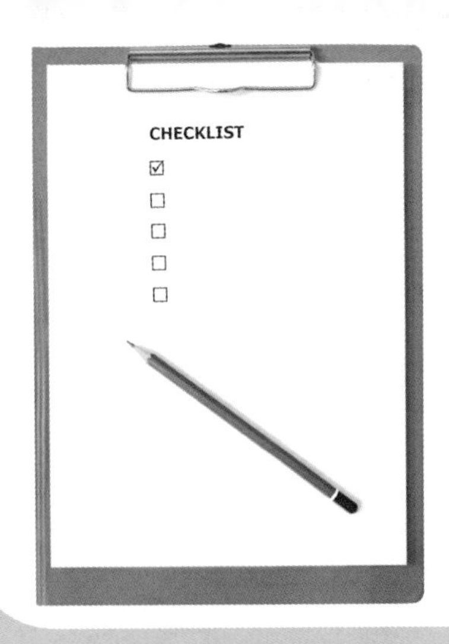

2.2 Start-up finance

One of the hardest things to do is to decide how you are going to get investment for your enterprise. And how can you keep your bank manager on your side? Being vague or cavalier about the real funds you need to set up your coffee or tea shop won't help your business succeed. For the first few months you may not even make a profit, so you will need to ensure you have enough cash to support dips and changes in trade as you find your feet.

In this chapter we'll cover:

- Funding options
- Equity finance
- Friends and family loans
- Dealing with banks
- Pitching for finance
- Paying yourself

FINANCE OPTIONS

By now, you have realised you will need money to start your coffee or tea shop, and quite a lot of it. There is no getting away from the fact that it's going to cost you a pretty penny to get up and running and will also involve substantial overheads. And you are possibly feeling concerned about the issue of raising funds during or just after a recession, especially one where the banks are taking the fall for it, and consequently lending a lot less. Indeed, it's a tough time for small and medium sized enterprises. Although the British Bankers' Association insists that lending by major banks was up by almost £1bn in the third financial quarter of 2008, there is no doubt that the financial squeeze is on small and entrepreneurial businesses. The credit crunch means that many lenders can't offer funding.

TIP

There is no reason why if you have done thorough research and planning, you shouldn't successfully access the finance you need to start up. It just means you will have to work harder to convince your bank and ensure your business plan is top notch – it's tough but it'll be worth it.

It's likely you will have three funding options for opening a coffee or tea shop. The first is to fund it yourself, the second to use a bank, the third is to seek equity investment from private investors (see page 94). It's highly unlikely you will raise venture capital finance (money invested by a venture capitalist who expects a good return) to start your first coffee or tea shop; you may do possibly to roll out a chain but not to start the first.

Funding it yourself

FROM THE EXPERTS:
Henry Rungan, Coffee Republic

We secured funding through a combination of private funding, business loan, investment and family.

Funding it yourself should be a fairly simple decision: either you can or you can't. There is no such thing as free money so for pure efficiency nothing makes better financial sense than resisting borrowing altogether. Of course it's an option few are blessed with. It's also an option some are distinctly uncomfortable with. Do you really want to invest your life savings in a venture when it's possible to borrow from a bank? Possibly not. If that's the case, the first question to ask is if you aren't convinced, why should any other form of investor be? The second is how much can you comfortably put in? Banks are likely to expect you to match whatever they lend you and you will do well to find an individual who will give you their cash to play with while you keep your own in the bank.

TIP

It can actually be sensible to fund start-up costs with a loan and save a slice of your own cash for running costs and future investment; borrowing for a loan will be less expensive than an overdraft or credit cards. There could also be tax advantages to structuring how much you invest yourself but you will probably need an accountant to help with structuring this.

Friends and family

Do you want to mix the two? Of course, it depends on the type of relationship you have, but the road to entrepreneurial success is often littered with the casualties of failed family/friend business partnerships. However lovely the idea and novelty seem of working with your father/best friend/cousin, it's best to think with your head and not your heart before your proceed. Are you prepared for the consequences of handling financial problems with your nearest and dearest? Money can put a strain on even the strongest of relationships – yours will be no exception.

If you go it alone, then consider that you will only have yourself to blame or congratulate with every success or failure. There will be no one else to blame and you always have your family as a sounding board for advice.

IN MY EXPERIENCE:

Shelagh Ryan, Lantana

Both family and friends have been incredibly encouraging and supportive. I think many of my friends are living out their own dreams of starting a café by just giving me advice and suggestions.

If you do take funds from friends and family, make sure you explain *all* the risks, get any investment tied up in a legally binding contract securing both your rights and state that no matter how much you will try to make this work you can't guarantee them it will. If after doing all this, both sides are happy then by all means go ahead. Funding from friends and family, when it works, is certainly a massive leg up and leaves you the freedom to save bank financing for a later stage when you are looking to expand and grow. And above all, remember that shareholder agreement (page 27).

Equity finance

> **TIP**
> Equity finance is where you pledge a percentage of your business in exchange for the money you require to start or grow.

Before we look at banks, which are how most of you will probably fund the opening of your coffee shop, it is worth mentioning equity finance. Private equity usually comes from one or more private wealthy individuals, commonly known as business angels, who are often experienced entrepreneurs with money to invest in other up-and-coming companies. Think of Peter Jones from *Dragons' Den*.

It's also possible to raise equity finance through organised public or private funds, which are usually run by either experienced entrepreneurs or investment companies. Private equity deals usually fill the gap between standard bank loans and venture capital deals, but can vary from anything from £10,000 to £250,000. Venture capital works on the same principle, but is run by large organisations and deals are usually in excess of £500,000, rarely for start-up businesses, even rarer for a new coffee or tea shop. The venture capital funding organisation will also usually place someone on the company's board. If you have run a coffee or tea shop, or have a proven track record in the sector it might be that you will find an investor willing to back you from day one.

Taking on an equity partner also provides a new sense of responsibility and pressure. With the money comes a need to create a substantial return in an agreed period of time, and once you commit to that decision, you must become more focused on generating that return than what works for you in a lifestyle scenario. That can be a very healthy motivation but it's only worth it if that's the type of business you want to run.

Keeping it to yourself

There is one thing all business advisers agree on. If you can keep 100% to start with, then do so. Those in the investment world will no doubt argue it's smarter to own 50% of a company worth £1m than 100% of one worth £100,000. The problem is that whatever you are giving away at the start won't be worth very much, so it's almost certain you will lose a chunky slice at what in a few years time might seem a meagre sum. It's far better to use debt finance and then re-finance once you are in a better position to bargain from and can offer a greater chance of reward for the investor's risk.

Bank or debt finance

Bank loans are a common type of finance for new businesses. Banks are likely to know your business model inside out and you won't have to try to convince them of a whole new concept or sector. However, banks also have very clear expectations of what they expect to see from your business plan before they'll give you money.

TIP

Be warned, banks will know coffee or tea shop models inside out and will see through any overly optimistic forecasts, dressing up of figures or holes in your business plan, so you will need to ensure your research is comprehensive and realistic.

While we've acknowledged that banks are less ready to hand out cash in the current climate, the situation isn't impossible. Just be prepared that their rates may be high, and the expectations of your business plan even higher. They'll want to see you have factored for all eventualities, your own income and been realistic about your anticipated revenues. Don't fake your figures – the banks would have seen it all before and will spot a bluff a mile away.

Choosing a bank

We always veer towards the familiar so you will probably turn to your current bank first. If you have a good relationship with your bank manager it's natural to want to choose their branch to open a business account with. However, even if you are keen to stay with your main bank, do shop around and examine the start-up packages on offer if only to check you aren't missing out on something available elsewhere. If you spot a deal, you can always negotiate with your existing bank manager to match it.

Different banks offer different incentives, such as so many years' free banking to open a business bank account, as well as pricing and organising their charging mechanisms differently. Some offer a greater level of service and usually offer lower interest rates or higher charges as a result, while other banks specialise in keeping basic costs low but offering little service. While there are savings it's likely you will ultimately derive more long-term value from finding a bank you are comfortable with, which makes the effort to listen, understands your business and ultimately, will lend you the money you need to start-up.

Also check what rates the bank is offering; with interest rates currently at the lowest levels in 315 years (0.5%), you may have to shop around for the best offer. It all depends what stance the banks are taking to fledgling businesses.

TIP

The banks will have clear criteria you will be expected to meet for them to be convinced they'll see a return on their investment. If you are at all unsure about your forecasts or figures it's worth speaking to a bank manager before submitting any loan application to see if you are on the right track or need to have a rethink. Bottom line: a good bank manager should be able to give you a clear explanation of your options and what is expected to meet any lending criteria.

Contending with bank managers

Make sure you meet the bank manager you will be dealing with. The relationship with your bank manager is crucial to your success, especially in raising finance. Managers will have a threshold of loans they can sign off and even though you will be assessed by the bank's credit and decisions programmes, having your manager onside will make a massive difference. Bear in mind that managers will vary within banks not just from bank to bank. If you like a package at one bank but don't click with the manager, ask to see another. Alternatively, check your manager is experienced in your sector and within your focus area; it could make a difference.

Depending on how much you want to borrow, banks will usually expect to see that you are matching what you are borrowing with your own money and could also ask for security against your home. This is something that puts many people off and can seem understandably frightening. If you reach this point and are having second thoughts, you are possibly not ready to start a business after all. What you are about to do is indeed high risk. However, provided that it works, it's also full of rewards. If you aren't convinced that the balance is in your favour you have to ask why the bank should.

> **TIP**
>
> If you can't offer the security the bank is asking for, you could apply for a loan through the government's Small Firms Loans Guarantee Scheme, which guarantees bank loans up to £250,000. Although notoriously bureaucratic and inconsistent in its outcome, the scheme is welcomed by all the main banks and did support more than £200m worth of loans in 2008.

If you are reluctant or unable to offer security or match the bank's lending, the other option is to lower the amount you want to borrow. Provided that you have a decent credit rating and can offer reasonable evidence you will be able to afford the repayments, banks will often give personal loans up to around £15,000, which can be used for start-up costs and repaid over 36–84 months.

Banks will also offer you credit card and overdraft facilities, but will discourage you from using them for anything other than cashflow management and short-term borrowing. That's not to say you can't use them however you see fit, but be very careful about borrowing anything you couldn't afford to pay back at very short notice or you could find yourself in trouble over a relatively small amount.

PITCHING FOR FINANCE

Regardless of how bad the economic climate gets, banks and investors will always lend money if they are confident they'll get a healthy return. Your challenge then isn't to beg but to present a compelling opportunity for them. It's on this premise you should base your pitch. Remember banks are investing other people's money so they need to, as far as is possible, guarantee a return. They are certainly not gamblers. Your job is to present a clear, low-risk proposition that demonstrates how the money will be spent and, crucially, how it will be repaid and when.

Preparation

Make sure you are 100% prepared. If you are making a presentation, be clear about all your facts and figures and know them off by heart. Practise at home.

It's likely that a bank will have already read your business plan by the time you get to pitch or talk through your proposition. View this stage as good news that the bank wants to talk further. However, think what else they might want to ask you. Critique your own business plan or ask others to do it for you with a view to pre-empting any questions that stand out.

TIP

A clear concise answer will reassure the bank that you are clear about what you are doing. Don't attempt to try to answer a question if you can't. All investors prefer honesty so be honest and admit you don't know, but suggest you could certainly find out.

Appearance

First impressions last. Dress smart. Forget jeans and t-shirts, even if it's the uniform you have vowed your coffee or tea shop will adopt. Your appearance can determine your success. Wearing a suit demonstrates a professionalism and desire to be taken seriously. Whatever your personal view, the majority of bank managers will still expect you to dress smartly, so neglecting to do so is risky.

Dealing with a 'No'

Rejection is something you should get used to quickly though. Sahar and Bobby Hashemi were refused by 22 banks before they managed to get their funding. So there is every chance several banks will say no before one says yes. See each rejection as a learning experience or rehearsal for the one that says yes. Find out why they've said no, the feedback might be useful. Don't despair, and don't argue with the decision either. You are never going to change their minds.

PAYING YOURSELF

Your business plan should include how and what you intend to pay yourself for at least the first year – and it's essential you include this in any borrowing that you take out. It's true that banks and investors want to see you are making massive sacrifices to see your business get off the ground, and if you can afford not to take a salary for the first few months, even year, they'll expect you to do this. It not only ensures all profits can be reinvested back into the business, but demonstrates just how badly you want to succeed. However, if you can't survive without taking a salary out of the business, whatever you do, don't pretend you can. Trying not to pay yourself and hoping you will somehow muddle through is irresponsible and wishful thinking. Everybody has to pay a mortgage or rent; everybody has to eat; everybody has reasonable living expenses – and lenders do understand that. Not paying yourself a wage will just mean you end up borrowing elsewhere and, conversely, lenders can actually view that as bad management. Saying you can live on £500 a month when your mortgage is £1,000 isn't going to help. Lenders also dislike it when they lend an initial amount of money based on forecasts they've been told are realistic only for the borrower to promptly return needing more. There are very few statistics for average earnings, but you can look at the average earnings in advertised retail manager posts to try to come in somewhere just below.

> **TIP**
>
> Include your wage as a cost of the business. But be realistic. If you are coming from a corporate background to escape the City rat race, wake up and smell the coffee. You are moving into hospitality and should expect to earn a hospitality salary.

Things to remember:

- Consider your finance options carefully. What's best for you, straight loans or giving away a share of the pie?
- Make sure family and friends are clear about what they are getting involved in before you accept any cash from them or they sign anything.
- Know your business model inside out, a bank will have seen it before and will see through any parts you have glossed over.
- Make sure you choose a bank (and a bank manager) who understands your business model and what you want to achieve.
- Be prepared when pitching. You need to know your figures inside-out.
- Be realistic. It's better to ask for the cash in advance than ask for help when you are in trouble.

2.3 Registering your business

In order to run your business, you need to register it. So let's take a look at some of the options that you can choose from. Some involve more paperwork; others are more suited to businesses of a certain size. The bottom line is that you are going to have to address this sooner rather than later if you want to have a legitimate business.

In this chapter we'll cover:

- Sole traders and partnerships
- Limited companies
- Registering as a limited company

 THE DIFFERENT LEGAL STRUCTURES

There are essentially three legal or accounting structures you can choose from when starting your coffee or tea shop. You can go it alone by being a sole trader, team up to form a partnership or operate a limited company. Choosing the right structure is important, so take the time to think it through carefully. Saying that, it is possible to switch between the different structures after you have started your coffee or tea shop. For example, you may start out as a sole trader, and then decide to register your business as a limited company or partnership. You will save yourself a lot of work if you establish the most appropriate business structure beforehand though. Below is an explanation of the different legal structures you can choose from when starting your coffee or tea shop and guidance on which structure is most suitable for your particular establishment.

TIP

If you can afford it, get a lawyer you can trust. It's their job to read the small print.

Sole traders and partnerships

Registering as a sole trader is relatively straightforward, record-keeping is simple and you get to keep all the profits after tax. As the name implies, as a sole trader you are the single owner of the business and have complete control over the way it is run. However, bear in mind that the law makes no distinction between the business and you as the owner; in simple terms, any debt can be met from your own personal wealth if the coffee or tea shop business runs into trouble. If you choose to run your coffee or tea shop as a sole trader you must also register as self-employed with Her Majesty's Revenue and Customs (HMRC) within three months of your trading start date, otherwise you could be fined and charged interest on any outstanding tax and National Insurance payments.

It may sound obvious but the business term for when two or more people combine to form a business unit is a partnership. As with the sole trader model, each partner is responsible for any debts the business incurs. Each partner is also self-employed and receives a percentage of any returns from the business, which they are then taxed on. The partnership, as well as the individuals within it, must submit annual self-assessment returns to HMRC and keep accurate records on business income and expenses.

Starting a coffee or tea shop as a sole trader or partnership venture may prove the easier option in the short term. There is less paperwork involved and you will not need to register and send annual returns to Companies House. It is also much easier to withdraw funds from the business as essentially, all profits make up your own earnings. However, think about whether you plan to expand in the future before you decide on the path you are going to take.

TIP

As a sole trader, besides the financial liability, it is much more difficult to grow the business and you may find it harder when dealing with creditors and suppliers.

Limited liability companies

Your next option is registering as a limited (Ltd) company, probably the best legal structure to go with if you have, as we've just suggested, any intention of growing your business. As well as offering you a degree of personal financial security, should your growing coffee or tea shop business run into money problems, it will also give it more credibility when seeking finance or credit. Registering your coffee or tea shop business as a limited company also makes tax and succession planning a lot easier.

If you expect your coffee or tea shop to maintain a healthy amount of trade and return high levels of profit you will definitely want to go with the limited company model. Profits will be subject to corporation tax, which currently stands at half the 40% income tax rate you could end up paying as a high-earning sole trader. Limited companies pay corporation tax on profits and company directors are taxed as employees in the same way that any other people you employ, such as baristas, are taxed.

A limited company is very different from a sole trader model where there is no legal distinction between you and the business. A limited company is a separate legal entity to the people that run it. Profits and losses belong to the company, and the business can continue regardless of the death, resignation or bankruptcy of the shareholders or directors. Your personal financial risk will be restricted to how much you have invested in the company and any guarantees you gave when raising finance for the business. However, if the company fails and you have not carried out your duties as a company director, you could be liable for debts as well as being disqualified from acting as a director in another company.

If you decide to register your coffee or tea shop as a limited company you will have to allow more time to deal with the paperwork; it is a much more administration-heavy process than running a business as a sole trader. We're not suggesting that you wouldn't anyway, but you would have to be highly efficient with your record keeping and auditing throughout the entire life of the business. Are you prepared for that if you choose this route?

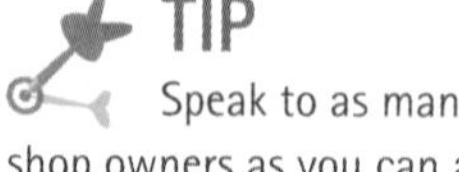

TIP

Speak to as many coffee or tea shop owners as you can and find out which route they chose and how appropriate it's been for them.

REGISTERING AS A LIMITED COMPANY

To register your coffee shop as a limited company you must submit the appropriate paperwork to Companies House, the official government register of UK companies. You can download more detailed instructions and the appropriate application forms from the website (www.companieshouse.gov.uk). What follows is a guide to the process, documents and requirements involved in turning your business into a legal entity.

Although you can register a limited company yourself, unless you have done it before you are probably going to need some legal advice, that is, the services of either a solicitor, accountant, chartered secretary or a company formation agent. Formation agents use their own software that works directly with the Companies House systems. If you want to register your company electronically (most are registered this way) you will need to have the specific Companies House electronic interface – hence the need for a formation agent. However, you can still deliver the physical documents directly to Companies House without the need of a formation agent or specific electronic interface.

Registration costs

Depending on the level of service you need, formation agent services can cost anything up to £200, but think of it as money well spent in terms of the valuable advice they provide on the compiling of the necessary documents and the right structure for your business. Companies House doesn't provide this service when registering, so if you aren't familiar with the process, get help to avoid making mistakes.

Alternatively, you could get assistance from an online registration company. The standard service usually costs £80–£100 including fees, but since some documentation needs to be posted, registration takes three to eight days. This option is usually cheaper than using a formation agent, although you won't receive the same level of personal service.

Finally, you can buy an 'off the shelf' company from an accountancy firm. You will receive a ready-made limited company that has designated company officers listed on the paperwork. You simply transfer your name and the names of any other company directors once you receive your documentation. The process can be completed on the same day and many accountancy firms will have several ready-made limited companies which they can sell to you. This is the quickest option, and, with the exception of registering the company yourself, can often be the cheapest too.

TIP

What level of service you go for depends on how confident you are and how much hand-holding you feel you need at this stage. That said, it's better to get it right at the beginning and avoid errors.

Company officers

Once you have agreed whether or not you need help in establishing your company you will need to decide on who the company officers will be, and what your business will be called.

Limited companies are required by law to have named company officers. Company officers are the formally named directors and company secretary as stated in the Articles of Association, one of the documents you submit to Companies House (this is explained in more detail below). It is a legal requirement for company officers to be in place at all times and for their names and current addresses to be written on the registration documents. If there is a change in company officers, Companies House must be informed straight away. All private limited companies must have at least one director and a company secretary. So before you think of asking a family member to become a director make sure you and your prospective team know what's expected.

Company directors

Company directors manage the company's affairs in accordance with its Articles of Association and the law. Generally, anyone can be appointed company director and the post doesn't require any formal qualifications. However, there are a few exceptions. You are prohibited from being a company director if:

- You are an undischarged bankrupt or disqualified by a court from holding a directorship
- You are under 16 (this only applies in Scotland)

Company directors have a responsibility to make sure certain documents reach the registrar at Companies House. These are:

- Accounts
- Annual returns
- Notice of change of directors or secretaries
- Notice of change of registered office

Directors who don't deliver these documents on time can be prosecuted and are subject to fines of up to £5,000 for each offence. On average, 1,000 directors are prosecuted each year for failing to deliver accounts and returns on time, so it is not a responsibility that can be taken lightly.

Company secretary

The company secretary's duties aren't specified by law but usually contained within an employment contract. For private limited companies, secretaries are not required to have any special qualifications. The main duties of a company secretary are to:

- Maintain the statutory registers
- Ensure statutory forms are filed promptly
- Provide members and auditors with notice of meetings

- Send the Registrar copies of resolutions and agreements
- Supply a copy of the accounts to every member of the company
- Keep or arrange minutes of meetings

Naming your business

As well as deciding upon your company officers, you will also need to pick a company name with which to register the business. We've given you some advice on choosing a name on page 65; here we discuss the legalities of it.

TIP

Take note! The name of your business does not have to be the same as the name of your coffee or tea shop! If you open three coffee or tea shops, all with different names, you can still run them as one limited company.

You will need to decide on your company's name before you fill out your registration documents as there are certain rules to consider. The name you choose for your company must:

- Feature the word 'Limited' or 'Ltd' at the end. For Welsh companies the equivalent 'Cyfyngedig' or 'Cyf' can be used, but documentation must also state in English that it is a limited company
- Not be made up of certain sensitive words or expressions (listed by Companies House) without the consent of the Secretary of State or the relevant government department
- Not imply a connection with central or local government
- Not be offensive
- Not be the same or similar to one that already appears in the index of names kept by Companies House

You can search the index of business names already registered on the Companies House website free of charge. If your chosen name is too similar to another, an objection can be lodged within 12 months following the incorporation of your company and you could be forced to change it. For more on the creative side of choosing your name, see page 66.

Documents to submit

When registering a limited company, four documents must be submitted to Companies House.

Memorandum of Association

This document sets out the following:

- The company's name
- Where the company's registered office is located – England, Wales or Scotland
- What the company will do – this can be as simple as: 'to conduct business as a general commercial company'

Articles of Association

Here is where you set out the rules for running your company. You must state how shares will be allocated and transferred, how the directors, the secretary and your meetings will be governed. And if you decide not to adopt the standard articles of the Companies Act in full (known as Table A) you have to submit your amended version when registering.

TIP

Once your company is incorporated you can only make changes if the holders of 75% of the voting rights in your company agree, so it pays to get this right at the outset.

Form 10

This document gives details of the first director(s), company secretary and the address of the registered office. Company directors must also give their name, address, date of birth, occupation and details of other directorships held in the past five years.

Form 12

This document is the statutory declaration of compliance with all the legal requirements of the incorporation of a company. It must be signed by one of the company directors or the secretary named on Form 10 or the solicitor forming the company. The signing of the document must be witnessed by a solicitor, a commissioner for oaths, a justice of the peace or a notary public. Form 12 must not be signed and dated before any of the other documents are completed, signed and dated.

Once all that's been submitted, your coffee or tea shop is a fully fledged limited company. But don't forget that the legal structure you choose when you start trading isn't set in stone. You can change this later on, as the business grows and changes – you can even float it on the stock market if it becomes successful enough!

Things to remember:

- Assess your business structure options carefully. It may be cheaper to stay as a sole trader but are the risks to your personal finances (and your nerves) worth it?
- When registering as a limited company make sure you have gone over your documents with a fine-tooth comb before submitting them. If you make a mistake you will have to submit them again, which will cause delays professionally and aggravation emotionally!
- Search the list of submitted business names on the Companies House website *before* you decide on one. It may not be available.

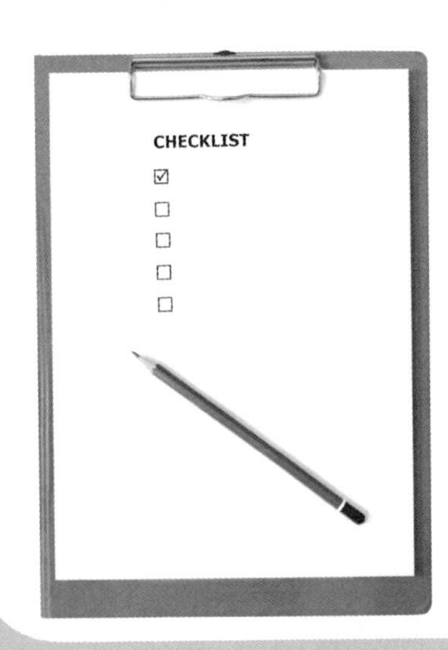

2.4 Getting legal

Once you have got the business set up there are a lot of smaller considerations you will also need to be aware of. While it's not the most exciting part of setting up the business, it's pretty much the most essential. The bottom line is that if you want to be running above board, you need to abide by a lot of rules and regulations. While some of the things you will need to know will become easier to understand as you put them into practice, it is a good idea, however boring, to commit some time to reading up on the various legislations that affect you.

In this chapter we'll cover:

- Money and credit cards
- Insurance
- The smoking ban and noise control
- Licensing
- Health and safety
- Environmental health
- Food hygiene
- Fire safety

MONEY ISSUES

Credit card or cash payments

Merchant status

Getting merchant status is necessary if you want to accept credit and debit card payments in your restaurant. Even today, some smaller cafés and coffee or tea shops get by by only accepting cash and cheques. But to make life easier for your customers you probably won't want to rely solely on this type of payment.

TIP

In general, transactions in a coffee or tea shop will be around £5. So it's worth investigating whether your credit card company will allow you to have a lower limit for accepting cards for those who don't have ready cash. Before you get a card machine though, think about how close you are to cash points, or shops that give cash back.

It's important you get your merchant status sorted out as quickly as you can. Customers are put off by inconvenience, and not being able to pay with a card can be seen as a nuisance. Only accepting cash will certainly save you on card processing fees but you could lose far more by customers choosing the shop next door if they don't have cash on them.

IN MY EXPERIENCE:
Simon Robertson, Leoni

We don't accept cards. There is a cash machine next to the café so it is quicker for the customer to use this than for us to use a card machine in the café.

When applying for merchant status you will be subject to some stringent security checks. Even without trading history you can still apply. However, acceptance is not automatic. High levels of fraud mean that credit card companies use various methods to ensure illegal activity is kept to a minimum. One of these methods is charge backs. If a charge is found to be fraudulent, the money paid by the credit card company can be taken back from you. This can occur up to six months after the transaction has taken place and it is then up to you to recover the fraudulent funds. The point is, since you can be held responsible for any fraudulent use of cards in your coffee or tea shop, your bank needs to know you will take adequate measures to prevent it.

The process of applying for merchant status involves getting in touch with your bank. The main high-street banks offer more or less the same uniform services. The process takes about a fortnight and as previously mentioned, new businesses do not generally have to prove trading history. However, you will be asked to provide your business plan. Longer-established venues will generally have to produce around three years' worth of accounts.

> **TIP**
>
> If you plan to take any food orders over the phone you will need to state this at the time of applying, as 'customer not present' transactions require special permission.

Transaction fees

In terms of price, it's a good idea to shop around if you are willing to look further afield than your business bank account provider. Most of the main banks charge roughly 3% per transaction, £15–£25 per month for the rental of the swipe machine and a one-off set up fee of £100–£150. That's the average cost, however, you can get these prices down with the right kind of negotiation. Don't be afraid to ask for a lower rate. The worst-case scenario is the bank saying no.

Cash forgery

Despite the rapid increase in paying with plastic over the past couple of decades, a lot of restaurants still accept cash. You therefore must be aware of forgery risks. Counterfeit notes are still relatively rare, but it pays to know how to recognise a fake.

Knowingly accepting fake notes is clearly illegal, however you are also responsible for making sure any cash you accept is genuine. Ignorance is not an excuse so you can't just turn a blind eye if you suspect customers have given you counterfeit money. Banks will not accept fake notes from you so you will lose out financially if you don't apply an adequate level of vigilance. When checking for fake notes, don't just rely on one method. Feel the notes in your hands and if in doubt, compare with one you know is genuine. The easiest way to check notes are genuine is with an ultraviolet pen. The pen causes a chemical reaction between the ink and the paper, but you will need to replace them regularly as dirty pens can be unreliable.

Tips for checking bank notes

If you don't have any kind of counterfeit-detecting device, a few elements to confirm genuine notes are:

- The paper and raised print
- The metallic thread
- The watermark
- The print quality
- The hologram

If you suspect you have received a counterfeit note you must report it to the police immediately. They will then give you a receipt and send it to the Bank of England. If it turns out to be genuine, they will refund you. For more information visit www.bankofengland.co.uk.

Refunds

Customers eating or drinking in your coffee or tea shop have the right to a certain standard of service. The law (Trade Descriptions Act) gives them the right to demand a refund or allows them to refuse payment in certain circumstances. It makes no difference if the customer has partly consumed or completely finished their drink; they still have the same rights under the aforementioned acts. For more on dealing with unhappy customers see Chapter 7.1 (*Surviving the first six months*).

INSURANCE

If you plan for the worst-case scenario, you can only ever be pleasantly surprised when it doesn't happen. You may not want to think about all the things that can go wrong with your coffee or tea shop, but making sure you have the right level of insurance

TIP

Generally, insurance requirements seem to be straightforward: public liability, employer's liability, buildings and contents etc. It might be worth speaking to a broker who will be better able to advise you on your specific needs.

cover is an absolute necessity. Some types of insurance are required by law, whereas others, although not compulsory, are essential if you want to protect your business against every eventuality.

Employers' liability insurance (ELI)

If you employ even a single member of staff you are required by law to have this cover, or you could face a fine. This type of insurance helps employers meet the cost of compensation for staff if they are injured while working. Policies generally start at around £10m worth of cover to include legal expenses. However, ELI doesn't mean you are untouchable. You must still honour all your health and safety obligations, carry out regular risk assessments and have all the appropriate paperwork to back this up.

Product and public liability insurance

Although not compulsory by law, as a coffee or tea shop owner, you are well advised to take out this kind of cover. By doing so you will be insured against claims made against your coffee or tea shop by members of the public. As your business relies on members of the public entering your premises and consuming the food and drink you produce, you need to protect yourself should anything untoward happen. However, you still have to make sure the food you serve meets certain quality standards; otherwise your claim is likely to be unsuccessful.

Premises insurance

Your coffee or tea shop's chance of survival will be severely compromised if the actual premises are damaged. You need to be covered against damage as a result of any number of unforeseen occurrences such as floods, fires, or malicious damage. If your premises are rented, you may not be responsible for taking out this cover, but if that is the case, you will want to make sure your landlord has taken care of it. Tenants are generally always responsible for shop fronts, however.

Contents insurance

As premises insurance only covers the physical building, you will need to make sure the contents of your coffee or tea shop are also adequately insured against damage or theft. This will cover stock, machinery, café furniture and anything else included in the policy.

Business interruption insurance

While covering you against the costs of repair and replacement, contents and premises insurance won't necessarily help with any income you lose while your coffee or tea shop is closed as a result of unforeseen events. This is where business interruption insurance comes in.

The legal requirements we've covered so far apply to most businesses. However, there is plenty of legislation which applies specifically to the hospitality trade. Before you open the doors to the first customer make sure you have covered ALL of the following regulations.

SMOKING AND NOISE CONTROL

In July 2007, a smoking ban was introduced in England, having already been established in Scotland, Wales and Northern Ireland. The ban made smoking in all enclosed public spaces and workplaces illegal. Under no circumstances can you allow customers or staff to smoke inside your coffee or tea shop. The smoking ban also extends to any company vehicles used by more than one person. The ban is enforced by local authorities and failure to adhere to it carries a fine of up to £2,500.

IN MY EXPERIENCE:

Simon Robertson, Leoni

We have always been a non-smoking establishment. We probably are now busier as a consequence of the ban. I know certain customers did not initially frequent our shop because they wanted a smoke with their coffee and so would go to a smoking café, that is not possible now as all cafés are smoke free.

A successful coffee or tea shop is going to have a great, buzzy atmosphere. While that's good for your business and your confidence levels, it's also your job to make sure it doesn't get *too* noisy.

However, as most coffee shops close at a reasonable hour, the only likelihood you would have of a complaint would be if you decide to have a live jazz trio in to perform and residents much prefer classical!

> **TIP**
>
> Music is something to consider. What sort of ambience do you want in your coffee shop? Think about how you are going to provide it, from the basic radio to a surround-sound music system. Remember that you will need a specific licence to play music, even the radio, check out page 207 for more details.

Under environment legislation, if noise from your coffee shop has a negative impact on the public, which includes nearby residents, you can be found guilty of causing a statutory nuisance. However, it is still useful to know that if a complaint is lodged against your business, the local authority can serve you with an abatement notice ordering you to reduce or stop any noise. If you are planning on it being a fairly lively establishment, you might want to consider a non-residential location.

> **TIP**
>
> For more advice on your responsibilities towards keeping local residents happy, contact your local authority for advice. You can find a list of all local councils at www.direct.gov.uk.

LICENSING

Most coffee or tea shops don't sell alcohol, but if you are considering it, you should be aware that the Licensing Act 2003, which came into force in England and Wales in November 2005, requires businesses to have a licence if they wish to sell or supply alcohol, or sell hot food or drink between 11pm and 5am. So, even if your coffee or tea shop doesn't serve alcohol, you will have to close before 11pm to avoid the need for a licence.

When applying for a new licence, or to change or add to your licence, you need to let other residents and local businesses know your intentions. You do this by putting up a notice on the premises for 28 days and by placing an advertisement in a local paper or circular. You also need to notify the police and environmental health service (see below).

HEALTH AND SAFETY

A coffee or tea shop business is essentially a people business. There are going to be a lot of them involved – whether staff or customers. So from the beginning, make sure you implement adequate health and safety practices. It can be time consuming and not what you want to be doing at 11pm, but grit your teeth and just get it done.

You are responsible for the well-being of every single person affected by your coffee shop. These people include:

- Staff
- Customers
- Any visitors to your premises, from the delivery people to the cleaner to the plumber

Before you or your staff start working in the coffee shop, you should conduct an assessment of the health and safety risks your business faces. You are required to have a formal policy based on this assessment. If you employ five or more people then this policy must be written down. As an employer, your legal requirements surrounding health and safety are as follows.

You should:

- Record and report all accidents
- Consult all staff on health and safety measures
- Ensure staff are aware of health and safety procedures and comply with them

Your local authority and the Health and Safety Executive (HSE) are the governing bodies that make sure you are meeting your obligations. However, they are not just there to enforce and punish you when you make a mistake. You can also ask their advice and even invite them to your premises to help you with your risk assessment and safety procedures.

> **TIP**
>
> For more information on health and safety and how to carry out a risk assessment of your business, visit the HSE website (www.hse.gov.uk).

ENVIRONMENTAL HEALTH

As we mentioned earlier in this section, it's a good idea to get a consultation from an environmental health officer before you agree on a specific property; as if the premises don't meet basic standards you will not be permitted to trade. However, if you decide on a property before you have spoken to an officer you must still register your premises with the local authority at least 28 days before opening your coffee shop. You are then subject to inspections every six months, although depending on your local authority it may not be as frequent as this.

There are a number of reasons why an environmental health officer may decide to call on your coffee shop out of the blue. It could simply be a routine inspection, or perhaps a response to a reported accident or complaint. Officers are permitted by law to enter commercial premises at any reasonable time. They are also allowed to bring assistance such as in the form of a tradesperson or police officer.

Environmental officers also have the right to demand all relevant information including the names of the company directors, maintenance records of any machinery and the ingredients and origin of any food.

At the end of a visit you can expect the following from the officer:

- A summary of what has been found and recorded
- A request for any further information needed from you
- Confirmation of any action you are required to take as a result of the visit (this can be in the form of a warning letter or notice)
- Confirmation of how long you have to take any required action
- An opportunity for you to make any comments

If you refuse to cooperate, or the officer feels they have been deliberately obstructed from carrying out their duty, you can be prosecuted and fined up to £5,000. If you disagree with any conclusions the officer comes to you have the right to take the following action:

- Ask to discuss the concerns directly with the officer to reach a compromise
- Ask to speak to the officer's team manager

TIP

Inspections can happen at any time and you won't get any notification that they are about to happen; but they are fairly routine.

- Write to the Director of Environmental Services detailing your concerns
- Complain to the local government ombudsman
- Appeal against any notice given to you

FOOD HYGIENE

So you have registered your coffee or tea shop with the local authority, but what do you need to do in order to prepare for an inspection? Although your shop isn't a restaurant, you still have to abide by the same hygiene standards as they do. The best way to get ready for an inspection is to never have to do any extra work for the environmental health officer's visit. In other words, run your coffee or tea shop like every day is inspection day.

The most important regulations relating to food preparation are:

- Regulation (EC) No. 852/2004 on the hygiene of foodstuffs
- The Food Hygiene (England) Regulations 2006 (there are equivalent regulations for Scotland, Wales and Northern Ireland)

These regulations set out the basic requirements for all aspects of a food business including premises, facilities and the hygiene requirements for you and your staff.

TIP
For more information regarding food hygiene in commercial premises, visit www.food.gov.uk.

You are legally required to put in place 'food safety management procedures'. With regard to these, you must:

- Permanently keep the policy in place
- Have up-to-date documents relating to the procedures
- Review all procedures if you change how you work or the food you produce

The regulations are designed to be relatively flexible, meaning smaller coffee or tea shops would only need to have simple procedures and documents relating to them, while larger establishments would have more complex procedures. The best way to ensure you are doing everything right is to make cleaning a part of your daily routine. Have a rota which all staff know about, clear instructions about the regularity and techniques for cleaning different equipment and, if you can do this, at the outset work environmental and cleaning standards into the layout for your coffee or tea shop – you will appreciate it in the long run. More detail on the regulations can be obtained from the Food Standards Agency (FSA).

TIP

Under the Trade Descriptions Act, the food your menu describes must be an accurate reflection of the food you serve. This includes ingredients and descriptions involving the manner in which any food was cooked. For example, if you claim the food is 'home-made' and it's not, you are breaking the law.

Food preparation

There are some basic guidelines to follow to comply with health and safety. All food must be stored and prepared in appropriate conditions, designed to prevent harmful deterioration and protect it from contamination. This includes all stages of preparation from the production of the raw ingredients to when they are served at the customer's table. There are four Cs to remember when thinking about food hygiene:

- Cross-contamination
- Cleaning
- Chilling
- Cooking

Cross-contamination

Cross-contamination is the most common cause of food poisoning and occurs when harmful bacteria are spread on to food from other food, surfaces, hands or equipment. The kind of harmful bacteria involved in cross-contamination usually come from raw meat, poultry and eggs, so you will need to take extra care when handling these foods, especially if you are making fresh sandwiches every day in-house.

Other sources of contamination to be mindful of are staff, pests, equipment and cloths. You should also watch out for both physical and chemical contamination of food, where items such as glass or packaging can fall into food, or substances such as cleaning products or pest control agents come into contact with it.

IN MY EXPERIENCE:
Simon Robertson, Leoni

The most common pest and most difficult to get rid of is the 'Can you make my cappuccino extra hot?' pest. Less common but equally irritating is the 'Can I have a skinny latte, 16oz, with Amaretto syrup and oh! – one of those double choc muffins as well' pest. We get the odd infestation of coach parties (usually 56 of them at a time huddled round one pot of tea) but not many. Other than these we are pest free.

Cleaning

It may sound obvious, but keeping clean – both your premises and your staff – is non-negotiable if you plan to avoid food poisoning. Think of your coffee shop's level of cleanliness as a reflection on you. You can't afford for it to be anything less than perfect.

TIP

Have a 'Now Wash Your Hands' poster in the toilets – a good reminder for staff and customers alike!

Chilling

Whether they are made in-house or bought in from an outside supplier, the following foods must be kept chilled:

- Food with a 'use-by' date
- Food that says 'keep refrigerated' on the label
- Food you have cooked and will not serve immediately
- Ready-to-eat food such as sandwiches.

You should check the temperature of your chilling equipment at least once a day.

Cooking

'Hot' food must be kept at 63 °C or higher. When food is reheated, it must be piping hot all the way through. In Scotland it must be reheated to 82 °C before it can be used or served.

More detail on the principles and legal requirements of safe food preparation can be found in the FSA guide *Safer Food, Better Business*, which can be downloaded from www.food.gov.uk. In this guide you will also find templates for cleaning schedules and staff training records.

Staff and premises

Any person working in the food-handling area of the coffee or tea shop is required by law to maintain a high level of personal cleanliness. You must also not allow anyone to enter a food-handling area if they:

- Are suffering from, or carrying, a disease likely to be transmitted through food
- Have infected wounds, skin infections or sores
- Have diarrhoea (in this instance, staff suffering from the condition must not return to work until 48 hours after the symptoms have disappeared)

Every aspect of your coffee or tea shop premises must be clean and kept in good condition. The layout and design of the coffee or tea shop must:

- Allow for adequate maintenance and cleaning
- Avoid or minimise air-borne contamination
- Provide enough space for you to carry out tasks hygienically
- Protect against dirt build-up
- Allow good hygiene practices
- Provide suitable conditions for handling and storing food

More details of the legal requirements for coffee shop premises can be found in Chapters 5.1 (*Finding premises*) and 5.2 (*Décor and furniture*).

Waste disposal

Think of the disposable coffee and tea cups, the teabags, the milk cartons and plastic spoons. Your coffee or tea shop will generate a lot of rubbish and you need to be aware of your legal responsibilities regarding its disposal. The law requires you to keep all waste tidy and safe. This means ensuring there is a specific area, away from the public where waste can be stored securely, and hygienically, until it's removed. Under the Environment Protection Act 1990 you must:

TIP

Failure to comply with statutory hygiene requirements could result in a fixed penalty notice or a court appearance.

- Arrange a trade waste collection agreement with the local authority or an authorised licensed-waste carrier (note: your business rates do not include payment for waste disposal).
- Keep records on the type of waste you give to the collector.
- Only put waste out on the street on the day of collection and in proper waste containers so it's contained.
- Not, under any circumstances, put commercial waste into litter bins. And don't be sneaky by trying to dispose of your rubbish via domestic waste collections.

FIRE SAFETY

TIP

Your local fire authority can give you more details on how to carry out the fire risk assessment and what details you need to include in your emergency plan.

The laws concerning businesses and their fire safety requirements have undergone significant reform in recent years. The Regulatory Reform (Fire Safety) Order 2005 came into force across England and Wales in October 2006. The order places emphasis towards risk reduction and fire prevention and means that fire certificates are no longer issued. Instead, you must carry out a fire risk assessment for your premises. The assessment should pay particular attention to those at special risk, such as young people, the disabled and those with special needs. You will also need to produce an emergency plan.

Things to remember:

Have you:

- Got the right insurance?
- Registered with your local authority 28 days before opening?
- Got the right licence under the Licensing Act 2003?
- Made sure your health and safety assessments and procedures are in place and staff are adequately trained?
- Arranged for a collector to dispose of commercial waste?
- If applicable, put food safety management procedures in place?
- Carried out a fire risk assessment?

“Espresso is to Italy, what champagne is to France.”

Charles Maurice de Talleyrand

“If man has no tea in him, he is incapable of understanding truth and beauty.”

Japanese Proverb

3

The beverage essentials

3.1 Coffee, tea and other drinks

This is what it all boils down to. If you want to start a coffee or tea shop the single most important thing is your product. And your commitment to it has to be absolute. We've already covered the fact that as an independent your strongest offering against the competition is a higher level of quality and service that the chains can never deliver – so this needs to be your number one priority. Consider very carefully the kinds of tea, coffee, drinks and food you want to offer, and be rigorous in your research. Not only is it important that you are armed with as much information as possible, but doing the research is also a crucial and exciting process in these setting up stages.

In this chapter we'll cover:

- History and background of tea and coffee
- Sources and types of beans and leaf
- Beverages to offer and how to make them
- Other drinks to consider
- Fairtrade and ethical issues

THE DRINKS

It's likely that many of your customers will choose your independent coffee or tea shop rather than the large chains because they are coffee or tea purists. So if you aren't already, consider becoming one! This way you can answer any customer's queries with confidence, and your expert knowledge will help build your word-of-mouth reputation. Luckily, we've done some of the research for you. So grab a nice hot drink and get reading!

COFFEE

History and background

Coffee has existed in many forms since the ninth century, discovered after an African famer noticed his goats were eating berries and then becoming rather excitable; he boiled the berries with hot water and coffee was born. Now it is a multi-million dollar industry, employing over 20 million people worldwide. Coffee moved from Africa to the rest of the world slowly, and it was when the Dutch planted some coffee in Indonesia during the 1600s that coffee became a global industry, with coffee houses opening all over Europe during the 1700s and the industry growing rapidly to what it is now.

Coffee is grown in equatorial climates. Brazil is the world's largest coffee supplier, producing nearly a third of the global coffee output. Colombia and Indonesia follow with 16% and 7%, respectively. Other countries produce a mere 1%–4% of the annual global coffee production.

The two main types of coffee bean are Robusta and Arabica. The coffee tree has dark green leaves and white blossom. Coffee berries resemble cranberries, and the two flat-sided seeds inside the berry form the coffee bean. Before the beans have been processed they are known as green coffee. Coffee trees can produce coffee for up to 25 years, and yield about 2,000 beans a year – this equates to 1kg of raw coffee.

Robusta

Where does it grow?

- Western and Central Africa
- Brazil

- South East Asia and Indonesia
- India

Key facts

- A strong plant, very tolerant of cold and moisture and resistant to disease.
- Grown at lower altitudes, 0m–600m
- High yield and high caffeine content (1.7%–4.0%)
- Accounts for a quarter of all coffee production

Flavour and use

- Strong, full-bodied and woody.
- Often used in blended and instant coffees

Harvesting and production

Robusta beans mature in about half the time of Arabica and yield almost twice as many berries. Robusta is often used to give body and depth to Arabica blends, especially espresso blends where it can add body and character.

Arabica

Where does it grow?

- Central America
- South America
- India
- Eastern Africa
- Papua New Guinea

TIP

Robusta berries don't fall off the tree when ripe, so aren't harvested immediately, which saves money.

Key facts

- Oldest species of bean, accounts for three-quarters of the beans grown in the world
- It is a more delicate coffee
- Grows at higher altitudes, up to 1,800m
- It's expensive because it has a lower yield, less caffeine content (0.8%–1.4%) and is labour intensive to produce

Flavour

- Subtle, acidic flavour
- Refined aroma and a caramel aftertaste

Harvesting and production

Arabicas are more expensive than Robusta – they are hand-picked and processed in the wet method (more on that later), and are also susceptible to frost damage, which means farmers factor in a replacement plant cost to production costs.

TIP

Ten per cent of Arabica produced a year is known as 'grand cru' beans. The phrase 'grand cru' refers to the quality of land the bean is produced on (it is the same for wine). It produces a superior quality coffee that can sell for up to £40 per kg.

IN MY EXPERIENCE:

Shelagh Ryan, Lantana

While I did ask people their opinions and got recommendations, ultimately I did lots and lots of research. Checking out reviews, taste tests, visiting suppliers, trawling the internet – anything I could do to get a rounded view of what products I was going to serve. And actually it turned out to be one of the most fun and interesting things I did before we opened.

Life of a coffee bean: from seed to shop

1. **Sowing:** Coffee seeds are sown in specially constructed beds, and at the first sign of leaves moved to shaded peat pots or foil bags.
2. **Growing:** Around five to seven months after this they are moved to the coffee plantation where they spend two to five years maturing, shaded from the severe equatorial sunlight by guamos trees.
3. **Harvesting:** Once the tree blossoms, it takes nine months for the berries to ripen ready for harvest. A time-consuming and labour intensive process, harvesting lasts between four and six months depending on the type of coffee, although this also varies depending on the climate.
4. **Picking:** There are three common picking methods:
   - **Hand-picking** – used for the highest quality Arabica beans, this method is also the most expensive. Berries are harvested only at the peak of maturity and selected for their ripeness and quality. In very hot countries the ripening process is so fast that workers will often visit the trees several times a day.

- **Strip-picking** – this involves workers pulling all berries, ripe and unripe, from the branch in one motion. The berries are collected on large cloths and harvested from the ground. It is commonly used for harvesting Robusta fruit and cheaper coffee.
- **Mechanical picking** – a lesser-used concept, common to Brazil, in which machines shake the berries from the trees; the berries are then harvested in the same way as strip picking.

5. **Processing:** There are two methods of processing the coffee beans, which involves removing the fruit, skin and husk of the berry to reveal the flat-sided seeds, which will eventually become coffee beans.
   - **Dry processing** – the oldest method of producing coffee, still used in Brazil, produces a less good quality of coffee. The berries are sieved to remove any excess twigs and leaves, then spread on cement or stone and dried for two to three weeks, being turned regularly. The dried berries are hulled using a peeling machine. The beans are then cleaned, sorted by size and bagged.
   - **Wet processing** – this involves removing the rest of the fruit before the berries have dried. It uses specific machinery and lots of water. While it is more expensive, it is commonly felt to ensure the quality of the coffee. The berries are cleaned with water and the ripe berries separated from the unripe berries. They are then hulled using a peeling machine similar to that used for dry processing – this pulls the fruit away under a strong stream of water. The beans are then fermented in more water, which removes a sticky film around the bean. It is this two-day fermentation process that gives the coffee its superior flavour. Following this the beans are washed again, dried on concrete blocks for five days, hulled by special machines, sieved to remove any foreign objects, sorted mechanically by size, and then selected by eye into different quality grades. At this point the coffee bean is green, and is known as green coffee – it can be stored for up to a year.
6. **Inspection and transport:** The final process before export is a sample inspection. A small portion of coffee from every bag is roasted, ground and tasted, and then given a quality seal by experts. It is at this point that it is exported globally to be roasted, ground and sold.

TIP

Less than 20% of beans are of high enough quality to be considered speciality coffee.

Types of coffee

The variety in flavour from coffee comes mainly from the country it is grown in, where climate and ground (or terroir) have a huge impact on flavour.

- **Brazil** – the biggest producer of coffee; Bourbon, Typica, Caturra, and Mundo Nov, are some of its key types.
- **Colombia** – renowned for its coffee, which has a strong acidity, a full body and is very aromatic. Hulia Supremo is a favoured, top quality coffee.
- **Ethiopia** – produces some of the most intense and unusual coffees. Ethiopian Harrar is particularly impressive, with a complex fruity flavour. Ethiopian Sidamo and Yirgacheffe are also well liked.
- **Guatemala** – a high-altitude coffee country, with some trees grown at over 5,000ft (1,524m); Huehuetenango is a wonderful coffee, with a rich smoky flavour and a peppery aroma.
- **Hawaii** – its Kona coffee, grown on the slopes of Hualalai, has a good reputation, which has earned it a solid price tag to match.
- **Jamaica** – produces perhaps one of the most renowned coffees, in part because of its price. Blue Mountain is loved for its mild and sweet flavour; it is also the base for Tia Maria liqueur.
- **Java** – this is where the Dutch began the cultivation of coffee trees, which led to its global exportation. Java coffee is heavy and strong in flavour. It is also a source of Kopi Luwak, renowned as the most expensive coffee in the world, selling for between £75 and £500 per pound. Kopi Luwak, at £50 a cup, is made from Indonesian cat's droppings and was recently sold in-store at retailer Peter Jones.
- **Kenya** – known among coffee enthusiasts to produce coffee that has a bright acidity, well known for its intense flavour, full body and pleasant aroma.
- **Mexico** – produces a solid coffee, with a mild flavour; usually used as a base for blending.
- **Yemen** – produces a coffee called Yemen Mocha, characterised by musky fruitiness and earthiness. The two key types are the fruity Sanani, and the heavier Mattari.
- **Panama** – its Gesha coffee, grown in the highlands of Boquete, is famed for its floral quality, and ability to reach high prices at auction.

- **Papua New Guinea** – producing sweet and floral coffees, with the original seedlings from Blue Mountain coffee; the aroma has fruity overtones of mango and papaya.
- **Sumatra** – produces two key coffee varieties, Mandheling and Lintong – heavy, smooth and complex.
- **Sulawesi** – its coffee is often used to improve the flavour of Sumatran coffee. Grown at high altitudes, it is a rich, full bodied coffee, with well-balanced acidity.
- **Tanzania** – less developed than its Kenyan neighbour, the coffee is usually bright in acidity, with Blackburn Estate from Ngorogoro Crater a highlight.
- **Uganda** – although it mostly produces Robusta coffee, the Arabica bean grown on the western slopes of Mt Elgon, known as Bugishu, is excellent.

Create your own coffee flavour

The art of blending: Various coffee varieties are often blended together, to create a flavour and aroma that can be produced again and again. It can also be used by coffee shops and food brands to create a specific type of coffee that is unique to them. Blends usually incorporate three to four different varieties of coffee, in varying ratios. Coffee is usually blended before roasting, but not always.

Roasting

One of the things that gives coffee its distinctive flavour is the roasting process, which can produce very different cups of coffee. During the roasting process the bean swells, the silver skin falls off and it changes from green to dark brown. It is at this stage that the coffee aroma really starts to develop. How you purchase your coffee, and what you want to use it for, will depend in part on how it is roasted.

The length of roasting usually depends on where it will be drunk. In southern Europe for instance the coffee is dark roasted, creating nearly

TIP

It is the caramelisation of the sugars in the coffee, during the roasting process, that develops its dark brown colour and distinctive aroma.

black beans, because it is intended to be drunk strong and black. A medium roast is preferred in the USA and Central Europe and will be the coffee you and your customers are most familiar with. In places such as Scandinavia, milder coffee is preferred, which is known as a blonde, or light, roast.

Roast know-how

- **Light roasts** – seven minutes. This is the subtlest roast, known sometimes as a Cinnamon Roast, in response to its colour.
- **Medium roasts** – 9 to 11 minutes. These have a strong body, and a good flavour and are common in the USA, hence their name American, or City, Roast.
- **Medium dark roasts** – 12–13 minutes. This brings the natural oils of the coffee to the surface resulting in a strong but not bitter flavoured coffee. These are known as Continental Roasts.
- **Dark roasts** – 14 minutes. The beans are blackened, which gives the coffee a thick, smoky flavour. It is often known as an Italian Roast.

Grinding and storing

Grinding and storing form the final process in getting the coffee ready to drink. Coffee must be used immediately after it is ground as the grinding process causes it to oxidise and lose its subtle flavour; so most coffee shops keep their coffee in the bean stage and have a machine which grinds the coffee as and when it is necessary.

Burr grinding is the most common form of grinding, and involves a machine which crushes and tears the beans between two abrasive surfaces, which create friction. This produces evenly ground coffee which in turn makes a smoother drink. Most machines will have a range of settings, making them suitable to grind coffee for espresso machines, drip filters and percolators. For more details about grinding machines, see Chapter 3.3 (*Essential equipment*, page 167).

Storage is obviously important as coffee spoils when it is exposed to air, heat, light or moisture. Coffee beans should be stored in airtight containers, in a cool place. Although some people advocate keeping coffee in the fridge, or sometimes the freezer, it isn't usually advised by the industry. And while you can store ground coffee in the same way as your keep coffee beans, but it really isn't advisable – as coffee is ground it releases its delicious aroma and flavour, and the longer it does this, the less tasty your coffee will be.

IN MY EXPERIENCE:

Tim Hume, Redroaster Coffee House

Our coffee menu has evolved from 'Seattle-faux-Italian' to incorporate our understanding of Italian and Spanish specialities plus the odd innovation of our own. It's safe to guess that double Caffé latte is our most popular since for volume it corresponds to the English taste but we make it strong so it tastes of coffee.

Tasting coffee

While you might be clued up on the different types of coffee, it's vital that you also start to understand what they really taste like, the differences between roasts and beans, and what really constitutes good quality coffee.

Pour yourself a small cup of coffee. Now first smell it, writing down any words that come to mind about the aroma. Use a spoon to gently move the coffee around, releasing the different aroma. Next you should taste it, taking a small sip, and as with wine, swilling the coffee around your mouth. Note down:

- **Flavour** – exactly what it tastes like, be as abstract and descriptive as you want.
- **Strength** – how deep is the flavour, give it a mark out of five if that helps.
- **Body** – this is its consistency, how thick, velvety, smooth or thin it is, and the acidity, which refers to the bitter, fruity taste in coffee, how strong is it?
- **Balance** – finally consider how structured is the taste, think of it from beginning to end, is there a harmony of flavour?

Once you have swallowed, think about the aftertaste, what is left on your tongue, how strong is the flavour, this will also help you determine the body. A full-bodied coffee will retain its flavour for up to a minute.

TIP

Keep a record of the different coffees you taste as you are planning and setting up shop, marking them out of 5 or ten for body, balance, strength, acidity and flavour and refer back to it often.

Some words to describe the different coffees

- Chocolatey, winey – Guatemalan, Kenyan
- Bright, dry, sharp, snappy – Costa Rican
- Caramelly, syrupy, earthy – Colombian Supremo or Sumatran
- Fragrant – Sumatra Mandheling and Kenyan
- Sweet, mellow, nutty – Whole Latta Java and Organic Mexican
- Spicy – Guatemala Huehuetenango

Drinks to offer

Now you have learnt about the origins and processes of coffee, it's on to the really fun stuff, and most probably the main reason why you decided to open a coffee shop: making and drinking the coffee. The most important thing is to ensure you know what you are talking about, and what your customers will want when they order from you. Most coffee recipes have a base of espresso, so perfecting your espresso skills first is vital, before branching out into more elaborate options.

There is ultimately a never-ending list of coffee drinks, and as your business and confidence grows you may start to invent your own. The list below is a good place to start, with some standard options, and several less common ones.

TIP

Espresso: A 1oz shot of coffee, made from 7g–8g of ground coffee; it takes between 15 and 25 seconds to brew.

Americano	One espresso shot, diluted with hot water. Not to be confused with a filter coffee.
Black coffee/ filter coffee	This is *not* made with espresso. It is commonly known as a filter coffee, made using a drip filter or percolator. Served without milk.
Café au lait	Another one without espresso, similar to a latte but the coffee element is provided by a measure of black filter coffee. A traditional French breakfast coffee.

Cappuccino	One part espresso, three parts frothed milk. There are also dry cappuccinos which have less foam, and no steamed milk.
Corretto	Espresso shot with a measure of grappa.
Doppio	A double shot of espresso.
Espresso	A single shot of espresso, a classic.
Espresso con panna	One shot of espresso topped with a small amount of whipped cream.
Frappé	Popular in Europe and Latin America, traditionally made with a cold espresso shot, and mixed with sugar, water, milk and ice.
Fredo	A latte, made with cold milk and shaken with ice. See below for details on lattes.
Granita	Espresso mixed with soft brown sugar and brandy, frozen, then crushed and served with whipped cream.
Hammerhead (also known as 'a shot in the dark')	A strong coffee made with a shot of espresso, topped up with drip or filter coffee, served in a standard coffee cup.
Iced espresso	A double shot of espresso over crushed ice.
Latte	A very milky cappuccino. One espresso shot, with five shots of steamed milk.
Lungo (long)	This allows twice as much water to go through the coffee grounds as for a normal espresso, it's a thinner coffee, but the concentration of caffeine is greater.
Macchiato	Double or single shot of espresso with a small amount of frothed milk on top.
Melya	Espresso mixed with powdered cocoa and honey. Can be served with cream.
Mocha	Basically a cappuccino, with chocolate syrup added to it, often whipped cream is added.
Ristretto (restricted)	A very concentrated espresso, achieved by allowing less water through than you would for a normal espresso. Strong in flavour, but lower in caffeine.
Romano	Espresso shot served with a twist of lemon.

Flavoured coffee

These are traditionally made using flavoured syrups, such as chocolate, cinnamon, maple, or nutmeg. They are either poured into the coffee or drizzled over the top, depending on what you are making.

Alternative coffees

It may be that you want to showcase a range of different coffees from around the world, or focus on a specific country's coffee; here are some innovative coffees from around the world.

- **Indian (Madras) coffee** – brewed in southern India, this is a filter coffee made using rough ground Indian coffee, drip-brewed for several hours and served with lots of milk.
- **Irish coffee** – a well-known after dinner drink, with brandy and brown sugar, and a cream top.
- **Kopi Tubruk** – thick Indonesian coffee, popular in Java and Bali, made by boiling the coffee grounds with a piece of sugar.
- **Oliang** – South East Asian coffee, blended with corn, soy beans, and sesame seeds.
- **Turkish coffee** – this coffee is also known as Greek coffee and is incredibly thick. Made in a brass or copper pan, it is unfiltered, and so served with the grounds still in it, along with sugar and spices.
- **Vietnamese coffee** – an iced drink, served with sweetened, condensed milk; the coffee is thick and strong.

> **TIP**
>
> You may initially want to start with a small offering of around five coffees; made well they can take some time, and irritated customers waiting to be served is not a good start! Once you and your baristas are confident about making everything on your menu, you can expand your offering.

Making the drinks

Mastering the art of espresso is probably one of the most important things you will need to learn as a coffee shop owner, as it'll be the basis of around 75% of the drinks you serve. Although it seems like a fairly straightforward process, a short stint of research will reveal that making a good espresso is an art in itself.

Step 1: Coffee grounds

Make sure you fill the espresso filter with exactly 7g of ground coffee or 14g if you are making a double measure. You should become adept at being able to see from just looking that you have the right amount of coffee. Level off the coffee, but don't press it down yet.

Step 2: Tamping

This is much more important for making great coffee than is given credit. Tamping involves packing the grounds together to make a solid pellet of coffee for the water to pass through at high pressure. Loose grounds mean the process will be uneven and the coffee won't be strong enough. Make sure you hold the flat-based tamping tool evenly in the palm of your hand, and take care not to knock the filter basket while tamping as this will dislodge the grains again. You need to tamp the coffee three times: the first time is fairly gentle, then use a finger to pull in any loose grounds. Then press down harder for the second tamp, sweeping any stray grounds into the filter, and do a final tamp which should be a strong pressure – around 30 pounds. Some people practise getting the right amount of pressure on some household weighing scales. On the final tamp twist the tamper to polish the coffee pellet you have made.

Step 3: Drawing

This is the stage when you pass water through the coffee. It should take about 20–25 seconds to pour a measure of espresso. Before you open, spend some time ensuring you have got everything correct. If the coffee comes out faster than 20 seconds your grounds are too fine, so adjust your coffee grinder's settings. If it takes too long, the reverse is true. If you have a pressure gauge on your machine it should show about 9bar during the draw process, and the water temperature should be stable and somewhere between 92°C and 96°C. The timing is the same for single and double measures.

Adding milk

Working with milk isn't simply about adding it to coffee; there is a technique to ensure the milk is smooth and velvety, and if you are thinking about branching into coffee art you need to spend a lot of time perfecting your technique.

Always begin with fresh, cold milk. Ensure the temperature is right, start at around 26°C–30°C, slowly building the temperature to 65°C–70°C. To heat and froth the milk, slowly turn on the steam and move the wand through the milk to the top. The milk will start to rise so make sure the wand is always about a centimetre below the surface. Try to create smaller groups of bubbles, don't let the milk over-boil or turn into foam. It should be soft and velvety, and when you pour it into the espresso it should mix and blend easily with the coffee.

TIP
Attending training programmes is vital to get hands-on experience of espresso making before you open; they will also help you learn about making different types of coffee, including heating and frothing the milk, and coffee art (for more details, see page 248).

Serving the drinks: which cup?

Contrary to popular belief it really does matter what you serve your coffee in, and some aficionados say the right cup is as important as the right glass for wine, as certain shapes and types release the aroma, and ensure the coffee cools at a slower pace. We'll cover more on cups and crockery on page 236, but it's a good idea at this stage to consider what coffee you will be offering and how this might impact the china you will need to buy.

Espresso is commonly served in small, thick cups, with a wide brim and a thinner bottom, as this forces the aroma to the top of the cup, which enhances the overall flavour. The thickness of the cup ensures the espresso stays hot for as long as possible; this is vital as heat also helps the aroma to travel. Iced drinks are usually served in tall, thick glasses, similar to a long cocktail. Lattes and café au lait are best served in tall or regular-sized mugs, and cappuccinos are often served in wide, low cups to allow the cream and milk to mix with the coffee. Thick glass cups or mugs are also popular as they keep the coffee warm and look impressive, especially if coffee art is part of your unique selling point (USP; see pages 45-46).

Almost all coffee is served with a saucer, especially the milk-based drinks, which are traditionally overfilled with cream.

TEA

History and background

Tea shops are becoming progressively more popular in the UK, especially with the increasingly large and diverse range of teas available, such as green and white tea, caffeine-free beverages and fruit infusions. According to the United Kingdom Tea Council, with 165 million cups of tea consumed every day, the UK accounts for 6% of world tea consumption. That's a large prospective market base, and whether you are running a specific tea shop, or considering what your tea offering will be alongside coffee, it's vital you give your tea as much thought as you did to your coffee.

IN MY EXPERIENCE:

Tim Hume, Redroaster Coffee House

We offer a wide range of real and herbal teas without considering ourselves to be specialists. Serving loose leaf tea by the pot is an important commitment to quality. Tea (quite rightly) has a considerable following and you cannot ignore it.

Legend has it that tea was discovered in ancient China, when leaves from a nearby *Camellia sinensis* tree fell into water that was being boiled for the then emperor, Shen Nung. The emperor, a keen herbalist, tasted it, found it to be refreshing – and tea was born. *Camellia sinensis* is an evergreen, tropical plant with green, shiny pointed leaves, native to China and India. Today it is grown all over the world, though it thrives in warm, humid climates in deep, well-drained soil, up to altitudes of 2,000m.

To some extent tea hasn't changed that drastically from its discovery 5,000 years ago. The four main types of tea we drink – black, white, green and oolong – are still made from the same tree and still infused with hot water to create a popular and iconic beverage. However, there have also been developments in various caffeine-free teas, and fruit and herbal infusions, which have turned the market into a vast and extensive industry.

Global tea

Tea is most commonly grown in China, Japan and India, and, because of the labour-intensive nature of tea production, most estates are still relatively small and often family-run, which means, depending on where you get your tea from, each box of tea can be totally unique. India is the biggest producer of tea, processing a staggering 850,000 tonnes of tea a year, a high percentage of which is black tea, such as Assam or Darjeeling. China produces tea with small leaves which is grown at high altitudes – it especially produces excellent white and green teas. Japanese tea production is some of the most inventive, and includes teas such as Sencha (steamed rather than dried) and Gyokuro.

Africa is the fourth largest exporter, and accounts for a large percentage of the global tea output – around 32% in total – though it is usually considered to be of inferior quality to tea from other producers. Countries such as Ethiopia, Uganda and Kenya produce strong, black teas with a golden glow and lots of flavour, often finding their way into the teabag market. In Malawi the colour of the soil has meant the tea is deep red, occasionally purple. South Africa is renowned for its Rooibos tea and also makes some popular golden teas. Because of its varying geography, Sri Lanka produces a range of different tasting teas, including bright, fresh teas grown at high altitudes, and darker, stronger teas grown lower down. Brazil's hot climate produces a golden, nutty tea, and Turkey also produces a large amount of tea, much of which is often used in iced teas because of its rich red colour.

Processing: from tree to tea

Teas are either caffeine teas or caffeine-free teas and can be most easily divided into six categories within this distinction:

Caffeine teas, all made from *Camellia sinensis*	Caffeine-free teas and infusions – made from other leaves, fruits and herbs
Black tea	Rooibos and honeybush tea
Green tea	Herbal and fruit infusions
Oolong tea	
White tea	

The key difference between these teas is the way in which they are harvested and processed.

Caffeine teas

Black, Oolong, green and white teas originate from the same tree, but what differentiates them is the way the leaves are processed, as well as the soil, climate and country the tea is produced in.

Camellia sinensis matures for five years before the leaves are ready to be harvested and, as long as the tree is well maintained, it can produce tea for 25 years. After this the tree is cut down and the trunk removed, forcing new stems to grow from the old roots – this process means one tree can produce tea for up to 100 years.

Picking

Tea picking season starts in Asia at the beginning of spring and lasts to the end of August, and in Africa picking is done all year. The leaves harvested earlier in the year – known as 'new tea' – are the best crop, producing a rich, strong tea. Tea flowers can also be added to the tea at the final stages, enhancing the aroma.

The tea is harvested traditionally, mostly by local women, who handpick the leaves, collecting them in baskets on their backs. White tea is made by picking only the youngest leaves, still covered in soft white hairs, or down; and black, green and oolong tea requires the first two leaves and a bud. This process, which is time-consuming (pickers can harvest just over half a kilogram a day), ensures that only the best leaves are collected. Machines are sometimes used, though this is only for less good quality tea as the technique results in broken leaves, which can only be used for teabags and lower graded tea. For more information on tea grading, see page 146.

Processing

The process of making tea involves a series of drying, wilting and rolling techniques which remove excess moisture and then allow the leaves to oxidise, before releasing their pungent oils and developing their flavour. While black, green and oolong teas are subject to a variety of these processes, white tea is merely picked, steamed and dried.

- **Wilting and withering** – the leaves are spread thinly and left to wilt at around 25°C–30°C, for between 10 and 15 hours. Often heated air is added to the process in cooler climates; leaves can lose up to 75% of their water content at this stage.
- **Rolling** – a rolling machine is used to twist and roll the leaves, releasing the natural oils in the leaves; it is at this point they start to develop their flavour. Sometimes this process is done by hand, for a higher quality of tea.
- **Oxidation** – this is the key point of production and the point at which the tea's eventual flavour is determined. The leaves are spread out in a cool area or room and allowed to oxidise, or take in oxygen. The leaves that are left the longest become black tea, those that oxidise for a shorter time, that is, undergo between 30% and 60% oxidation, are either oolong or green tea. Some producers will escalate this process by tumbling or rolling the leaves, known as 'bruising'.
- **Drying and firing** – these are the finishing stages of the tea production process, where the leaves are usually baked, or occasionally sun or air dried. This stops the oxidation process, and must be done carefully as over-cooking or burning can ruin the leaves.

Grading tea

Tea is graded depending on the size and texture of its leaves. The full details are intensive, and complex, but this guide should give you a clear idea. A good thing to remember is that the tea in ordinary English teabags is at the bottom of the scale and provides a hugely sub-standard level of tea.

Fine Tippy Golden Flowery Orange Pekoe (FTGFOP)	The best, highest quality loose-leaf tea, well-rounded, pure, clean to taste, with a bright, fresh colour. It has an abundance of tips (the down-like hair from the youngest tea leaves).
Tippy Golden Flowery Orange Pekoe (TGFOP)	A good quality loose-leaf tea, which includes the golden tips of young tea buds. It has a solid flavour and aroma, and is used for Assam and Darjeeling teas.

Golden Flowery Orange Pekoe (GFOP)	Still good quality at this level, with some golden tips, however, it has considerably smaller leaves.
Flowery Orange Pekoe (FOP)	Common loose-leaf tea, readily available across the globe.
Orange Pekoe (OP)	Has quite large leaves, but no tips, commonly from Sir Lanka or South India. A low range tea grade.
Broken Orange Pekoe (BOP)	Broken leaves, which reduces the quality, can sometimes be found in high-end teabags.
Fannings /Dust	Scrapings from the production floor, used extensively across the world to fill teabags. The taste, flavour and quality is hugely inferior.

Blending tea

Nowadays nearly 90% of the tea we drink in the UK is blended. Black tea is traditionally blended to make some of the teas we now enjoy on a daily basis. Blending is a unique art, done by expert tea tasters, and each blend is a closely guarded secret of its producers. The key point of blending is to create something balanced and memorable, which means that every batch must taste exactly the same. These days blending is done by the use of computer, which works out the exact measurements needed for each tea, and then mixes the tea together in a large blending drum.

Common black tea blends are made by mixing up to 35 different teas together, and you will know them as English Breakfast, Afternoon Tea, and many of the branded teas such as Yorkshire Tea, PG Tips and Tetley's. Some black teas are also mixed with perfumes, oils and other flavours to create a unique type of tea, such as Earl Grey, which is mixed with citrus and bergamot oils, and Lapsang Souchong, which is roasted over pine needles.

Green tea mixes use lotus, jasmine, rose, vanilla, mint, citrus flavours and a range of spices to create an infinite variety of interesting and unique teas.

Tasting tea

Being a tea taster is vocational in every respect, taking at least five years to train, as well as being a lifelong learning process. Tea is tasted similarly to wine, or even coffee, swilling it around the mouth and spitting it out, as well as considering aroma, appearance and other things such as the tannins and astringency of the tea.

Some unique and interesting tasting terms include:

- **Agony of leaves** – how the leaves curl and roll when boiling water is added to them.
- **Astringency** – how dry the tea makes your mouth feel.
- **Bright** – the fresh look of the tea, almost clear enough to act as a mirror.
- **Body** – the texture of the tea, and the depth of its taste.
- **Chesty** – when the tea has retained the woody flavour from the chest it was packed in.
- **Fruity** – usually reserved for oolong tea, especially fruity and citrus in flavour.
- **Fung** – a bad thing, meaning that that tea has become damp and tastes almost fungal.
- **Malty** – common to Assam tea, a milky, rich flavour.
- **Pungent** – used for teas such as Earl Grey or Lapsang Souchong when the aroma is so strong you can taste the tea before you have drunk it.
- **Wild** – refers to the rare, unique tasting tea, made using leaves grown at the end of the tea season.

Types of tea

Black tea

The most common, and cheapest of all teas, drunk across the globe, it contains the most caffeine, and is the tea subject to the most extensive processing of all four teas. It preserves its flavour longer than green and oolong tea.

Types of black tea

- Assam, Darjeeling, Sri Lankan Ceylon, Lapsang Souchong, Nilgiri, Yunnan
- Blends such as English Breakfast, Earl Grey and Afternoon Tea
- Some black teas are also blended with citrus fruits or herbs to create a sweeter blend

Flavour and appearance

- Usually a strong amber in colour
- A rich, hearty brew, used for numerous blended teas, and iced tea

Oolong tea

Typically grown in China, Japan and Taiwan, oolong, which means 'black dragon' in Chinese, is often 'bruised' after wilting and fermented for a slightly shorter time than that of black tea. Owing to their Chinese origins, these teas have some of the most inventive and unique names.

Types of oolong tea

- Tie Kuan Yin (Tea of the Iron Goddess of Mercy)
- Shui Hsien (Water Sprite)
- Wuyi Yan (Bohea Rock)

Flavour and appearance

- Oolong tea is often brown, but can be a subtler golden colour
- The taste can be either woody or flowery as well
- It is best drunk without milk

Green tea

This differs from black and oolong as it isn't oxidised, merely withered, rolled and dried; some green teas are also hand-rolled into tea pearls, which capture the flavour and release a wonderful aroma when boiling water is added. Green teas have a quarter of the caffeine of coffee. They are grown most commonly in China, although some of the best come from Taiwan.

Types of green tea

- Gunpowder
- Chun Me
- Gyokuro (Precious Dew)
- Sencha

Flavour and appearance

- Huge variety of colour and flavour, ranging from pale, transparent tea, through pale green to a warm golden colour
- Green tea is fresh and citrus tasting, often quite bitter

- Wet leaves first with a splash of cold water before adding hot water
- Milk should not be added

White tea

The least processed tea, white tea is not oxidised or rolled but simply withered and dried by steaming. It is produced in much smaller quantities than the other three teas and is traditionally quite expensive.

Types of white tea

- White Peony
- Silver Needle
- Narcissus
- Chaicha

Flavour and appearance

- A stunning silvery grey in colour, white tea has a soft, sweet flavour and is often mixed with fruits or spices
- Can be brewed for up to 10 minutes but the water should not be boiling as this can make the tea bitter

Caffeine-free tea

Caffeine-free tea has had a renaissance in recent years, particularly as the health benefits of avoiding caffeine become more and more apparent. It makes an interesting addition to any café menu, and can often be a big part of the identity you are working to create, particularly with more bohemian, global-culture coffee and tea shops.

Rooibos tea

Rooibos tea – meaning 'red bush' tea – is native to South Africa, which is still the only country that produces it. Rooibos is produced from the *Aspalathus linearis* plant, in the Cedarberg region of the Western Cape province and is harvested in the same way as black teas, with oxidation and drying. Some green Rooibos is also produced, in which the oxidation process is skipped. Caffeine-free, with a syrupy, earthy aroma and a light, sweet flavour, Rooibos can be drunk with milk and sugar, and is popular for its health benefits as well as its taste.

Honeybush tea

Similar in many ways to Rooibos, honeybush is known as Heuningbos in South Africa. The plant's flowers smell strongly of honey, and the tea itself is sweeter than Rooibos, but similarly light and golden in colour.

Herbal and fruit tea

Herb and fruit infusions are not considered teas, and are often referred to as infusions or tisanes. They are made using the various parts of natural plants, spices, flowers and fruits, such as stems, leaves, nuts, buds, blossoms, roots and herbs. They are drunk without milk and are sweetened by the natural sugars in the plant. Typical infusions include: camomile, lemon grass, ginger, peppermint, jasmine, rosehip, blackcurrant and lemon. Often these are blended together to create a variety of flavours.

Tea varieties

The variety of teas you serve in your tea shop says a lot about your identity; and even if you are considering tea as a second product line after coffee, you will also want to make sure what you offer says a lot about who you are. The different varieties of tea are far too numerous to mention in their entirety, and it's imperative you undertake some of your own research to work out exactly what you would like. Here we've listed a selection of some of the most common, and some more interesting, types.

Afternoon	A lighter blend, made with Darjeeling, and usually some Oolong or Ceylon tea, it is sometimes scented with jasmine.
Assam	While usually more common in a blend, pure Assam tea is malty and rich with a warm golden brew.
Camomile	Sweet tasting brew, made with delicate flowers, it is calming and soothing.
Chai	A traditional milky Indian tea, with spices and sweetener. Made with black tea and infused with cardamom, cinnamon, ginger, cloves or pepper, it has recently become popular in America as a kind of 'tea latte'.

Darjeeling	The 'Champagne of Teas', as only tea grown high up in this stunning Himalayan area can be classified as Darjeeling. The tea is pungent, spicy and smooth, with a green, golden hue.
Dragon Well	A renowned green tea, known as Long Jing in China, it is a rich, smooth green tea.
Earl Grey	A black tea blend flavoured with bergamot and citrus oil. Popular as an afternoon tea, it can be drunk with or without milk and is very popular in the UK.
English Breakfast	Strong black tea blend, known also as 'morning' tea, designed to give a kickstart to the day, usually made with Assam, Ceylon and Keenum Chinese teas, often with some African teas added.
Fruit teas	Common berries and fruits used in infusions are redcurrant, rosehip, blackcurrant, raspberry, strawberry and blackberry. Lemon is the most common citrus tea and is often mixed with ginger to make a really fresh, strong flavour. Make sure to look for teas that use the actual fruit and don't have flavourings.
Genmaicha	A unique Japanese green tea, mixed with roasted grains of rice – incredibly healthy.
Iced tea	Made with black tea, iced tea is a great refreshing summer option; it is served with ice and often flavoured with syrup such as vanilla, peach, apple or lime.
Jasmine	Traditionally a Chinese tea, it has a subtle sweet flavour and is often made using one large jasmine flower which opens to reveal a stunning bloom when hot water is added.
Lapsang Souchong	A rich smoky tea, fire-dried over pine needles. It has a heady, indulgent aroma and is a delicious alternative to Earl Grey or English Breakfast.
Lemon grass	A refreshing tea, with antibacterial and antifungal properties.
Nilgiri	Green in colour, this Indian black tea is intensely strong and aromatic, with a rich flavour.
Pu-erh	A unique Chinese delicacy, made by fermenting the leaves in the ground for up to 50 years. It is strong, rich and has a very distinctive flavour – an acquired taste!

Rose Grey	A vanilla and rose flavoured black tea, summery, sweet and light tasting, it's a unique and interesting alternative to afternoon tea.
Rooibos	Classic and well-known caffeine-free alternative from South Africa, it is sweet and subtle in flavour and can be enjoyed with or without milk.
Russian Caravan	Made with Lapsang Souchong, Oolong and Assam, it is a strong, flavourful tea, often a popular alternative to coffee.
Sencha	Delicate and aromatic, this green tea is steamed rather dried during processing.
Silver Needle	Wonderful white tea, a perfect example of the subtlety of the leaves, it is sweet and delicate.

If you are stuck for what to offer initially it might be an idea to stock one of each type of tea, such as English Breakfast, green tea, white tea, Rooibos, Peppermint, Fruit and Camomile – this gives you a broad range of teas, and allows your customers variety without overwhelming them.

Making and serving tea

Once you have decided what tea you want to offer, you will need to think about how it's made, and what you will serve it in.

Bag or leaf?

For tea aficionados there is no debate, loose-leaf tea is the only way to go, promising a far superior brew, in flavour, aroma and colour. However as a busy tea shop owner you might find teabags a quicker option. Make sure you consider what works best for you, and what suits the ethos of your shop. For London-based teashop Yumchaa, serving only loose-leaf tea is an intrinsic part of its identity.

> 'Creating great teas is driven by our desire to make tea (chaa) that tastes Yum. To ensure the highest quality tea blends we use quality ingredients and make only loose leaf tea, sticking firmly to our No Teabagging policy!'

Making tea

The tea must be fresh, so ensure you not only store the tea in a sealed container, in a cool dry place but also stagger your stock purchasing so your tea is not sitting around for several months. A lot of tea is ruined by the maker adding too much tea and too little water; good quality tea has an excellent depth of flavour so ensure you are clear on what you really need - this will also help your profit margins! A lot of shops and cafés measure their tea, but this can be time consuming, so, as with coffee, train yourself and your baristas to be clear about the amounts you need, or keep it simple and use teabags.

Water quality and temperature is the second consideration. If you can find a way to reduce the hardness of your water, or use filtered water, do it - it can often mean the difference between a bitter, chalky tea and a smooth, fresh brew. Many tea brands now make teas that can withstand harsher water so if you do live in a hard water area investigate this option too.

Whereas black tea needs boiling water to release the flavour, the more delicate oolong, green and white can be damaged by very hot water, so you should wet the leaves with cold water first and then add hot, but not boiling water. All teas should be allowed time to brew, but green and oolong tea need less time than a black tea - it's a good idea if you are serving your tea in a teapot to let the customer know how long to brew it for to ensure they get the best cup possible.

Serving tea

If you are using teabags you may decide you want to serve tea in big mugs, which can work well, with a homely 'builder's tea' approach, or you can use large cups and saucers. Alternatively, especially if you are running a tea shop, or choosing to have tea as a large part of your offering, you will want to look at teapots - which could range from large family-style pots, smaller assorted sizes, or the 'tea and cup' combination with a smaller tea-for-one pot on top of a large, wide-brimmed cup. The options are endless and will largely depend on what you are serving, and how much of it you expect to serve. In the beginning it might be an idea to keep your options open and purchase the bulk of your teapots and mugs a few months into service.

TIP

If you are serving a variety of herbal and fruit teas you may want to consider the aesthetics of the tea, and consider glass mugs, cups and teapots that allow customers to see the wonderful colours and shapes of the leaves, buds, fruits and flowers.

Additions

Adding milk to different teas is partly a matter of taste, and partly a matter of tradition. Help your customers by giving them the option, and gently advising them of what is best: adding milk to green tea will ruin it, but adding milk to Rooibos creates a creamy, sweet drink. Don't let your desire for quality be compromised here. This can often be overlooked in the quest for the perfect tea or coffee. Do also check out your local dairy suppliers. You will be surprised at how much milk you will be using – and how much it will cost you.

Sugar, or other sweeteners are also important, and aside from standard sugar you might set yourself apart by offering lemon slices, honey, vanilla, cherry and other flavoured syrups.

> **TIP**
> Whatever you decide, make sure you consider the serving aspect of milk and sugar. Will you give each customer their own milk and sugar? In which case you will need a lot of trays – or have a central station where they can add their own.

OTHER DRINKS

Of course you will also need to consider some other drinks, aside from tea and coffee – especially as in the summer or during holidays these can be lucrative offerings. Some to consider are given below.

Hot chocolate

This is typically included in any coffee shop menu, and is a great option for children. You can offer anything from powdered hot chocolate to rich, melted chocolate with milk. Think about how your offering fits with your ethos, as well as considering the time it takes to make each drink. Think also about toppings – are you going to offer marshmallows or whipped cream to

> **TIP**
> If you are planning on making your coffee shop family-friendly, why not offer a kids-size hot chocolate complete with sprinkles and a cookie for a fixed price?

make your hot chocolate that bit different? Can you afford to be adventurous and offer something really rich and exotic – hot chocolate with chilli perhaps?

Smoothies and juices

Smoothies and juices can be a lovely thing to offer, another great option for children and a delicious summer treat. Decide whether you will:

- Buy these already bottled and made
- Serve them in glasses or in self-serve bottles from a small fridge
- Juice and blend your own. (Making your own juice and smoothies adds a nice authentic twist but can take time and needs to be carefully managed so that you don't end up with too much wasted stock)

If you will be making smoothies, developing your own flavours is a nice idea, but try to get a balance of dairy (milk, yoghurt and ice cream) and fruit-based options, and invest in a good smoothie-maker. Smoothies can take time to make, and use up a lot of produce, so do your research into whether having ready-made batches is better, or whether you should make them on demand. This is something you can adapt as you start to learn more about what your customers want. However, making your own is also quite expensive – if you aren't planning to make these drinks a core part of your business it might be an idea to buy them in.

Some nice smoothie recipes include classics such as yoghurt, vanilla and banana; chocolate with strawberries; and mango and orange. Other interesting flavours to play with are cinnamon, winter berries, peach, ginger, mint, cherry, spices, coconut and lemon. You could also theme your juices and smoothies into things such as: superfood berries, indulgence, warming, tropical. Don't forget that you can use green and black teas to make iced teas and smoothies too; and you can also make savoury options such as vegetable juice or tomato smoothies.

Fizzy drinks and water

The final consideration is the more standard drinks that you do need to offer if you want to cater for everyone – coke, lemonade, even water. Make sure you have the capacity to serve these either from a small fridge, or from the counter, and think about whether your water offering will be glasses of tap water for free, or bottles of water. However, don't ignore the traditions of some fizzy drinks – ginger ale, old-fashioned lemonade and tomato juice often do a roaring trade in the summer, and if 'homemade' is your forte then you can even make some of these yourself.

Alcohol

Serving alcohol – such as bottles of beer and small bottles of wine – can be a nice touch, especially if you plan on serving a wide selection of food, or being open for evening meals. However, if your food selection is limited it may be something not worth investing in, as most people would simply go to a bar or pub if they wanted an alcoholic drink, rather than come to a coffee shop.

If you do want to serve alcohol for your customers to drink on your premises, you will need to apply for a personal licence, which allows you the right to sell alcohol – your name will appear on the licence. Getting this licence can also be handy if you are planning on having entertainment as the licence covers both this and alcohol consumption. Check with your local authority about the legal specifics, and see page 117.

BEING ETHICAL: FAIRTRADE, GREEN AND ORGANIC

With our tea and coffee we believe that quality and trading fairly go hand in hand. It's only by forging strong relationships with the growers and by paying them premium prices that we can ensure a continued supply of the best quality. Our tea and coffee buyers spend many weeks a year overseas finding the best tea leaves and coffee beans the world has to offer.

Recently we have become more aware of the plight of coffee and tea farmers, of the damage food miles are doing to our environment and the excess of pesticides, additives and genetically modified produce in our food and drink. This has led many of us to become more concerned about what we eat and drink and where it comes from.

For coffee and tea this is not only a big deal ethically, but it can also be a big deal financially. Eco-conscious customers are becoming more aware of the provenance of their food, as well as whether it is organic or ethically sourced, such as fairtrade, and you must consider this when sourcing and purchasing your supplies.

Fairtrade

The Fairtrade movement started in 1992 and works to ensure a fair deal for the poorer farmers and growers in regions such as Latin America, Asia and Africa. Before Fairtrade was established, the gap between the money paid to farmers, and the profits gained by large multinationals in the Western world was, quite literally, vast. Fairtrade works to both ensure a fair price to farmers and growers for goods such as coffee, tea, wine and chocolate, as well as upholding certain standards to guarantee fair wages, living and working conditions.

Fairtrade is popular with the public too. In 2007 Marks & Spencer converted all of its tea and coffee to Fairtrade, which led to a sales growth of 6%, against a market growth of 1.5%. And a recent survey by Mintel found Fairtrade to be one of the fastest growing sectors (including organic), with 265% growth since 2002.

Whether you source specifically Fairtrade produce, or use a supplier who has good ethical credentials, is up to you. However, if it's something you feel strongly about, or you know your customers will (and nowadays more than one in two people in the UK recognise the FAIRTRADE mark), you need to consider the extra hike in price that it might incur. Having said that, in recent years this has become less of an issue, with many Fairtrade products retailing for less than their non-Fairtrade competitors. That said, for decisions such as this it is important to make sure you have thoroughly researched your customer base (see page 47).

> **TIP**
> For more information on Fairtrade and coffee and tea, visit www.fairtrade.org.uk.

It may also be wise to think about how Fairtrade will affect your marketing and public relations (PR), as well as your overall identity. The Fairtrade Foundation allows you to use its logo and branding on any promotional materials and website. Some coffee shops choose to promote the information on their boards, menus and price charts, while others simply source fair or ethically traded produce as standard. There is no right way to do it, so work with what feels right for your coffee or tea shop.

IN MY EXPERIENCE:
Simon Robertson, Leoni

It is important to me that the coffee beans and tea we use are produced and traded fairly and ethically. To ensure this I use a reputable coffee/tea supplier. In some cases I have visited the farmers who produce our coffee beans. The important issue is the traceability of ingredients; can the supplier prove that the coffee or tea comes from ethical sources?

Green and sustainable

The other consideration after being ethical is the more sustainable and green aspects of what you source. One key way to ensure you are doing this is to try to source as much as you can locally, and work with suppliers who have made an effort to think about food miles and the way they transport their food. You can also do your bit for the environment by recycling as much as you can, using recycled or biodegradable goods where possible.

Organic

Is organic necessary?

In the current economic climate, many consumers see organic produce as 'nice to have' rather than 'must have'. It may be well worth doing some market research with your prospective customers *before* committing to an organic supplier.

It's still a hotly debated issue whether or not organic food is actually better for you and the earth or just has a superior taste. Either way, organic food is big business and increasing numbers of people go out of their way to find all-natural produce. But as we've said earlier, remember that not everyone will want to pay the higher prices for their ethically and environmentally resourced food and drink.

You could choose to make being an all-organic coffee shop your badge of honour, or part of your identity, or you could decide to source only your coffee and tea organically, getting everything else a bit cheaper. Either way there is a financial consideration to make, so spend some time doing a few numbers to work out the difference it will make to your profit margins.

TIP

For more information about organic food, visit www.soilassociation.org.

Things to remember:

- Coffee spoils easily and loses its flavour immediately after it has been ground, so organise regular deliveries and only grind the amount you need.
- Tea comes in many varieties these days – set yourself apart from the competition by having a unique and interesting tea menu.
- Don't forget cold drinks and other beverages; hot chocolate, juices and smoothies are great sellers, especially with children.
- Eco and ethical products are big business these days, but make sure your customers will be prepared to pay higher premiums for them.

3.2 Finding suppliers

Getting your suppliers right is a key part of your business, and it's also a huge learning curve. While you may hope to decide exactly what coffees and teas you want to serve, and then set about finding the right supplier, this might not be the best way to do it. If you work at the relationship a supplier can be your best friend – someone who knows your business, can help source and suggest new products, and advise you on other things such as training, new brands and equipment. But if things go sour, they can turn into your worst enemy . . . So while you are deciding what drinks you would like to serve, spend some time looking and speaking to suppliers, as this will inform your decisions just as much.

In this chapter we'll cover:

- Finding a supplier
- Meeting and choosing a supplier
- Supplying your own produce

FINDING A SUPPLIER

Finding a supplier needs a two-pronged approach. Firstly, ask other coffee shops and local hospitality businesses if they will recommend anyone, and just as importantly whom they would avoid, and the reasons for both. Remember that one coffee shop's needs may be the opposite of yours and a supplier they couldn't work with could be just the person for you. Equally, listen to why they like their supplier – what criterion is it that seals the deal? Is it the speed of their delivery; the friendly service they offer; the diverse range of their products; the fact that they are a local company; their very low prices; that they offer training courses or that they have an expert team of buyers? What do *you* want from your supplier?

Secondly, do your own research to find suppliers. Simple internet searches, industry magazines and local papers or directories are a good place to start; you can also try searching for a specific type of coffee and tea online and then look at what comes up for a supplier. Think also about what's new, popular and what will work for you. The kind of coffee and tea you serve, and the supplier you have, go hand in hand, so think about it in tandem.

Websites with supplier information

- www.caterer-directory.com
- www.tea.co.uk/tea_directory.php
- www.britishcoffeeassociation.org

Finally, look for a supplier who roasts their own coffee. This not only ensures better quality and a consistent roast, but also means you can work with them to develop your own blend.

MEETING YOUR SUPPLIER

IN MY EXPERIENCE:

Raymond Voce, Royal Teas

I was lucky to inherit a very good coffee and tea supplier. We have had taste tests and were given information by them on each of the coffees they provide us with. We have a good relationship with them and they are always on hand to help if necessary.

Once you have whittled your choice of suppliers down to several that you like, arrange to meet them. This is crucial; at this meeting you are looking to establish that this is a supplier you can work with, someone whose products correlate with the idea of what you want to offer in your café, as well as ensuring that quality and price are at a level that suits you. Take along some questions that you want to ask, and don't be afraid to ask them.

TIP

The best way to strike up deals with local suppliers is to visit them yourself. You can foster a much closer relationship if you try to know them personally, and it shows you are taking the time out to understand how they work. Visit them, or go over and have a chat at trade fairs and markets.

Products

- What do they offer – and what does their catalogue of products say about them? Has it changed recently? Do they have a wide range, or have they concentrated on the quality of a small selection of products? How often do they update and change their range?
- Taste – make sure you try the coffees, teas and anything else you are considering purchasing, and others; take your time and discuss this with the supplier.

Delivery

- Ask about costs.
- Ask about times of delivery, regularity, flexibility – what if you need several deliveries, or might change your order and requirement from week to week, especially in the first six months?

Knowledge and experience

- Do they understand the industry of coffee and tea shops; do their buyers and tasters have a good knowledge (at least four years' hands-on experience) in tasting coffee?
- Are you confident they know enough about the kinds of teas and coffees you want to serve to provide you with everything you need?

Passion and personality

- Do they love their product; can they share your enthusiasm about it?
- Patience – will they be responsive to the fact that this is a new business and there are things you still need to learn; can they help you fill in some of the gaps in your knowledge?
- Are they someone you can work with on a weekly basis – will you be able to resolve differences, discuss pricing and quality? Is there a rapport there?
- Openness – who are their customers? How is the business going? And how happy are they to share this information with you?

Progress

- Will they constantly be open to updating and improving what they offer?
- Will you be able to source and discover new products with them?
- Is training important to them?
- Are their buyers constantly improving their knowledge and developing their range?

Price

- What is their attitude to pricing, does it come before the product?
- Are they flexible?
- Is their pricing worryingly low?
- Do they offer special deals and one-offs?

Location

Location is also important, and most coffee shop owners advocate that local is better. If your supplier is also the person roasting and blending your coffee, it makes sense to find someone whom you can work with regularly over time to develop coffee and tea that suits you best. Equally, convenience is another crucial advantage of using local suppliers. If your coffee comes from the other side of the country, what happens when you unexpectedly run out? Local suppliers are far more willing to accommodate extra orders, not to mention quicker!

What else can they offer?

Other things include training, equipment sales, hire or maintenance, other products, advice, information and support.

The key thing in these meetings is establishing a rapport with someone who has a quality range of products at a price that suits you. While this might sound like the Holy Grail, it is achievable, especially if you are honest and realistic with yourself about what you want, and need.

Obviously a lot of it is about personality, and think about what works for you. For instance, if you are good at cutting a deal and bargaining, work with a supplier who is happy to haggle with you regularly. If you find the 'getting a good deal' side of purchasing more challenging (and you should be realistic that there will be elements of this throughout running a shop) find a supplier whose prices you are happy with, who is unlikely to suddenly hike up costs, and most importantly is someone you feel comfortable discussing this with.

TIP

Remember that there is always room for negotiation on price even if you are a small outlet. Don't be afraid.

IN MY EXPERIENCE:

Tim Hume, Redroaster Coffee House

You should firstly get the right product at the right price and secondly buy it from someone who understands the needs of your business. As far as our suppliers are concerned, we like to deal with other small businesses with whom we can build relationships. Some of them have supplied us since we set up.

DO IT YOURSELF

Don't forget that there is also scope for you to provide some of your produce yourself. If you are a small coffee shop for instance you may find, especially to begin with, that it's easier to select and buy some of your own produce from local markets. This is a great way to be sure of what you are paying for, and keep up your quality standards. Raymond Voce at Royal Teas says: 'I prefer to choose and pick up my own fresh produce because I have had too many bad experiences with suppliers delivering wilted lettuce or bruised fruits.'

There is more information on dealing with suppliers in Part 7 (*Up and running*, page 285).

Things to remember:

- When asking for word of mouth recommendations, make sure to ask why they would recommend someone. While one coffee shop owner may care about price, you might want quality.

- Meet your potential supplier and make sure you can develop a rapport with them – they need to be the person who will help you out when something runs out in the middle of a busy weekend.

- Don't forget local traders and markets – they could provide you with a lot of the produce and stock you need, without delivery costs.

3.3 Essential equipment

You have chosen your products and found a supplier; now you need to make your coffee and tea! Choosing your equipment depends on a number of factors, budget, customer numbers, as well as style, décor and space, so there is a lot to think about. Also, things such as coffee machines are an expensive purchase, but one of your most important – not only will they make hundreds of coffees a day but they form the heart of your counter and can even contribute to your identity and branding.

In this chapter we'll cover:

- How coffee machines work
- Coffee machine brands
- Purchasing and leasing
- Grinders and accessories
- Hot water urns, teapots and strainers
- Maintenance and cleaning

We'll deal with the smaller, but equally important, things such as crockery, cups, saucers, plates and teaspoons, in Part 5 (*Setting up shop*).

COFFEE MACHINES

A coffee machine is one of the most important purchases you will make, or certainly one of the purchases that you should expect to get the most use out of.

Basics of a coffee machine: what's what?

- **Portafilter** – the basket, filter, handle and spouts that you remove from the machine to fill with coffee and reattach.
- **Steam-wand** – the small metallic spout that sits flush from the machine, this pushes steam out and is used to heat and froth milk.
- **Pressure gauge** – this measures the pressure of the water tank, as well as the pressure of the water that is forced through the coffee, which should be between 9 and 10 atmospheres.
- **Controls** – also known as the keypad, the buttons you press and the dials you turn to work the machine.
- **Water-tank and boiler** – holds and heats the water.
- **Drip-tray** – the tray beneath the machine that catches the excess milk, water and coffee.

First of all, consider:

- The size of the beverages you are going to serve; this will influence your choice and size of machine.
- Whether your supplier provides you with a warranty and a replacement model if your machine needs a service? You don't want to be left high and dry.
- The amount of tea and coffee you expect to make each day, and what machines can cope best with the kind of usage you anticipate.

Second, spend some time researching the machines out there, and the different costs, but don't get too hung up about getting the 'perfect machine'. Crucially, make sure you understand the way coffee machines work, and that you can work the one you are purchasing – not only so you can produce consistently great coffee, but also because maintenance is the biggest issue for any espresso machine. Understanding how it works can help prevent day-to-day problems or servicing charges.

IN MY EXPERIENCE:

Tim Hume, Redroaster Coffee House

The basic advice is to buy a machine you are happy with, but mostly don't worry too much about getting the last word in technology – worry about making coffee properly using the equipment you have.

Some things to look for

Semi-automatic

The choice available to any commercial property is the automatic bean-to-cup machine, or the semi-automatic traditional espresso machine. Bean-to-cup refers to an automatic machine that measures out the amount of coffee you need, grinds it from beans, pours the designated amount of water through and sometimes even froths the milk for you. An automatic machine requires very little training or knowledge and while it might ensure a consistently good cup of coffee, and reduce your staff numbers, as it's fast and efficient, it doesn't allow enough flexibility to make a range of drinks. These machines are also notoriously hard to maintain and break down more easily than traditional espresso machines. For these reasons most coffee shops will nearly always have a traditional, semi-automatic espresso machine, which allows you to control water, steam, heat, and the weights and measures of coffee.

Temperature control

Some machines now have steam chambers to ensure temperature is not lost during brewing, while others have devices which can stabilise the brewing temperature – think about what you require to meet the needs of your customers, and discuss everything with a number of different suppliers.

Boiler

The bigger the better, as this provides a more steady supply of hot water and steam for hot milk. The size of the boiler can range from 5 litres to 20 litres. But remember that increasing the boiler size also means it will take more power to run the machine (2,000 watts–5,000 watts) and the weight can increase by up to 20kg, as of course will the cost!

Maintenance and aftercare

One key thing to remember from the experts is that it is not so much the machines you buy, but the aftercare service, maintenance and the availability of parts that matter. Make sure this is one of the first things you discuss with your supplier, and work with them to get a good deal. Most offer at least 12 months' aftercare, but be clear about what that entails and what's included.

Aesthetics

Don't forget the look of your coffee machine. This is very important as it can really serve to reinforce the identity and décor in your coffee shop. Many suppliers do machines in a range of colours, and some have even branched out into covering them in leopard print, faux diamante covers or retro patterns. Also think about where your machine will be. Some coffee shops have their machines on a back-shelf facing the customer, but many choose to have them on the coffee bar itself, with the back of the machine to the customer, which means the back of your machine needs to look as good as its front.

Size

Not only should you consider where your coffee machine is going, but you should also think about how much space you can afford for it to take up – which is why you might well decide to buy your coffee machine after you have identified and bought your premises, and worked out the spacing and layout design.

Extras

Remember that you will also need things such as frothing jugs, steam-wands, water filters, latte glasses – a lot of machines come with these now, but you need to be sure what is and isn't included.

Some recommended brands from the experts

- **Fracino** – good quality espresso machines, made in Birmingham. Only UK-made machines, reliable, parts are easily obtainable.
- **Gaggia** – traditional, well-known brand that makes a range of shapes and sizes.
- **La Marcozzo** – handmade in Florence, with two boilers ensuring steam and hot water constantly.
- **La Spaziale** – renowned Italian brand, with a steam chamber to ensure the stability of the brewing temperature.
- **Planet** – robust and simple machines, made in Treviso, Italy.
- **Rancilio** – good looking, sleek Italian machines, variety of sizes and options.
- **Sanremo** – another Italian brand, whose options include Capri (small and compact), Amalfi (for taller drinks), and Milan (with a retro look).
- **Synesso** – these machines have an adjustable temperature gauge for brewing different coffees. Made in Seattle, Washington.

Remember the list in the box is just some suggestions; you can also do some research of your own – visit local coffee shops and look at the machines they are using. Online research usually brings up just specific suppliers, but there are plenty of blogs and online information resources with discussions on espresso machines and their various benefits. Your supplier will also be able to point you in the direction of a brand and type that will suit your business.

Purchasing

Purchasing a coffee machine can be a fairly straightforward process if you have done your research. Also, make sure you are prepared for the cost, which could be anything from £1,500 to £10,000. However, there is often a lot included in that, such as:

- Delivery
- Aftercare, warranty and maintenance agreements
- Grinders (occasionally)
- Coffee, tea and syrups

- Jugs, steam wands, filters
- Cups, saucers and glasses
- Discounts on further services

Finding a supplier is fairly easy – you could go to your current coffee and tea supplier (which is one of the easier options), look in industry magazines, or get recommendations. In general terms, most machines obtained from and recommended by distributors are generally good; those available off the shelf or from the back of a mailshot catalogue are not. When purchasing the equipment, get the distributor to prove the quality of the machine by trying the coffee the machine produces and more importantly, trying a second coffee and comparing it with the first one.

For more information on choosing a supplier, see page 162.

Coffee machine contacts for the UK

- Bravilor: 01628 776060; www.bravilor.com
- Café Bar: 0800 515446; www.cafebar.co.uk
- Café du Monde: 01322 284804; www.cafedumonde.co.uk
- Drury Tea & Coffee Company: 020 7740 1100; www.drury.uk.com
- Espresso Warehouse (Clover): 0141 420 2422; www.espressowarehouse.com
- Fracino: 0121 328 5757; www.fracino.com
- Mulmar: 020 8905 1060; www.mulmar.co.uk
- Sanremo: 0870 774 0163; www.sanremouk.com

Leasing

If the outlay of an espresso machine is rather daunting so early on, you could think about leasing the machine, which offers many benefits. Leasing basically involves renting the machine for an agreed period; you can often then buy the machine at a discounted price further down the line. It's beneficial if you are trying to reduce start-up costs, and can also help with things such as maintenance and repairs. Most companies are flexible about the length of time you can have the machine for, many don't require a deposit and you can often get barista training, telephone support and even tax benefits.

Tax benefits and leasing

While you might initially pay more for leasing a machine – as you will have some interest to pay – the tax relief you get from it can be up to 40%, meaning you often save money in the long run, as the total cost of your purchase, capital and interest can be offset during the lease period, with your payments deducted as a trading expense.

Look for an independent leasing company, with a good track record, ask for current customers and testimonials, as well as agreeing to a trial period and clearly set down maintenance and service agreement – including how quickly they will repair or replace the machine, and if there is any contingency for loss of business due to a broken machine.

OTHER EQUIPMENT

Coffee grinder

While your coffee machine is the most crucial thing you will buy, you will also need a good coffee grinder. The recommended grinders are called 'burr' grinders, and they are either flat or cone shaped. Conical burr coffee grinders have more surface area so can often release a larger amount of flavour from the beans, and they often last longer than flat grinders too.

Frothing jugs and steam-wands

You should get a couple of jugs with your machine, but if not, your supplier will be able to provide these as extras, though you should only need a maximum of three or four jugs that you can rotate while in use. Steam-wands usually come attached to the espresso machine, but as your skill improves you may wish to invest in a top quality steam-wand which can help with latte art by producing a really smooth foam.

Urns

While you might be happy using the hot water spout on your espresso machine to make tea, you may also prefer to use a hot water urn. This is a fairly simple machine that heats water and keeps it warm for several hours. They are usually made of stainless steel and you can buy them from the same supplier as your coffee machine and tea equipment. They cost anything from £300 to £1,000, depending on the kind of capacity you need, which ranges from 2 litres to 5 litres.

Teapots and strainers

It's a good idea to have a range of different-sized teapots to serve tea in depending on what your needs are. Make sure you choose something easy to wash, and that is also easy to replace if broken. Quite popular now are the single person teapots, made to sit on top of a wide-brimmed teacup – they are a very neat option and available fairly readily.

Maintenance and cleaning

Cleaning an espresso machine regularly is the single most important thing in producing a good espresso; it will also seriously lengthen the life of your machine. Your supplier will be able to show you the exact specifics of cleaning your machine, and barista training courses will also do this, but there are a few basics it's good to know from the outset.

1. Clean the portafilter regularly, ideally two or three times a day. The filter and the basket become contaminated with damaging coffee oils by making just one espresso, and if they are not suitably cleaned it can lead to rancid and thin tasting espresso. Scrub it quickly with a scrubbing cloth, and rinse with water; and at the end of the day soak the filter in hot water for 20 minutes.
2. Backflushing is essential. Ask your supplier to show you how to do this, and make sure it becomes part of your daily routine. You should also do it once a week with a special coffee detergent.

3. Baristas often talk about purging the steam-wand, which simply means to allow some steam to run through it after it has been used. The steam-wand should also be wiped after every use and a small pin used each day to pick out any dried milk from the holes. It should then be soaked in hot water at the end of the day.
4. Water build-up: check and replace water filters or cartridges on a monthly basis, and descale the entire machine once a year.

Things to remember:

- Your coffee machine will be the most expensive piece of equipment you buy – so take the time to make sure you know exactly how they work and what you need.
- Teapots are a great way to stamp your identity and develop your brand, shop around till you find the perfect thing for you.
- Leasing can be a cheap and efficient way to source your equipment if you don't have the capital to purchase everything initially.
- Cleaning is essential to prolong the life of your coffee machines and urns – make it a regular part of your daily routine.

3.4 Pricing your drinks

We've already looked at the specifics of working out pricing on pages 84–86, but when considering what beverages to sell, it is something that shouldn't be far from your mind. Exactly how much you intend to sell your cups of coffee and cappuccino for will depend in part on your profit margin, operating and start-up costs. But there are other considerations too – such as competition, identity and pricing bands – so pricing always needs to be at the forefront of your mind.

In this chapter we'll cover:

- Average prices
- What to consider when pricing
- Pricing against your competitors

 DECIDING YOUR PRICES

You want to make a profit, yet if you aim for too much, you will alienate customers and lose business. People know how much they should be spending on a cup of coffee. And if you have done your research properly, you will have a good idea of price points too. Initially, you should compare against your competitors and subsequently in line with rising costs to keep your profit margin. It's pointless trying to test what the customers will bear. Price rises are usually far less traumatic than you can ever expect.

Equally, refer back to the market research and customer base analysis you did and look at the kinds of prices your customers will be paying. Be realistic about this and if you are going to set relatively high prices, make sure your customer knows why. For example, if a strong part of your coffee or tea shop's profile is the emphasis you place on fairtrade ingredients and the time and skill that may go into hand-made cakes.

IN MY EXPERIENCE:

Shelagh Ryan, Lantana

Prices are based on what it costs to produce the product but we are also mindful of what our competitors are charging. We want Lantana to be part of people's daily rituals rather than a special treat so we have priced accordingly.

Competitor prices

Considering your competitors, especially the chains, is vital. You will need to make sure your prices can compete with them, both in terms of offering the same quality for less, charging the same and offering more. Equally if there is another independent in the area, your prices will have to do something different to theirs – either undercutting them with deals and cheap prices, or delivering excellent quality at a price to match.

We've put in a range of prices from the four independent coffee and tea shops as well as one of the big chains featured in this book to give you an idea of how prices can vary – or be rather similar across the board. Remember when you are thinking about pricing and looking at this chart that so much else comes into consideration. Look at location for instance – Lantana is in an enviable part of busy, wealthy Central London, Leoni is in a more rural, northern location where the overall cost of living and going out is less. Equally Redroaster is in the tourist hotspot of Brighton, but without the London price tag.

	Costa (medium drink)	Leoni	Royal Teas	Lantana	Redroaster Coffee House
Cappuccino	£2.35	£1.40	£1.50	£2.40	£1.90
Latte	£2.35	£1.70	£1.50	£2.40	£1.90
Black coffee	£2.00	£1.30	£1.40	£2.20	£1.70
Tea	£1.60	£1.45	£1.10	£2.00	£1.70
Hot chocolate	£2.35	£1.70	£1.50	£2.50	£1.90
Espresso	£1.70	£1.30	£1.30	£1.30	£1.30

You simply cannot price your coffee or tea shop's offerings in a vacuum. You must consider all the local and external factors that affect your pricing, including:

- Identity and your unique selling point (USP)
- Profit margins and turnover
- Quality and type of produce
- Location
- Competition
- Local demographics
- Current economic climate
- Public awareness of standards, hygiene and quality
- Fashion trends and fads of the moment

IN MY EXPERIENCE:

Simon Robertson, Leoni

I could charge more. I could make more profit per cup but if I sell fewer cups what is the point? The difference at Leoni is that we offer a better product for a similar price. So our profit per cup is more or less the same as our competitors but we are, as mentioned, very busy and in difficult financial times that is a real advantage.

Eating in and takeaways

Remember you will also have to vary your prices for sitting in and takeaway. Most coffee or tea shops charge that little bit extra to sit in and finish your beverage – considering the costs of crockery, cleaning and staffing implications – so when you are comparing against others in the market, check across both sets of figures. Sandwich bar Pret a Manger charges the VAT cost for eating in, while other cafés add anything from 50p to £1.50 to eat in. Again think about the experience you want customers to have, and what they'll be likely to pay for. That said, you don't even have to charge them extra for eating or drinking in – just make sure it's profitable for you if they do.

Coffee and tea shop chain prices

- **Starbucks**: Medium cappuccino £2.29; single espresso £1.40
- **Costa**: Medium cappuccino £2.35; single espresso £1.70
- **Caffé Nero**: Medium cappuccino £1.80; single espresso £1.25

According to a recent report, you will pay an average £1.48 for a medium-sized cappuccino in an independent coffee shop compared with £2.29 in Starbucks.

Pricing to sell

Knowing what a cappuccino costs you and the percentage of profit you would like to make is rarely all it takes to make your coffee or tea shop's proposition viable. You have to have a customer base or market willing to buy at the prices you are selling at. To a certain extent your prices will be determined by the quality of ingredients used, and the level of service or coffee drinking experience you offer your customers when they choose to visit you.

TIP

Remember your obligations under the Price Marking Order 1979, which states you must display your prices clearly at the entrance to the coffee shop.

If you do decide to price below your competitors you will need to work on keeping your overheads rock bottom. As we've mentioned earlier, while the economic climate may work in your favour with customers opting for a coffee or tea rather than three-course meal, the beverage has to be affordable, and on a regular basis if you are going to survive.

Things to remember:

- Try to get the balance between not seeming too pricey and making your drinks too cheap to attract the kind of clientele you want.
- Always consider your competitors' prices.
- Don't forget to think about current trends and seasons when pricing.

“There are few hours in life more agreeable than the hour dedicated to the ceremony known as afternoon tea.”

Henry James

“Man does not live by coffee alone. Have a Danish.”

Author Unknown

4

Menu planning

4 Menu planning

If your attention is primarily focused on your drinks offering, it's still a good idea to offer something tasty to accompany your brew. Or you might have opted for a more food-based coffee or tea shop, in which case this section is another must-read. You can keep it simple by offering basic cupcakes and muffins, go one step further with soups and ready-packed paninis, or offer a more substantial meal. If you decide to do all your baking or cooking on the premises, you will need to incorporate certain equipment into your shop and architectural plans. Alternatively, you may want to save money by reaching an agreement with a good local baker or deli who can supply you with food on a daily basis.

In this section we'll cover:

- The simple stuff
- Expanding your food range
- Suppliers
- Food preparation
- Pricing

THE SIMPLE STUFF

Cakes, muffins and biscotti

As a beginner you may want to start simple, and sweet things are the automatic and easiest choice to offer. Most people will often choose to have a sweet treat with their coffee and tea, and it can be a great way to get customers to spend a little more money – both through ordering a slice of cake, and staying longer to order a second beverage.

There are a range of things you can offer, from some which are an easy sell, requiring little extra effort, to homemade indulgent cakes, which take more work but can be a big selling point. It may be that you know what you want to do, and have factored it into your plans and finances from day one – or it may be that food is something you are much less sure about, reluctantly toying with it, or trying to offer it as easily and quickly as possible. If this is the case start with something simple and work up from there; you can always run promotional weeks with homemade cakes or freshly baked biscuits and see how they sell before committing to do something full time.

Bites and nibbles

The first (and easiest) step is to offer simple pre-packaged biscuits, biscotti, cookies, cake slices and muffins. These are easy to offer as they don't require much extra storage, display or plates and cutlery to serve them with. Buying ready-made produce is a good way to test the water. Keep a clear note of what people are purchasing and listen to their discussions at the counter – why have they chosen a cookie over a muffin, or why haven't they bought anything. Do they prefer homemade food perhaps?

Displaying and serving

Pre-packaged biscuits, cake slices and muffins won't usually require refrigeration, and many products come with a serving stand or rack with the company's branding on, so make sure you ask. The way you display the food will have a lot to do with how popular

> **TIP**
> Usually the wrapping and packaging will suffice as a temporary plate, so you won't need crockery or cutlery to serve pre-packaged food, and they are quick to clear away as well.

it is. You can either have a separate section, shelf or racks for muffins, cookies and biscuits, or display them close to the till so customers can add them to their order at the last minute. You may decide to have them as an integral part of your counter display, and draw attention to them on your menu or pricing boards. You may also want to make sure all your staff always ask each customer if they want a cookie or a muffin with their coffee.

In-house baking

Cakes and other homemade produce such as brownies, flapjacks, scones, tarts, muffins, doughnuts and pies are popular classics, and numerous coffee and tea shops advertise their homemade cakes and pies as a key part of their identity. Baking in-house can also be a great way to set you apart from the local competition, especially chains. There are extra considerations you will need to have, such as space for a kitchen, and understanding the health and safety protocols you will have to abide by. Spend some time deciding what you would like to offer and how it ties in with the theme of your coffee or tea shop. Research recipes, look at cookbooks and check out magazines for ideas, as well as visiting other local coffee and tea shops for ideas. Perhaps go back to your own cultural roots and devise a patisserie menu around them, whether Caribbean, Jewish or Persian. This again could give your coffee or tea shop a distinctive flavour.

Try to get a balance between classics and some more interesting cakes; some customers will come in specifically for your homemade cakes, where others will be tempted by something that sounds new and interesting. Also make sure to decide if you want to offer the same five or so flavours all the time, or if you want to vary your offering from week to week depending on what products and suppliers have on offer or what is seasonal. Perhaps you could even theme your cakes each week: a Valentine's indulgence cake in February; pumpkin, ginger and chocolate swirls for Halloween; mulled fruits at Christmas; and summer berries in August.

TIP

Remember that baked goods have a short shelf-life. Whether you are baking them yourself or having them delivered in, don't keep them longer than two to three days. You will also need to factor in baking time to your daily routine.

Displaying and serving

If you are deciding to serve homemade produce it's a good idea to have thought about this before you design and build your counter and surrounding space, as this could affect your layout. The way you display your baked goods is up to you but the most crucial thing is that they should look appetising, and that customers can clearly see what they are and what they cost.

Working with local bakers

If you are looking to buy in cakes or cake slices it might be a good idea to develop a relationship with a local bakery, cake maker or deli, which can provide you freshly baked cakes and pies on a daily or weekly basis; this can be good for offering great food with minimal fuss at your end. You can either buy them in direct, and sell them for a profit, or you can work out a mutually beneficial arrangement, where you give them a percentage of what you sell, meaning you can buy the cakes at a low cost price. This is an especially good option if you want to gauge how popular cakes would be in your coffee shop.

Some things to think about:

- Do you want to make the cakes self-service? Or will your staff need to factor in the time to serve the cake slices?
- Will you pre-slice them?
- Will you display them in their own cabinet to the side of the counter or have them plated up on the counter?
- Will you draw attention to them on your menu and pricing boards? Or will you have individual tags with prices on?
- Will you serve them on plates, and will you offer a fork with them?
- What about offering cream or crême fraiche?

EXPANDING YOUR FOOD RANGE

If food has always been part of your plans, or you have found that it is one of the most successful aspects of your business, you may want to diversify and extend what you do, bringing in a breakfast or higher spending lunchtime crowd.

Ready-made: sandwiches, paninis, salads

As with the sweeter treats, the first option might well be to buy in ready-made sandwiches and salads, which can be easily picked up from a self-service fridge by customers. At the very most you might be expected to provide a plate and some cutlery, which could even be disposable.

You may also decide to serve paninis and soups, which might be ready-made but will need to be toasted or heated up and served with plates or bowls and cutlery. Make sure you have factored in the space for this, either behind the counter or in a separate kitchen area. Also think about whether the customer will wait at the counter while you do this, or whether you offer table service, and how you will manage customer flow during the busier periods. This will also mean checking out health and safety rules and regulations, and you will have to think about extra staffing.

Making your own: cooking in-house

The final option for food is to prepare and serve your own, offering pre-made or made-to-order dishes.

Ideas for making your own food to sell

- Sandwiches
- Salads
- Jacket potatoes
- Wraps
- Dips and pitta
- Soup
- Tarts and quiches
- Meat and fish skewers
- Scrambled eggs
- Smoked salmon
- Cured meats
- Nachos
- Fried breakfasts
- Cheese platters and ploughman's lunches

- Risottos and pastas
- Currys, stews and stirfrys

Display-based food

Foods that don't need to be cooked to order, such as sandwiches, cured meats, cheeses and wraps, can be made in the morning and displayed in a refrigerated glass counter; you and your staff would then serve these directly to the customers. This can mean you don't need a menu, and can change your offering on a daily basis. It also makes for quicker service during busy periods and will mean you don't need to employ a dedicated member of kitchen staff. Even some pastas and risottos can be made ahead and heated up when necessary. To read more about purchasing and using refrigerators, see page 235.

Menu-based

Foods such as soups, jacket potatoes, fried breakfasts, risottos, skewers and steak sandwiches, which require cooking or warming to order, can also be offered on a menu in a coffee or tea shop. Customers can either order the food at the counter with their hot drinks or you can offer table service (as long as you have the staff to manage it). Your menu can be something as simple as a few blackboards with daily specials written on each morning, or something more permanent. It's probably a good idea to start by offering a range of different foods to see what is the most successful before committing to a permanent menu; that said you can always offer daily specials around your core things such as sandwiches, soups and quiches.

IN MY EXPERIENCE:

Raymond Voce, Royal Teas

During the week, our freshly homemade soups and lunches are the most popular items. Weekday lunch times are very busy and are where we will do most of our business, hence the type of meals we will serve. The weekends are busy all day and we serve mostly cooked breakfasts all day. Weekend and weekday afternoons we sell a lot of our cream teas.

SUPPLIERS

As with the suppliers for your beverages, look for local companies or suppliers who understand the needs of your business. If you plan to sell pre-packaged food try to find a company with a recognisable reputation, or one whose produce matches the kind of coffee or tea shop you are running. Look for food with a selling point such as unique flavours, organic ingredients, quirky names and branding. Research other local coffee shops and cafés to see what the top-selling brands and foods are, and make sure you meet the supplier and do taste testing.

Think about going local for your bakery and savoury supplies as well. Can you get the things you need – flour, eggs, bread, milk, butter, meat and fish, sugar, fruit and vegetables, chocolate – from local markets or farms?

TIP

Advertising your produce and ingredients as local is always a positive thing, and it means you can get new supplies quickly if you run out.

Consider your supplier's delivery days, how fresh their products are, how they fit in with your identity, how long the food will last and what you need to serve it – will you need refrigeration facilities, and can your supplier help with display stands? Also, if the bakery or deli you choose has a good local reputation you can promote that as part of your advertising and marketing.

Make sure you also find a supplier who can be flexible to suit your needs, and will understand if you change your order often, as demand grows and falls depending on the season, for instance.

IN MY EXPERIENCE:

Shelagh Ryan, Lantana

Our meat is sourced from a butcher who uses British organic products. Our coffee is from Monmouth and our tea is from All About Tea. All our cakes, salads and tarts are made by our chefs at Lantana. I asked other cafés who they used, went to lots of food markets and trade events, and researched on the internet.

FOOD PREPARATION

Offering something that requires some form of cooking is a serious undertaking and will add several new dimensions to your business, as well as give you many more things to think about. Here we discuss the key considerations that you should look at before even deciding to serve food.

Kitchen area

To bake cakes, prepare sandwiches or cook a meal you will need a working kitchen with an oven, hob, sink, fridge, freezer, dishwasher and preparation areas, all of which will need to be approved by a health and safety officer. While the area itself doesn't have to be particularly large, there will be certain criteria you will need to adhere to such as: size and specification of food preparation areas, fire safety, environmental health regulations and food safety standards. As a first step contact your environmental health office for further advice, and see page 219 for more information on layout and kitchen design.

Staffing

Employing staff will have huge implications on your outgoings, so make sure you will make enough money from your food offering to cover these costs, as well as make a profit. Think about the fact that you will need to put aside more in the budget for staff, whether that's for needing them to do slightly longer hours to prepare the food in the morning and thoroughly clean up in the evening, or needing an extra set of hands during the breakfast and lunchtime rush. You may need to employ a chef or cook to prepare and serve your food on a daily basis. You will also need to decide whether you offer some form of waitress service, which might require more training and a change from an exclusive counter or bar service.

Serving the food

You will need to know how you are going to manage orders and serve the food. Think about the crockery and cutlery you will need, and that it will also need to be cleared from tables and washed each day.

Will you focus on a self-service approach or a more laidback table service offering? Equally, are you going to target the local offices as a key market and provide takeaway meals and sandwiches? If so, you will need a series of disposable boxes, tubs, cutlery and cups.

Cleaning

This has been covered in the sections above but we're summarising it here again as it is of prime importance. While you will already have a solid cleaning regimen for each day, adding food to your menu means adhering to another set of key health and safety rules, and cleaning will take up a large percentage of your time. Make sure you can spare this time, or spare the funds to pay staff the extra hours it takes to clean or employ a cleaning service.

PRICING

The profit margin you will make on food is around 40%–60%, so consider this when deciding what to charge. Cookies, muffins and biscotti are meant to be a quick, sweet treat – rather than a meal. Make sure your prices reflect this, as it must be something reasonable that your customers can pick up quickly.

Cakes and baked goods can go for a bit more, especially as you will need to factor in the other costs it involves to produce and serve them. Your prices should also reflect the quality of the cakes you are making. Bear in mind that all this will tie in with the kind of atmosphere and ethos you want to create. For lunchtime and breakfast foods you will find that local cafés and coffee or tea shops will charge anything from £2.50 to £7.50. If you are expecting large lunchtime takeaway custom, then you will need to keep your prices towards the lower end of the scale, but if you expect most of your customers to be tourists or people with time to spare, then they'll want to sit in and enjoy the atmosphere, allowing you to charge a little more. Check page 178 for more information on pricing.

TIP

Be sure to write up any dishes that have nuts in them. With so many people suffering from allergies nowadays, it's crucial that you know exactly what ingredients are in the dishes you are offering.

IN MY EXPERIENCE:
Tim Hume, Redroaster Coffee House

We had a Spanish employee whose English wasn't great. When doing sandwich making she seemed to think all the French-bread orders were takeaways because she kept wrapping them rather than serving them on a plate. At the end of the shift someone mentioned to her that the baguette orders were not takeaway unless it was said so. She said, 'Well I do what they say. They say "bag it", so that's what I do.'

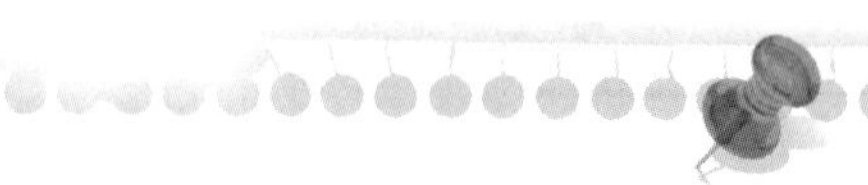

Things to remember:

- Food is just as crucial as your beverages, so make sure you give it the time it deserves.
- If you are unsure of what to offer, start with simple, sweet treats and keep track of how successful they are.
- Hot food that you prepare on the premises is a much more serious undertaking – make sure you have thought about staffing, kitchen equipment and capacity, and the impact on your profits.
- Food preparation laws are very strict – do your homework well.

“Wouldn't it be dreadful to live in a country where they didn't have tea?”
Noel Coward
“Chocolate, men, coffee – some things are better rich.”
Unknown

5

Setting up shop

5.1

Finding premises

The premises you choose will have a massive impact on the look, feel and general atmosphere of your coffee shop. It's probably the most important single decision you have to make in the whole start-up process, and it's the one thing you can't change your mind about once you have taken the plunge, so think it through carefully. Things such as location, cost, size, identity and competition will all come into your decision, and you may have to learn that you need to compromise on some things and what these may be, and what is absolutely imperative. So be sure you are clear on your unique selling points (USPs) before you start.

In this chapter, we'll cover:

- What you need from a property
- Location
- Commercial classifications
- Leasing versus buying
- Professional advisers

WHAT ARE YOUR PROPERTY NEEDS?

At this stage you should already have a clear idea in your mind of what you need and want from your coffee or tea shop premises. You will already have decided on the type of clientele you want to attract, the kind of atmosphere you want to create and the food and beverages you are going to serve. All these decisions will have a bearing on where you locate your coffee or tea shop, what size it needs to be and how much you are willing to pay.

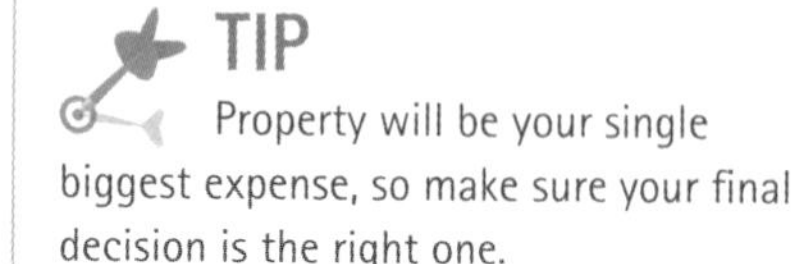

LOCATION, SIZE AND LAYOUT

Location and size to some degree go hand in hand, especially when it comes to your budget. If you expect a lot of your business to come from foot traffic you will need to be in a busy urban area, with lots of passing trade and tourists. However, properties such as this are expensive and the amount of square feet you will be able to get will be less than if you choose a more suburban or rural location. Equally, you may have envisioned a spacious, airy coffee and tea shop with room for large sofas and coffee tables covered in newspapers, which means you might be more restricted on the kind of location you can afford. The important thing is to be a bit flexible, visit a range of properties, big and small, in busy and quiet locations – and be open-minded. You will soon discover what you are less prepared to compromise on, and what you can work around.

Location

Choosing a location for your coffee or tea shop involves far more than just picking a postcode. You will need to think long and hard, not just about the area you choose, but also about your budget and the type of coffee or tea shop you want to open and the type of location which will fit that vision. Finding a good location is easy. Finding a good location that is not over-priced is nearly impossible. The first thing to decide on is whether your coffee or tea shop would be suited to the high street, a shopping centre or retail park or somewhere more tucked away.

FROM THE EXPERTS:
Bettys Café Tea Rooms

The first Bettys opened in Harrogate in 1919 and we now have six café tea rooms all in Yorkshire. Despite countless requests we've firmly refused to open branches outside Yorkshire because of our commitment to keeping Bettys small and special.

The high street

An obvious choice due to the high levels of passing trade. You will be noticed on the high street and therefore might not have to rely as much on advertising or promotion. However, rents will be comparatively high, property will be harder to obtain and you will need to be pitching to the same types of customer as other coffee or tea shops in the area to succeed. You will also need to bear in mind what position you have on the high street. Being located at the wrong end of the street, or even the wrong side of the road can have a massive impact on trade.

Shopping centres, retail parks, supermarkets and bookstores

There are some obvious advantages to setting up somewhere that you can capitalise on an already established customer base. Retail parks and shopping centres have a lot of passing trade, and people are usually making a 'day of it' and want to take the time out to grab a coffee or a bite to eat. Parking is also likely to be easy for your customers as almost all shopping centres and supermarkets have their own car parks. In bookstores people often want to take the time to buy a book or magazine and read it over a coffee, so you have the benefit of customers who aren't in a rush. Having your coffee or tea shop in a local bookstore can also help you establish your identity. Equally, setting up in a larger shop or centre means you have the benefit of their marketing and PR machine, which will help you establish a name quickly.

However, on the down side, rent will again be comparatively high, your coffee or tea shop may well have to conform to the type of outlet the shopping centre is looking for, and unless they open late, or there is a cinema or some other form of evening entertainment in the centre, you may find evening trade is slow or even non-existent. If there is evening entertainment and you want to take advantage of it, you will have to re-think your staffing timetable to ensure you can physically be open at night.

Tucked-away location

The obvious advantage to opening your coffee or tea shop somewhere less prominent is lower property costs – you can quite simply get more for your money. Quiet secluded areas are likely to attract a different type of customer to that of the high street or retail park sites. Coffee aficionados will travel longer distances and seek out hidden coffee bars with a great reputation, and the main bulk of your business will come from people who are looking for something different from the chains, and are happy to walk a short distance from the main high street to find a great cup of coffee or tea and a good atmosphere.

It's likely that you will have fewer customers than a shop on the high street, but they will stay longer and spend more. However, be aware that you may find it hard to pull in these customers initially and will have to work a lot harder to get noticed by customers and local residents. This is where marketing and PR comes in. See page 255 onwards for more information on raising your profile in the local community and beyond.

IN MY EXPERIENCE:

Raymond Voce, Royal Teas

I have never been interested in running a high-street café. The footfall may be great but I enjoy seeing the same faces and building a rapport. There is a sense of satisfaction that people come back again and again.

Size

While the size of the property you will buy is intrinsically linked to its location, you should know roughly what sort of size and square footage you need, or how many covers (people seated) it can accommodate, as this will help you when going through property advertisements. You need to be clear about whether you need a large seating area, a kitchen, space for internet access, a performance area or a small retail section for instance. What may seem a great little spot on the high street wouldn't be that great if you can only do takeaway coffees from it when you would prefer to serve breakfasts and lunches every day. Information about the number of covers can vary, and will also only be available if the property is already a café or restaurant.

A rough guide to coffee or tea shop size

- Small: 15–45 covers, 500sq ft–10,00sq ft
- Medium: 45–100 covers, 1,000+sq ft
- Large: 100+ covers, 2,000+sq ft

Facilities and layout

Think about what you need from your coffee or tea shop, what is already provided and what you would need to add yourself. When viewing properties, take the layout into careful consideration and try to imagine your service area fully staffed and a bustling sitting space decked out with tables, chairs and a lot of customers in need of a caffeine injection.

TIP

Remember that you will be viewing existing businesses for sale, as well as empty spaces that might not have any of the facilities you need. Bear in mind what the pros and cons are of each and be realistic.

Make a list of all the rooms and spaces you might need. Then consider which of these is vital, how much it might cost to add things that aren't there, and assign to each thing either an 'essential', 'desirable' or 'bonus' tag. A kitchen is pretty essential, office space is more desirable, and a performance area is a bonus, for instance. You should also have a think about what you will need from each area.

- **Counter and standing/queuing area** – think about how big it needs to be, the kind of service you will offer, where people will queue.
- **Seating area** – how many covers do you need, what size will your tables be, do you want to put sofas in?
- **Kitchen** – how much cooking will you be doing, is the kitchen in a logical place for serving your customers?

- **Stock room** – is there one? And do you need one? How much stock will you need to store, what about access?
- **Office** – is there space for this, is it secure?
- **Toilets** – are these up to scratch, if there aren't any, how much will they cost to put in?
- **Staffroom** – how many staff will you have initially, is this space and luxury you don't need?
- **Other areas** – shop space, internet space, performance area – how vital are these, are they deal breakers?
- **Outside areas** – does the outside space fit into your vision, is it easy to access, how hard will it be to maintain?

Other factors to consider

Once you have decided what kind of location, size and layout you want for your coffee or tea shop there are still plenty of other factors you could consider to get the best deal for yourself.

Parking

How easy will it be for your potential customers to access the shop? Are there plenty of parking spots nearby? You need it to be as convenient as possible for customers to pop in.

TIP

If you will be near numerous 20–30 minute stopping bays think about serving quick sit-down coffee, or having an efficient takeaway service.

Security

Is the property secure? Will you be able to safeguard against break-ins and theft?

IN MY EXPERIENCE:

Tim Hume, Redroaster Coffee House

We have a digital monitored alarm system. Following a break-in two years ago we increased security by for example, adding a steel plate to an external door and installing a stronger safe.

Competition

What other coffee or tea shops are in the area? Are they attracting the same kind of clientele you are after? If there is a chain a few doors down it might not be the best location, as people will often look for what they know and head to Starbucks. However, if you are surrounded by the kinds of shops and restaurants with a similar ethos to you – independent, boutique, quality and individual – you could well have an edge over the chains. Also, being located within a cluster of coffee and tea shops means there will always be plenty of prospective customers choosing where they want to have their cuppa.

> **TIP**
> If you aren't sure of your location, spend some time in the area, seeing how busy your competition is, and whether there is a 'you-shaped' gap in the market.

Proximity to staff

If you want to attract the right level of loyal talent for your coffee or tea shop, make sure the location is both accessible and attractive for your staff. And that the kind of staff you will need are available in this area. For instance, if you want a young, student vibe from your employees, you will need to be near schools and universities, and not in a village with a largely elderly population.

Do you like it?

It's a balance of emotion and business sense when you choose your property, but remember you will be spending an awful lot of time in it, particularly during the first few months. You need to be in an area that is easy for you to get to, somewhere you actually look forward to going each morning and somewhere you feel safe closing up at night by yourself.

Customer base

Is it there? This is absolutely vital and ties in with the competition point above. If you believe there is a gap in the market for your independent coffee shop, make sure the gap isn't there because no one wants or needs a shop like that in the local area. Do some research into the disposable income of the local residents. Can the market afford the luxury of coffee and cake more than once a week? Is it a business or residential environment? Equally in a rich and wealthy neighbourhood, will they appreciate your cheap and cheerful coffee shop? See Part 1 of this book for more information on identifying the market.

Outside space

How much outside space is there, and is it manageable? Outside space is a big draw in the summer, and is a clever way to easily increase your capacity during the hotter months; however it does require its own maintenance and there are often legal implications if your outside space spills onto the street, so do consider these.

TIP

If you are moving into a pre-existing coffee or tea shop site, find out if there is a good reason why the previous owner is moving on. Where are they moving to? What was their experience of having a coffee or tea shop in the area?

COMMERCIAL CLASSIFICATION

Before you negotiate the lease or purchase of a property you must check what commercial classification it currently falls under. If the property does not already have the correct classification for a coffee or tea shop you will need to get planning permission from your local authority. You will need to be cautious at this stage: planning consent might not be granted if the local authority feels the change of classification would not benefit the area.

Factors affecting planning permissions

When giving permission to start a coffee or tea shop, your local authority will take into consideration several factors such as:

- Is there a need for that type of business in the area?
- What are the traffic and parking requirements?
- Are there any likely causes of nuisance such as noise, smells or environmental hazards the business may cause?
- What are the trading hours?
- Objections (if any) from other occupiers and residents in the area.

Local authorities classify properties into various types and make sure there is an adequate balance of different types of commercial property in any one area. Shops are classified A1, A2, A3, and you need to be sure of your classification because this will dictate what you are able to do. There are numerous grey areas concerning this – if you plan initially to serve cold food, but may want to upscale to hot food later on, you need to make sure you have a classification which allows you to do this. The box below should give you a brief idea, but it is vital you speak to your local planning department, which is part of your local council.

- *A1*: **Shops** – post offices, travel agents, hairdressers, funeral directors, dry cleaners, sandwich shops.
- *A2*: **Financial and professional services** – banks, building societies, betting offices, and other financial and professional services.
- *A3*: **Food and drink** – pubs, restaurants, cafés and hot food takeaways.

TIP

While most cafés that are making and serving food to be consumed on the premises come under the A3 classification, if you are selling cold food such as sandwiches and cakes to be consumed off the premises you may only need an A1 classification. Check with the planning office to be sure.

An A3 classification will most likely be the one you need, and they are the hardest to obtain, and the most expensive, so it does have a bearing on the rental or purchase value of your chosen premises. Simply put: premises with the A3 classification cost more. And if you ever decided to change your A3 classified premises from a coffee shop/café to a bar or takeaway you would need planning consent. However, changes from bar or takeaway to coffee or tea shop do not need prior consent as long as the permitted development rights have not been excluded in relation to your specific property.

You will need a 'premises' licence if you are going to have any live performances (of music, for example); and you will need a PRS and a PPL licence if you are going to play recorded music (including the radio). Licences are available from your local council and cost anything from £100 to £635, depending on the rateable value of your property – which is a professional view of the annual rent a property could achieve if it was available on the open market.

What a licence will cover

- Sale or supply of alcohol
- Provision of regulated entertainment - plays, films, indoor sports, live music, playing recorded music including radio, dance
- Provision of late night refreshment - food and drink between 11pm and 5am

LEASING VERSUS BUYING

You may not be in a position to even choose whether you rent or buy your business property. If you don't have the capital to put towards buying a property, you will be left with the option of renting. However, even if buying is a financial option, you should still weigh up the pros and cons of buying or renting first.

Buying

For many coffee or tea shop entrepreneurs, the idea of owning your own property is just too much of a pipe dream. However, with so many changes, and dips and dives in the property market, you may be able to get yourself a bargain. Shop and ask around. A good deal may be within your reach, but remember that with every property purchase comes the associated costs, such as stamp duty and solicitor fees. Can you afford one?

Should you buy?

Ask yourself the following questions before you decide to buy.

- Is the coffee or tea shop in the best location you think you can ever afford?
- Do you plan to keep your coffee or tea shop the same size indefinitely?
- Do you have either a sufficient deposit and the budget for a mortgage, or enough cash to purchase the property outright?
- Do you plan on staying in this area for a long time?

If you can't answer yes to all of the above questions, buying isn't for you.

There are, of course, several advantages associated with buying a property. Firstly, as we've mentioned, with the decline in the property market, you may be able to get premises for much less than you had anticipated. Secondly, you will own it, have the freedom to do with it as you please, and not have to answer to a landlord. Another major advantage with owning your own premises is you will have a major asset, either to secure loans against or think of as an investment.

As with any property purchase, domestic or commercial, you will need to carry out the appropriate checks before you agree to buy. Bring in a reputable surveyor, get the place checked with the environmental health officer, find out what your business rates will be.

TIP

Do as much research on the building and area as is physically possible, because if something's not right with it once you have got the keys, it won't be easy to just pack up and move on.

Leasing

Leasing is a lot more common than buying, simply because it gives you that little bit more flexibility in both a physical and a financial sense. If you expand more quickly than anticipated, you can move at relatively short notice, provided that you negotiated the right kind of contract when you took out the lease. Also, if there are a limited number of properties on the market to buy (and again, the current economic climate will dictate this) then you will find your options are far more open when looking for leased property.

A lease can be negotiated for any length of time that you and the landlord agree on, but typically will last anywhere between three and 25 years. The landlord will be looking for a reliable tenant who will run a successful business and consequently be able to pay the rent on time. You may be asked to present a business plan and have your financial history checked out.

On the flip side, you have just as much right to do your own checks on the landlord. If possible talk to the current or previous tenants. Find out why they are moving on. If their business failed was it because of the location, something wrong with the property, or even as a result of

TIP

If you don't have any trading history, be prepared for the landlord to ask for anything up to a year's rent in advance; bear this in mind when budgeting.

a difficult landlord? These are the kind of things you will want to know *before* signing a lease.

Thinking . . . and thinking again

It's easy to get burned when it comes to property deals and the best way to protect yourself is to ask all the right questions, get everything agreed in writing and above all, check your contract. Then check it again. Here are a few things to consider before signing a lease:

- What kinds of rent are similar businesses in the area being charged, and are yours a fare rate in comparison?
- Is the length of lease suitable? If it's too short your coffee or tea shop will lack security, but if it's too long and you don't have a break clause, you may find yourself stuck.
- Is the building sound and in a state of good repair? It's advisable to bring in expert help to check there are no serious faults.
- Will the landlord offer a rent-free period if there are repairs to be carried out?
- Do you need planning permission before you can build or alter the premises according to your designs?
- Who is responsible for insurance? What's included in the rent, and what cover will the landlord expect you to take out yourself in addition?

This above list is purely a guideline. It's not exhaustive and we recommend you have a solicitor or property expert to check the small print for you.

➡ PROFESSIONAL ADVISERS

Estate agents

Whether they deserve to be lumped in the same boat as used-car salesmen is debatable, but if you find an agent or company that is helpful and trustworthy then that's half the battle won. Having said that, it's always a good idea to shop around. With the internet at your fingertips you can search for properties that suit your requirements and rule out ones that don't.

Once you have got yourself on a few estate agents' books, speak to them regularly. Make sure they know exactly what you are looking for so they don't waste your valuable time by showing you round unsuitable properties. Helpful estate agents can also do more for you than put you in contact with landlords and property owners. An estate agent who specialises in commercial property may be able to put you in touch with other professional advisers such as solicitors, surveyors and architects.

Solicitors

Getting the right help on-board at the beginning is essential to avoid problems. It's better to have someone steering you clear of problems early on rather than hiring them to put out fires further down the line.

If possible, get someone on-board who specialises in the coffee and tea shop trade. If they've overseen countless similar sales and leases in the past, the chances are they'll spot any problems or concerns with your deal a mile away. To find a specialised solicitor, contact the Law Society. You can search by location or sector at www.lawsociety.org.uk.

TIP

Don't sign *anything* before it's been carefully looked over by an independent legal expert in the property sector.

Builders, architects and decorators

Choosing an architect or builder who comes highly recommended is the best way to find someone trustworthy and capable of doing a satisfactory job. Go through organisations such as the Federation of Master Builders (www.fmb.org.uk). Ask friends or other coffee or tea shop owners for advice, or ask for examples of previous work so that you can see for yourself what the finished results will look like. Visit your favourite coffee or tea shops and ask who did the work for them.

You may not be an expert when it comes to building terms, how long things take or how much it's all likely to cost, but it's up to you to do your research and arm yourself with as much knowledge as possible. The more you know, the less likely you are to be taken advantage of.

TIP

Before you make your final decision, look at what other businesses are around, talk to people, attend a local traders' association meeting, speak to the local tourist board. You may still misjudge your clientele but as long as you are flexible and adaptable you can alter and improve your service once running.

As a final check before you sign a lease or agree to a mortgage, make sure you have considered all of the following:

- Have other coffee shops been successful in the premises? If not, why not? Can you succeed where they've failed?
- Is it the right size to meet the projections in your business plan?
- Does it have the fittings you need – counters, kitchen etc – if it doesn't what will you need to add and can you afford to?
- Does the kitchen meet the required standards for food hygiene as well as health and safety? Has the environmental health officer given it the thumbs up?
- Is the property security friendly? Is it easy to break into? Does it have a burglar alarm, and if not, how much would it cost to add one?
- Is it protected against pests such as insects or rodents? Is there somewhere to dispose of waste without attracting unwanted visitors?
- Are there any major structural problems or damaged areas?
- How much are you likely to pay in business rates?
- Are you really certain it's the best possible place for you to locate your coffee shop?

Things to remember:

- Think carefully about your property needs before you even start viewing properties. You need a clear idea of exactly what you require before speaking to agents. Decide what is vital and what is a bonus, what can you compromise on and what is non-negotiable.
- Weigh up the different options for locations.
- Remember to check the commercial classification of any property you are interested in.
- Don't rush into buying if leasing is more suited to your finances.
- Find a solicitor and estate agent you feel comfortable with.

5.2 Décor and furniture: decking it out

A major hurdle is over – you have signed the lease and collected the keys, so now what? Now comes the hard, but fun, job, of getting your coffee or tea shop ready to open. There are several things to think about, so taking a measured approach is best – you will need to write lots of lists, have a clear timeline for things to be completed, as well as contingency time for when things take longer than expected. That said, try to have fun with it as well – this is when you will start to see your vision take shape, so enjoy it!

In this chapter we'll cover:

- Things to consider before you start
- Décor and layout
- Signage
- Dressing the window

BEFORE YOU PICK UP A PAINTBRUSH

Your best planning skills are needed for this stage of the setting-up process. Every aspect of the coffee or tea shop's physical appearance and functionality has to be thought out before you start drilling into walls or choosing cappuccino makers.

IN MY EXPERIENCE:

Raymond Voce, Royal Teas

Space is an issue. It could be improved but it would cost and so we make the most of how it is. When I first came to the café the bar was at the front and a very regular crowd would sit around it. It appeared to be very cliquey and therefore unwelcoming. I moved the bar to the back and opened up the entrance which wasn't met with approval from the regulars but was the right decision. We want to welcome everyone, not just a select few.

Environmental health officer

Bring in one as soon as possible if you haven't done so already, to talk you through what you need to do to meet legal requirements for your coffee or tea shop. This is vital, as the design of the kitchen is non-negotiable and you will need to work the rest of your layout around this. You also need to inform your local authority's food hygiene department, which will inspect your shop after opening and on a regular basis.

Contact your local council for details of your environmental health department. Contrary to popular opinion, environmental health officers are not the enemy and can actually be very helpful when you are first starting out. The government's food safety department also offers very good advice.

TIP

Bringing an expert in during the planning stage could end up saving you thousands of pounds and even prevent delays in opening.

Utilities

TIP

Contact consumer champions *Which?* (www.which.co.uk) for up-to-date and independent advice on everything from the most cost-effective electricity companies to warnings about the worst cappuccino makers. (There may be a small charge for this service.)

Another area to think through carefully is utilities. It's tempting to leave things as they are if the premises already have water and electricity set up, but the current suppliers may not be the most cost-effective for your business. There are deals to be had if you just have the patience to shop around for them. A few hours invested in comparing prices may save you a considerable amount in the long run.

TIP

Find out from your landlord or the previous premises owner what the situation is for running water and electricity before you get the keys. You won't be able to do much without working utilities and it may be something you can sort out before the handover.

DIY versus contractors

Your business plan should have already helped you decide whether you will be doing a DIY job or hiring professional decorators, architects or builders. Even if you decide to do the work yourself, it's a good idea to get some professional advice before you start as there may be some issues you haven't considered. If you decide to bring in contractors, think about the following before choosing whom you will hire, so that you can give them a true idea of what they need to offer you, and to avoid being taken advantage of:

- The kind of atmosphere you want to achieve
- The colour scheme/design theme you are leaning towards
- The layout of both the coffee counter and drinking/seating area
- The price you are prepared to pay

Don't accept the first price and package you are offered. Don't be afraid to haggle and definitely get as many different quotations and pitches as you can to compare *before* you make a decision. Trouble over builders or designers can cause delays in opening or going over budget. For extra reassurance it's worth going via trade bodies such as the Federation of Master Builders. It may cost more, but at least then you can be more confident of a professional service.

IN MY EXPERIENCE:

Tim Hume, Redroaster Coffee House

Although we had experience before of designing a coffee service counter that was tight and worked well, this time we were not so successful. We left too much space behind the counter and inadvertently got some other measurements wrong. The outcome was that we have a slightly awkward and inefficient work area. Because it more or less works it was not seen as the priority to change when we refurbished this summer, but it is the next project.

Timing

Work out a timescale that seems manageable with your architect or builder but be prepared for delays and setbacks. The key issue you will have is deciding how long you can afford to pay the mortgage or rent while you aren't earning. For a basic refurbishment you could be looking at anything from three weeks to two months, and if you are doing more structural changes the time could move to three or even four months.

The main things that hold up building work are delays in getting materials, coordinating electricians and plumbers, and problems fitting large pieces of furniture, such as counters or built-in shelving that haven't been measured properly. Try as much as you can to be prepared for the building and decorating portion of setting up. Anything you can already have ordered and organised is vital. Equally, be realistic, things will go wrong and there will be set backs, so build this into your timing. Finally, while building work is going on, don't assume this means you can't do anything – now is the time to source and research suppliers, purchase your crockery, cutlery and other supplies and equipment, go on barista training

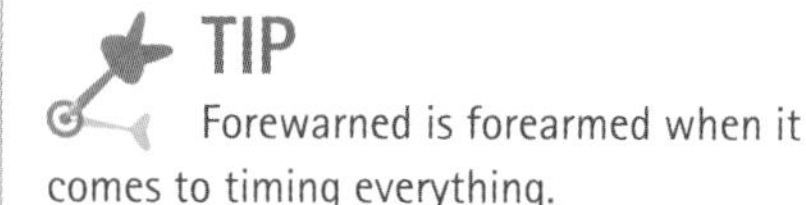

TIP

Forewarned is forearmed when it comes to timing everything.

courses and practise making the perfect espresso. You can also use this time to familiarise yourself with the legalities of running a business and even start looking for staff.

LAYOUT

Now's the time to go back to the list of all the areas and spaces you needed, which you wrote before you bought or leased the property. You will have more of an idea of what you have and don't have, and what you need. Consider each area and what you will specifically need from it – this will help if you are doing some major building work, or even if you are just starting to decorate and buy furniture.

Counter, standing and seating areas

- What kind of service do you plan to have? Counter, table or both?
- What percentages of your service will be takeaway? If lots, how will you deal with queuing?
- How much food will you serve? How big will your tables need to be?
- Will your seating area have small chairs and tables or large sofas?
- How near the door should the counter be?
- How wide, high and deep will your counter be?
- What will you keep behind the counter – crockery, stock, equipment?
- Where will the till go?

Kitchen

- Does this need to be accessible from behind the counter?
- Will it be easy for your staff to serve food from the kitchen?
- Can you have it on a different floor from the main coffee shop?
- Is there space in it to keep all the stock you need to?
- Is it easily accessible via a back door for deliveries?

Stockroom

- How much stock will you be storing on a weekly and monthly basis?
- Can you have the stockroom in a convenient place, near the counter?
- Is the stock room well located for deliveries?
- If space is an issue, is it a luxury you don't need? Would a 'stock area' suffice?
- Can it be safely locked at night?

Office

- Do you need an actual office space, or can you do the books from home?
- How will you keep it secure?
- Can you equip it with everything you need and still have enough space for everything else you need?

Customer toilets

- Are the toilets easily accessible for everyone – from elderly people to pregnant women, small children and those with disabilities?
- Can you ensure they are far enough away from the food preparation and service areas?
- Will you have several cubicles or one toilet each for men and women?
- Where is the best place for toilets based on your plumbing and electrics?
- Can you provide a baby changing area?

Staffroom

- What do you need to provide for staff? How many staff will you have?
- Do you need separate toilets for staff?
- Will they be coming from far away, and will they need somewhere private to change?
- Do you need to provide lockers?
- Where will they take their breaks and can they eat in the staffroom?

Other areas

- Are you planning to offer internet, evening performances, an art gallery, a shop, a bookstore or anything else?
- Can you afford this space initially?
- Is it better to have this near the front of your coffee or tea shop, or at the back? Or on another floor?
- What power points and plumbing access might these need?
- Will you have a separate counter for these areas?
- What will the seating be like?

Outside areas

- How big do you need this to be?
- Is the current area enough, or is it too big?
- Can you ensure people won't leave this outside area without paying?

- Or that you customers won't be hassled by street sellers?
- Can you provide shade in the summer, and a safe place to smoke?

Crucially, you have to have an overall concept of how the café is going to look. Think about what your unique selling point (USP) is and how the design needs to fit into that. Tim Hume at Redroaster Coffee House wanted a slight 'factory' aesthetic for his coffee shop, to tie in with their major selling point of roasting their own coffee. That said, you also need to make sure your coffee or tea shop is comfortable, so make sure to get the balance between aesthetics and practicalities.

Counters and seating areas

TIP

Try to avoid positioning tables too close to the front door; you will know yourself how annoying it is to be constantly interrupted by a blast of gale force wind or a crowd of people cramping your style, and your space.

Think about the best place to position the coffee bar in terms of how you will arrange the tables. In small premises you need to be as economical with your space as possible, so the counters, the types of chairs you use and even the shape of your tables will affect how many covers you can seat at any one time. Raymond Voce from Royal Teas decided to move his counter to the back of the tea shop, which encouraged more customers in, and at Bettys in Harrogate the café offers waitress service, which reduces big queues at the front of the shop.

IN MY EXPERIENCE:

Raymond Voce, Royal Teas

I like that people can see into the café and we always have different artists displaying their stuff. If you like, the window frames to passers-by a moment in the life of our café, a glimpse of a scene of friends chatting, relaxing and enjoying delicious food.

Toilets

IN MY EXPERIENCE:
Simon Robertson, Leoni

It is quite amazing how people are influenced and make a judgement on a business based on the cleanliness of the toilets and for good reason. If an establishment can't be bothered to clean what the customer can see what state are the places the customer can't see, i.e. the kitchen?

There is no law that says you have to provide toilet facilities for customers, especially if public facilities are close by; however it's rare to see a coffee or tea shop without one now, and if you can spare the space it's worth doing.

Toilets: the small print

A few rules do apply when providing toilets in coffee or tea shops, such as:

- All cubicles should have a door.
- All toilet areas must be separated by a door from all food preparation areas.
- The toilets and washbasin should not be visible from the public areas, either by having double doors or modesty screens or by arranging toilets and urinals in such as way as to hide them from view.
- Toilets must be well ventilated.
- Toilets should be accessible for disabled customers.
- There should be separate handwashing facilities for your staff, as they should not be using the same sinks that are used to handle any food, whether it's a panini or a biscotti.

TIP

How are you to going to handle passing shoppers who want to use your toilet but aren't going to buy a coffee? Will you have a customer-only policy? A polite notice can do the job.

The basics for any toilet are fairly common sense: keep it simple, and keep it clean. Look for a good, reliable cleaner if you aren't already getting a member of staff to do it for you. And keep the toilets well stocked with toilet paper, soap and hand drying facilities. You will also need to make sure locks and doors are in good working order at all times, or you may have some rather desperate customers on your hands. Toilets should be checked throughout the day to make sure there are no nasty surprises awaiting customers. A good rule is to have a quick check once an hour, especially when the coffee shop is busy.

DECORATION

Colour

Relate colour to the kind of atmosphere you want to achieve and be sensitive to the kinds of moods and emotions that certain colours create. In crude terms, reds and oranges would create a lively and bustling shop, and blues and greens work for more relaxed and chilled-out establishments.

Avoid very bright colours as it can have an unpleasant impact on your customers (like a migraine). However, likewise, too much white or cream can make people feel they are in a hospital or ubiquitous shopping mall.

TIP

If you have got a very small customer area, avoid colours that are too dark on the walls as this may make the room feel even more cramped. Don't forget that plainer walls can be complemented with brighter or stronger colours in other areas such as furniture or upholstery. And mirrors can also add a real feeling of space.

Lighting

This is something you will need to consider carefully, to ensure the balance between enough light for your baristas to see to make the drinks and food and handle money, and a mellow vibe across the rest of the coffee or tea shop. Don't write off the option of various floor and table lamps, and dimmer switches that allow you to change and alter the lighting depending on the time of day, or the weather. You should also consider the lighting for any window displays, internet stations or art if you plan to have some on the walls.

Furniture

Before you buy your furniture it's important to strike a balance between what you want design-wise, and what's suitable and functional for your coffee or tea shop. Think about comfort, shape, size, durability and cost, and as always, keep the USP in your mind – why are people in your coffee shop, what are they doing there, what will they be drinking and how will your furniture reinforce this?

Sofas and coffee tables

You will need to decide on whether you want sofas and armchairs, or a range of tables and chairs. If sofas are a key part of your vision, make sure you have got enough space, and that they don't restrict the amount of covers you can have at any one time. It can be quite nice to include a few sofas towards the front of your coffee shop – the sight of a few friends curled up on a sofa with a hot mug of tea will definitely attract people in during a cold day. You will also need coffee tables to go with these. Again be sensible about space, and consider whether if people want to eat, the tables are big enough to accommodate this.

Chairs and tables

If space is limited, or you intend to serve a lot of food, chairs and table are the way to go. You can usually fit more people in this way, and the ability to move chairs and tables more easily makes for a flexible space, which can be handy if a large group comes in, for instance, and you need to create a table of 10 quickly. It is also popular with people who might decide to use your café to work from, or have meetings in.

Stools and bar tables

Don't forget it might also be nice to include some higher tables and bar stools, for a coffee bar at the front of the shop where people can sit and watch the world go by; these are quite popular, especially in an urban location where people tend to stop to enjoy a coffee alone.

Matching or mismatched?

Whether you decide to go for matching furniture or not will often depend on the atmosphere and identity you decided on earlier. Having matching furniture might be a good move if you aren't too confident with your interior decorating skills, or you have created the image of a clean, fresh tea shop, smart and relaxed. However, non-matching furniture is quite fashionable at the moment – visit a few gastropubs to see the effect. They can create a more bohemian and unique look, and it can also work out cheaper, especially if you are looking at second-hand stuff.

Booths

If you are going for static furniture such as in-built booths, shop around when it comes to designers and carpenters. It's always worth getting more than one opinion or quote for the work.

Extras

As any good interior makeover show will tell you, it's important to 'dress' the room as well; don't forget the little details, pictures, artwork, photos, cushions, vases, throws, candles, statues, lights and lamps, book shelves and books.

Sourcing furniture

There are lots of ways to source furniture, either through a supplier or from local or nationwide shops – some smaller coffee and tea shops do use places such as Ikea and Habitat to kit out parts of their café.

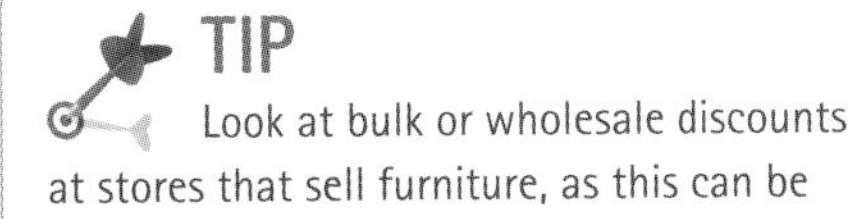

TIP

Look at bulk or wholesale discounts at stores that sell furniture, as this can be quite a pricey option.

Suppliers

As with your coffee and tea supplier, industry magazines, word of mouth and the internet are a great place to start – just type 'coffee/tea shop furniture' into Google and the results will reveal several good companies with a range of modern and old-fashioned furniture solutions. Try to go with companies that have experience in coffee or tea shops as they'll be able to advise you of what's popular at the moment, and will suggest options you might not have thought about. If you can, try to visit suppliers to see some of the furniture on offer. Take the time to sit down at the tables, try out the chairs and touch the furniture – do you want smooth and sleek, or rough and rustic? Also ask questions about durability, how quickly certain surfaces get scratched or damaged, and consider guarantees and how easy it would be to replace things that get broken.

Second-hand

Furniture buying is one area you can save money without compromising on quality or style. Buying second-hand may give you not only a better class of furniture for your money, but also some antiques that may even fit in with your design theme.

Reclamation and restoration yards

There are numerous reclamation and restoration yards across the UK, some of which are veritable treasure troves of unique and interesting furniture and fixtures at great prices – including doors, fireplaces, door handles, wooden flooring, tiles, chairs and tables, sideboards etc. You may even find a unique old-fashioned tea or coffee shop counter. Sometimes the furniture needs some form of restoration, which you can get done, or attempt yourself, but often it's just a case of cleaning and polishing something.

Window display

Are you going to have one? If part of your unique offering is the fantastic cakes you serve, then perhaps you should think about how best to tempt customers on the street. Could a dedicated and regularly changing window display be part of your coffee shop's 'culture' and a talking point amongst customers? Window displays can be fun – whether it's getting creative with a coffee sack and beans or theming it for a major festival or celebration.

FROM THE EXPERTS:
Bettys Café Tea Rooms

Our shop staff and Bettys small creative marketing team work together to decorate our window – the displays change frequently reflecting the seasons and yearly celebrations (such as Christmas and Easter). Our summer and Christmas displays are the longest – otherwise they change nearly every month.

SIGNAGE

Like everything else suggested in this chapter, your signage is wholly dependent on the kind of look and feel you want for your coffee or tea shop. Be sensible and choose what best suits the type of establishment you are running.

Signage can usually be done reasonably economically if it is done with taste; perhaps £2,000–£3,000 at the most. An awning with your logo on would double this, but would usually be worthwhile, especially if you have space for eating outside. Durability has to be a consideration, so use a well-established sign-writing company. You will usually find that they know what they are doing and will not over-charge.

IN MY EXPERIENCE:

Tim Hume, Redroaster Coffee House

We have elevated lettering at a high level with the name 'Redroaster Coffee House', an awning with our logo and an illuminated menu board. In the next period we are to have an additional advertising board on a projecting side wall for which we have quotes ranging from £500 to £1,000 depending on materials (painted wood to cast metal). Also we would like to have barriers round our pavement seating area with our logo on them but we are looking at money we don't want to spend just yet.

Sandwich boards can work well outside if you want to inform passing potential customers of coffee/tea offers or a new muffin/cake you are promoting. Be careful of spelling mistakes though, and make sure you have included any exclusions or exceptions when advertising special offers.

Design for signage should match up with the choices you made when considering the identity and the name of your business (see Part 1 for help on this).

TIP

Check if your local council has a colour palette you have to choose from; protruding signs can be a no-no as can sandwich boards if they obstruct the pavement.

IN MY EXPERIENCE:

Raymond Voce, Royal Teas

I am just about to buy a canopy for the café. It will have the website address printed on it and will cost around £1,200. Got to think of that kerb appeal.

Security

Once you have spent your cash on good equipment, be smart and make sure it's secure. No ifs and buts, no shortcuts. You will regret being cheap with security if you get burgled. Spend the money properly when it comes to locks, bolts and secure doors and windows. If it doesn't look impenetrable it will just attract thieves. An alarm is a must, and preferably one that alerts a security company rather than just making a loud noise. You will pay a monthly fee of at least £40–£50 for this service, but it will be well worth it for the peace of mind.

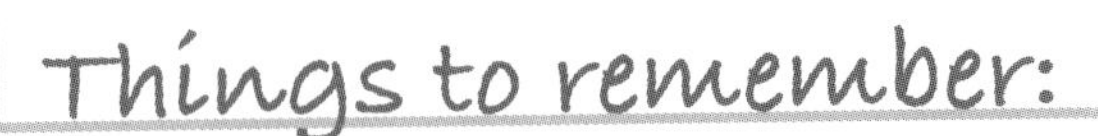

- Consult an environmental health officer. It could save you a lot of time and money, not to mention prevent you from having to correct mistakes down the line.
- Check your utilities are due to work before you move in. You may arrive to a water-less, electricity-free property.
- Make sure your toilets are accessible to everyone and meet all the legal requirements.
- Don't be tempted to decorate solely to your taste. It's your customers that need to feel the most comfortable.
- Think about locations, seasons, window displays and signage together – it should be as unified as possible.

5.3 Serving equipment needed

We've already covered how you will serve your coffees and teas in Part 3, so by this point you will have a good idea of what you will need. But when you start purchasing it's good to do as much as you can in bulk, so have a complete list of everything you will need (see page 233). You don't want to be overstretched when it comes to having enough cutlery or chinaware, but at the same time, if you don't get your estimates right you may end up over-buying.

In this chapter we'll cover:

- Purchasing equipment
- Sourcing your equipment
- What you will need

➡ PURCHASING EQUIPMENT

IN MY EXPERIENCE:
Simon Robertson, Leoni

The till was left over from the previous business (a butcher's shop) and was very basic. The till had to be re-programmed; but it was a simple case of changing sausages to espresso.

Here we'll go into detail about all the bits and bobs you will need to equip your coffee or tea shop. It may seem a bit overwhelming at first, but bear with us and approach this methodically. By this point, your shop should be a reality, and you are very nearly ready to open.

Top tips to remember when buying equipment

- Remember, you can gradually add various types of equipment. They can be very expensive and at the beginning you need to keep expenditure to a minimum. Who knows how long it is going to take for the word to get around that you are great?
- Buy only what is absolutely necessary. You can buy second-hand or perhaps lease to keep your costs down at first. There are plenty of companies both online and listed in business directories that will lease you equipment, allowing you to work out what you use most, and what apparatus you think you should return.
- Avoid buying unnecessary gizmos and gadgets which you think might come in useful at some point.
- Be economical, but don't go for the cheapest options on the market. You really do get what you pay for, so it may well be worth the splurge at the beginning to avoid spending twice when the cheap bargain version stops working after two days.
- See what you have already; if you are buying or leasing an established coffee or tea shop business, the likelihood is that they'll have many of the things you already need including coffee machines, cups and saucers, chairs and tables – see what's included, or at least what you would like to be included, and try to get a deal. Often people will be more than happy for you to take unwanted equipment and furniture off their hands.

WHAT YOU WILL NEED: A COMPREHENSIVE LIST

Serving

- **Cups and saucers** – coffee cups, tea cups, saucers, mugs, glasses and plastic cups for children. If you plan to serve small, medium and large coffees and teas, you will need different sized cups and mugs.
- **Teapots and coffee pots** – you will need a variety of sizes for tea, and will also need jugs or pots to serve hot water in for those who want to dilute their tea.
- **Takeaway cups** – you will have to provide these, in a variety of sizes. Consider recyclable and green options, and don't forget about lids.
- **Plates and bowls** – this will vary hugely depending on what food you are offering; for cakes and sandwiches you will need smaller side plates, and for bigger meals you will need dinner plates and bowls for pasta and risotto.
- **Cutlery** – will you offer disposable or metal cutlery? Either way you will need knives, forks, dessert spoons and teaspoons. You will also need cake-cutting knives or slicers. For the general cutlery you will need to decide if this will be given out at the counter with meals, served with table service, or collected by the customer from a central service station.
- **Napkins** – unless you want to match these to your décor (and there are some wonderful designs out there now) basic white napkins are the best way to go; as with cutlery decide if you will give them out at the counter or from a central self-service station.
- **Extras** – depending on what you will do and what you will leave up to the customer you will need a variety of chocolate shakers (for sprinkling), syrup bottles, sugar sachets, milk jugs or portions. Go through your menu to create a list of all extra ingredients you offer.

Display equipment

- **Refrigerator units** – under-counter fridges, self-serve refrigeration or 'serve over' fridge units. See page 235 for more information.

- **Assorted bottles, jars and bowls** – for biscotti, muffins, biscuits and cookies.
- **Plates, trays and bowls** – for cakes, brownies, sandwiches, pastas, risottos and wraps.
- **Décor extras** – flower vases – small, if you are going to use them on your customer tables, and large if you are using them on the counters or windowsills.
- **Menus and menu holders** – think about whether menus will be small enough to sit in little stands on the tables, or can be kept in holders on the walls. Or will you just use blackboards above the counter? See pages 185-194 for more on menus.

Kitchen and cooking equipment

- **Knives** – a selection of chef's knives, including a few good bread knives if you are making sandwiches.
- **Baking equipment** – mixing bowls, measuring scales, whisk, cake tins, greaseproof paper, wire racks, cooling trays, cake tins.
- **Cooking equipment** – strainer, saucepans, roasting tins, and chopping boards.
- **Food storage** – Tupperware, cling film, tin foil, tins and jars.

Cleaning equipment

- **Hand cleaning soap** – for staff.
- **Washing-up scrubbers and brushes**.
- **Mops, buckets, detergents**.
- **Vacuum cleaner**.
- **Toilet goods** – toilet roll, hand soap, handtowels.
- **Sanitary bins for the ladies**' toilet – you usually get these from a company that deals with the servicing, and empties them on a regular basis.
- **Rubbish bins** – separate for food and recyclable waste; bin liners; rubbish bin for the toilet.

Electrical goods

- **Espresso/coffee machines** – we've covered this in detail in Part 3 (The beverages essentials, see pages 167–175). Don't forget that you will also need milk jugs and steam-wands.

- **Hot water urn** – You will need to decide if you need one of these or can use the hot water from your espresso machine. If you do purchase one make a note of the space you have and the kind of litre capacity you might need; ask a supplier if you aren't sure. See page 174 for more information on these.
- **Fridges** – these may have already been installed in your kitchen but you may also require one under or behind the counter for keeping milk and other chilled goods in and one in which to keep and display the food you are serving. Prices for refrigerated units and counters start at £800 and go up to £2,500 so take your time and make sure you have bought the right unit for you.

Display fridges

You will probably need a refrigerated unit to keep and serve your chilled food and drinks from. If you are serving sandwiches then a stand-alone self-service fridge would suffice. You can have an open cabinet, or a more upright fridge with clear doors. What you choose will depend on whether you are serving more drinks or food-based items, and the space requirements for your coffee or tea shop.

If you are offering salads, cakes and other lunchtime items that you and your staff will be serving then you will need something known as a 'serve over' fridge counter, a refrigerated unit that also acts as a counter. Customers can see your produce and your staff can serve it to them. These often come in different heights, widths and sizes so spend some time thinking about this, and making sure to incorporate it in your counter design.

- **Dishwasher** – an industrial dishwasher, rather than a domestic one. You may want to have a small counter top one for mugs and glasses, as well as a larger one in the kitchen for plates, bowls and saucepans.
- **Oven, hob and grill** – this will come with the kitchen design; try to get something big and sturdy enough to last the distance.
- **Sandwich toasting machine** – these are quite useful to have behind the counter if you plan to heat up paninis for customers regularly.
- **Microwave** – useful in the kitchen; make sure it is robust enough to survive six to seven busy lunch periods a week.

Paying equipment

- **Tills and card machines** – you will need at least one till for your coffee shop depending on its size and scale of operation. Smaller establishments can get away with a basic system, while more complicated operations will want to go with a more advanced electronic point of sale (EPoS) system. This is another area where you can choose to either lease or buy.
- **EPoS**: The more sophisticated EPoS systems will have computerised touch screens which can keep track of exactly what's been ordered and give you accurate up-to-date figures on what your most popular drinks are. However the cost of these can run into the thousands and you may find that a standalone system which provides paper printouts is more than adequate for your operation. For details on how to apply for merchant status to receive credit card payments, see the Chapter 2.4 (*Getting legal*).

CUPS AND SAUCERS: GETTING THE BASICS RIGHT

It is vital that you choose cups and saucers that suit your brand and identity, but are also easy to clean, and replace. You need to choose something practical and aesthetically pleasing. Bear the following points in mind to make your life easier.

White's alright

You could decide to get your plates, dishes and cups in plain white, especially if you aren't sure about the rest of your colour schemes yet. They are easy to replace when they break, and you can still add some individuality with different shapes and sizes. Ultimately, people will remember what's in the cup, not what's on it.

Branded is nice

It can add a real touch of class to your establishment, and if you have a strong logo and branded identity then personalised coffee and tea cups can work well, just remember they may take longer and cost more to replace.

Free cups

Numerous coffee and tea suppliers will also throw in several branded mugs with the type of coffee or tea you have purchased (you will have seen Illy mugs in coffee shops, for instance), and these are often at the right shape and size for the different drinks you will serve. They also add quite a nice continental touch and, if you have gone for a well-known and liked brand of coffee or tea, it's another piece of excellent and subtle marketing. You can usually buy more from them if you need to.

Colours and sizes

There is a wealth of china patterns and designs out there, as well as cups of all different shapes and sizes – and something a little bit different and unique can really reinforce your identity further; though, as with branded cups, replacing them can be slightly more challenging, or expensive.

Mix and match

You may decide that you want to source different mugs from second-hand, antique and charity shops. This can be quite fun, and different, but be careful about your sizing as you will need to keep it uniform to ensure each customer gets the same-sized drink for their money.

Sizes

This is crucial. Not only will you need to decide how big your small, medium and large coffees and teas are – and this is entirely up to you – you will need different-sized cups for espresso, lattes and cappuccinos.

Takeaway cups

Obviously essential, though just because they are eventually going to be thrown away doesn't mean you shouldn't give them some consideration. Various companies now offer generic takeaway cups, usually with some form of interesting design. If you are planning a considerable amount of takeaway business you might like to use these as another form of marketing or PR and get them branded, though this does cost more.

How many do you need?

The ratio for cups to customers is 1.5 times the number of seats or covers for plates/cups etc; though remember this means each type of crockery. So if you have 20 covers you will need 30 cappuccino cups, 30 latte mugs, 30 espresso mugs, 30 plates, etc.

However, you can start off with less in the beginning, especially if you have issues with storage – but make sure you keep on top of the clearing of tables and washing cups. You don't want to have run out of things to serve your drinks in by 12pm on the first day. Raymond Voce at Royal Teas also says: 'Get lots of cutlery – you will need it.'

SOURCING YOUR EQUIPMENT

We've already said above that most coffee and tea suppliers also have a great range of coffee and tea equipment, including cups, mugs, saucers, spoons etc. If you have got a good relationship with your supplier then this could be a good option. Otherwise spend some time looking through industry magazines and websites, and send off for some catalogues – most companies will also happily send samples of their china and cutlery now, so you can get a good feel for what you like.

Discuss the delivery costs, the speed of re-orders for replacing old stock, and what the minimum order is for china and cutlery – as this could affect whether you can use them on an ongoing basis. For larger items, especially electrical goods, make sure you deal with the issues of maintenance, service and guarantees, especially the speed that they'll replace or fix something – a broken espresso machine or a fridge on the blink can have a seriously detrimental effect on your business.

Things to remember:

- You don't need to buy everything all at once, you can add equipment as and when you need it.
- Think carefully about the cups and saucers you choose as this can be one of the most crucial parts of any coffee or tea shop's branding.
- Take your time choosing your supplier.
- With bigger electrical equipment always ask about maintenance and guarantees.

5.4 Recruiting and training staff

The people you employ to help run your coffee or tea shop will have just as much influence over its success as the quality of the beverages you serve, so it's crucial that you get the right team on board. Recruitment is tricky, and if it's your first time employing staff you might not get it right initially, although it helps if you can! You will need to consider how many staff you need, what roles they'll have and what kind of training they'll need, as well as what you will pay them.

In this chapter we'll cover:

- Your staffing needs
- Finding staff
- Recruitment
- Interviewing
- Paperwork
- Job roles
- Training
- Wages

WHAT ARE YOUR STAFFING NEEDS?

Your business plan should not only have included an idea of how many members of staff you will need to run your coffee or tea shop, but also should have taken into account what you can afford. Ask yourself the following questions:

- How many people will you need and what roles will they perform?
- Will you be recruiting baristas, or taking on those duties yourself?
- Will you employ a dedicated cleaner or will this fall under the remit of other staff?
- How many days/hours will your staff work? Which staff will you need to double up on to make sure you always have the right number of employees working on any given day?
- Which members of staff will work part-time and whom will you need to employ on a full-time basis?
- What will be your emergency policy if a barista is unable to work?
- What kind of training are you prepared to give them – will you train them yourself? How much time can you spare? Or can you afford to send them on a barista training course?

IN MY EXPERIENCE:
Raymond Voce, Royal Teas

When I started off there was only me working at the café. When we got a little busier I hired someone to help me over lunch times. Later I needed this person all day and so it went. What I am saying is, do not employ a bunch of people who are going to spend a great deal of time sitting around. Staff are your biggest expense.

Once you have established exactly how many members of staff your coffee or tea shop needs you will have to make a decision on what you can afford to pay them. You will need to strike a fine balance between being practical and not stretching your budget too far and being realistic about what you need to pay to attract the right kind of talent.

WRITING RECRUITMENT ADS AND SHORT-LISTING

Before drawing up a recruitment advertisement you need to have worked out the duties and level of responsibility included in the role. You need to define the vacant position accurately and be clear about exactly what type of person you want for the role.

Get the recruitment process right and you will greatly reduce the risk of attracting the wrong kind of people. Mess it up and you won't even find a suitable candidate to pick from a pile of 100 CVs, let alone be able to spot them at interview stage.

TIP

Are you going to hire qualified, professional baristas or local people whom you can train yourself?

IN MY EXPERIENCE:

Tim Hume, Redroaster Coffee House

We tend to select from unsolicited CVs and referrals from existing staff – we're sufficiently well known to receive a large number of these. We have advertised occasionally in the past, but haven't received very rewarding results when we did.

WHERE TO ADVERTISE?

Think about the kinds of staff you want and focus your attentions on avenues that will attract them. Local schools, colleges and universities are good if you need Saturday or part-time staff and you can usually put a note on their noticeboards for free. Local newsagents, restaurants and supermarkets are also a good place to put an advert. If you can afford to pay for an advertisement try the local paper, or an online portal. The local job centre is also a good place to approach, especially in a climate such as this, where employment opportunities are few and far between.

The key point is to try to ensure you invest time, rather than money, in the recruitment process, as it can be extremely expensive. You don't want to eat away at your start-up funds by spending money on recruitment advertisements that aren't attracting the kind of staff you want and need for your coffee shop; even a note in the window or on one of your A-line sandwich boards could be enough.

INTERVIEW STAGE

Once you have received some CVs and whittled them down to around 10 or so, depending on how many staff you require, you will need to run interviews. It's best if you can do this at your coffee or tea shop, although if it's a building site at the time, you can usually hire some space in a local office or business centre, or reserve a table in the back of a restaurant or pub.

Interview tips

- Set aside around half an hour for each interview; if you decide to do second interviews you can make them longer.
- If you aren't confident you can ask the right questions, have a friend or colleague along with you to ask the questions you might not have thought of.
- Start the interview by settling down the interviewee with a cup of tea or coffee, and tell them a bit about yourself, your background and the coffee or tea shop itself and your plans for it. You can even give them a quick tour if you feel it's appropriate.
- Be prepared: interviewing can be as nerve-wracking for the interviewer as the interviewee and it's up to you to keep the conversation and questions flowing, so have a variety of questions and topics written down.
- Read their CV before they arrive – and then get them to fill in any gaps and clarify anything that interests you, especially something you don't like the sound of, or that sounds too good to be true.
- Write notes, and be specific – and keep them in order. You will be amazed how quickly one interview merges into the other and you forget who said what.
- Be aware that some people are just bad at interviews but might be your ideal staff member, so if they are quiet, take the time to find out the key information you need.

- Give them an opportunity to ask questions, and remember what they asked, as this often says a lot about them. Did they ask about money, or hours, or why you started your coffee or tea shop, or career progression? These sorts of things give invaluable clues as to what they see this job being.
- Present them with a few problem-solving scenarios to see how they would resolve them.
- Ask them some more abstract questions about their hobbies, passions in life, what they know about tea and coffee, how their friends might describe them, and what their one strength and one weakness might be.

During the interview process not only will you need to find out whether you can work with this person, and whether they have the skills you need, but there are also some legal implications you should remember. It's natural to want to find out as much about the candidate as possible but there are certain questions that you simply must NOT ask, or you could leave yourself vulnerable to discrimination claims. These include:

- **Race** – avoid questions about ethnic background or country of origin, even if it fits with your coffee or tea shop's theme. There will be time to get to know someone's background if you decide to take the candidate on. Avoid the subject during the interview.
- **Gender** – there are the obvious sexist comments to avoid, but something you may slip up on is asking about families. Avoid asking about a candidate's future plans to have children etc.
- **Disability** – obviously there are certain disabilities that would prevent certain coffee or tea shop roles. However, if it only involves certain adjustments to enable a disabled person to do the job you should consider them as equally as all other candidates.
- **Age** – this is also crucial, be careful of using words in your advertisement or during interviews that could imply you want people of a certain age – words such as 'fresh' and 'energetic' can imply someone young for instance. Also be careful about how you approach the issue of levels or years of experience, as it can alienate the younger candidates who haven't had the time to get as much experience as someone older.

Once you have made an offer, the next step is to check references. The usual format is to make the offer verbally over the phone or in person, and follow this up with a written document or contract that the person will need to sign. Once you have checked their references, you can confirm their start date and begin the administrative process of taking on an employee.

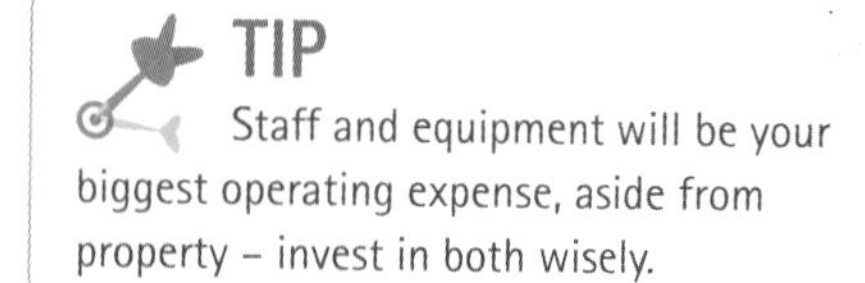

IN MY EXPERIENCE:

Simon Robertson, Leoni

We will consider employing people firstly based on their character and personality; this is after all how a customer will initially rate a member of staff. Attitude and appearance are also important. Should the above appear to be satisfactory then we will ask the person to come for a trial at the coffee house. We can usually tell within a day if the person is suitable. If they are suitable then we will employ on a specified trial period then hopefully as a permanent member of staff.

THE PAPERWORK

Becoming an employer for the first time can seem a little daunting. There is a whole raft of administrative duties you will now be responsible for, and neglecting them is not an option. Your first point of call should be the HMRC (0845 60 70 143) to request a new employer starter pack. It contains everything you need to set yourself up to recruit staff.

Nearly everyone who will work in your coffee or tea shop will count as an employee, which means you need to be aware of your obligations for tax and National Insurance contributions. You must keep detailed records of every single member of staff right from the very beginning. All of the following types of staff count as employees in the eyes of the taxman:

- Directors
- Full and part-time workers
- Temporary or casual workers

Even if a worker claims to be self-employed and will pay their own tax and National Insurance, as an employer it is your responsibility to confirm that. HMRC offers guidance on how to do this in the starter pack. Of course, making sure your employees' tax is in order isn't the only obligation you have. You should also know your legal responsibilities regarding:

- Statutory sick and maternity pay
- Working time and pay regulations
- The national minimum wage (NMW)
- Redundancy pay
- Employing foreign nationals
- Part-time workers' regulations

WAGES

Unless you have family working for you in your coffee or tea shop, it's likely that your staff will be local and temporary.

IN MY EXPERIENCE:

Tim Hume, Redroaster Coffee House

We pay above minimum wage. Our starting rate is £6 per hour (except for school students where it is £5 per hour). Our general rate is £7 per hour. Some employees with more responsibility are paid more than this.

To a certain extent you can choose how much you pay your staff. However, you have to stick to the NMW. This is the minimum amount per hour you can pay any person who works for you. The amount, which is regularly updated to take into account things such as inflation, is set by the central government and there are tough penalties for not paying your staff in line with it, including risk of prosecution.

As long as tips are not paid directly through the employer's payroll system, you must pay your staff minimum wage, which at the time of writing is £5.73 per hour, for workers over the age of 22 (as of 1 October 2008). The NMW is constantly being revised and it's up to you to make sure you are aware of any changes. Check Startups.co.uk for the most up-to-date rate.

When you employ others it is also your responsibility to make appropriate National Insurance contributions on their behalf. See the section in *Managing the Books* (page 297) for more information on your tax and National Insurance obligations as an employer.

IN MY EXPERIENCE:
Raymond Voce, Royal Teas

We presently pay between £6.15 and £8.20 per hour. On top of this the staff will share the tips. If it is a day I am working they receive a greater share because I don't take any. Because of our flexible nature and the fact we pay above the minimum wage we keep staff much longer than most café-type places. I would guess that many business owners would want to pay staff the minimum they can get away with; I, on the other hand want to pay the staff as much as I am able to. Some people would think this foolish but it is only fair in my opinion.

TRAINING

Certain members of staff you hire will undoubtedly have had the right kind of barista training and will have general know-how about food hygiene; and there will be other members of your staff who may need to be trained up to completely comply with the minimum legal standards. Either way, both kinds will require some form of training, even if it's just a short induction into how you plan to do things, as every business is different.

The first step is to get your staff trained to use your coffee machines – if your staff don't know how to make the basic hot coffee beverages, you are going to look amateurish, foolish and will ultimately risk your business. Your supplier will be able to assist you with courses if you aren't confident you can give staff the time to ensure their espresso skills are top notch. Much of this will need to be done before you open. Learning on the job is all well and good but come opening day, you will need staff who are on the ball and working together smoothly.

You may also have decided that quality coffee and tea, and a knowledge of both, is essential to your coffee and tea shop's identity, in which case you may want to provide staff with a starter pack of information about the origins and different types of drinks, and some key information on the types of tea and coffee you will be serving so they can answer any customers' questions. (It could be similar to the information we gave you on coffee and tea in Part 3, or you could ask them to read it!)

TIP

Before you open, why not have friends and family round so that your team have a chance to put all their skills into action before paying customers arrive. That way you will be able to identify any areas where more training is required, and whether you are in a position to provide the training yourself or assess whether outside help is needed.

BARISTA TRAINING

What is a barista?

The word 'barista' derives from Italian and essentially means 'bartender'. Baristas are coffee shop staff skilled in the art of espresso making. Among coffee aficionados the term is often used for someone who has reached a certain level of skill.

Something to seriously consider before embarking on your own coffee shop is barista training. There are varying degrees and levels of coffee making training courses, from beginner to advanced and even competition level training. (This is taken extremely seriously, with an annual World Barista Championship.) A basic barista training course should cover areas such as:

- The production of coffee
- The importance of fresh coffee
- Using grinders
- Understanding espresso coffee machines
- The barista's menu
- Milk steaming technique
- Cleaning procedures
- Coffee art training – this is creating patterns with milk on top of cappuccinos and latte's, the most popular designs being the rosetta and the heart latte

IN MY EXPERIENCE:

Simon Robertson, Leoni

It might be possible during training to make one good cup, however producing good coffee consistently takes practice. I have made coffee for over 12 years and still haven't perfected it, nobody ever will. There is always something to learn.

Useful websites for barista training information

- www.absolutecoffee.co.uk
- www.bestcoffeebeans.co.uk
- www.caffesociety.co.uk
- www.gaggia.uk.com/training
- www.ukbaristachampionship.co.uk
- www.worldbaristachampionship.com

Things to remember:

- Try to keep a flexible approach to staffing numbers when you first start. You may need to keep some staff on stand-by while you get a feel for the average number of customers you will have.
- Work out exactly what you require in each role before you start recruiting for the job.
- Consider whether you need to use an agency or pay for a job advertisement; you can put an advertisement in your window for casual staff such as cleaners or waiters.
- Be careful not to fall into any interview traps regarding questions about personal or family life. It could land you in hot water and contravene employment law.
- Look into barista training courses for your staff to make sure their skills are up to standard.

“Coffee smells like freshly ground heaven.”

Jessi Lane Adams

“You can never get a cup of tea large enough or a book long enough to suit me.”

CS Lewis

6

Marketing and PR

Marketing and PR

Marketing and PR are some of the most important things for any independent coffee or tea shop – in this competitive industry you need to make sure you are telling everyone how great you are, and ensuring potential new customers know where you are, and why they should visit you. It can also be invaluable for keeping customers and getting new business. In this chapter we'll take you through the process of getting ready for the launch and achieving the right level of publicity so that customers are queuing up on a regular basis.

In this chapter we'll cover:

- What marketing is
- How to form your own marketing strategy
- How to measure the success of your marketing plan
- Opening and launches
- Public relations (PR)
- Ideas for offers and promotions
- Getting onto dedicated independent coffee and tea shop websites and business directories
- Advertising

WHAT IS MARKETING?

Marketing is a solid combination of word of mouth, advertising and press coverage that ensures you are constantly in the public eye and developing your identity and your brand. If carried out effectively it will not only ensure that your coffee or tea shop is seen and heard but it will also give it the flexibility to adapt to changing customer demands and an ever-evolving business environment.

If your coffee or tea shop venture is going to be successful, it needs you, as the owner, to have a clear vision of where you want it to be in one, five and even 10 years. Marketing will help you understand who your potential customers are; place and price the product compared with the competition and also position the company in the marketplace. It will also help identify future opportunities for self-promotion.

TIP

If your marketing is going to be effective, take the time to know your customers: their drinks, their first name; getting them involved in any menu decisions is a big plus to your business.

You can never be certain what people will and won't do but the best preparation is to research the existing market and learn how people currently behave. Learn and adapt accordingly.

Marketing plans

These can be as small scale or grandiose as you want. However, as we previously mentioned, it's a good idea to think about what you want your coffee or tea shop to achieve in a certain timeframe: a year, two years or even five years time compared with where it would be *without* a marketing strategy.

TIP

It may be worthwhile to do a customer survey regularly – enough to give you a real insight into your customer base, but not too often: that gets annoying.

Tips for devising your marketing plan

- Start by setting clear objectives – where do you want your coffee or tea shop to go?
- Define your target market and identify your potential customers.
- Decide on the brand and the values you want to communicate.
- Plan your promotion strategy.
- Set a budget.
- Devise a schedule.
- Decide how the strategy will be measured, for example, increased sales, direct responses, coverage in local press etc.
- Implement the programme according to the schedule.
- Monitor and evaluate results as an aid for future marketing decisions.

Measuring success

If you have got several ideas on the go at the same time, it's going to be a challenge to work out which ones are being effective. If you aren't sure which marketing technique is giving you the best return on investment then why not try them one by one, then calculate any increase in customers or turnover for that period.

Of course the successes of certain promotions are easy enough to measure because you can count up how many customers make use of the offers. However it's important to remember that you need to bring in more custom as a result of the promotion than you spend on your marketing. It's no good offering discounted rates, or free cups of coffee or tea, if it will just fill up the seats but result in lower profit margins than a half full early morning coffee or tea run.

Opening

First impressions

No matter how well you plan, there are always going to be mistakes made in the first few weeks of opening. You can't re-do a first impression and reputations in the coffee or tea shop trade can be made and broken by word of mouth recommendation or criticism, so think carefully about how you want to open your doors for the first time.

Soft opening

A good method for testing the waters, training your staff and ironing out any obvious kinks in your operation before properly launching is to have a soft launch. This is where you can open a few afternoons a week and let passing customers come in and have a cup of coffee or tea perhaps for a discounted rate. The point of this is you won't have advertised your shop as open yet, so you shouldn't be inundated with customers.

IN MY EXPERIENCE:

Simon Robertson, Leoni

The opening of Leoni was a 'soft opening'; I opened when we were ready and over a period of weeks made improvements to certain things and adjusted aspects of the business until I felt the café operated correctly. We at that point ran some adverts in the newspaper to let people know we had opened.

You could also consider offering discounted coffee or tea while you launch; it will mean you can make a few mistakes and learn from them without too much complaining from your customers.

TIP

Use this opportunity to get your customers to fill in a questionnaire on the coffee, food, service, price, general atmosphere. Ask them to rate each of these factors from 1 to 5. We've mocked up an example on page 334.

Launch party

If you are confident you have got everything ready, you and your staff are ready to meet the public, and you want to thank your family, friends and local residents for their support, it's worth considering inviting them for a coffee or tea tasting launch. It's good for morale, a good training exercise for your staff, a positive way to introduce yourself to the community, and a great way to generate some interest in your coffee or tea shop. Invite local figures such as the mayor, local councillors, any local celebrities and make sure you have the local press out in force. Put flyers through the doors of local residents, telling them about the launch and inviting them to join you for some free coffee or tea and cakes.

Offer little tasters of what you will be serving – espresso-sized cups of perfect lattes and green teas, bite-size pieces of chocolate brownies and carrot cakes; mini sandwiches and homemade houmous to nibble at. Get your staff serving the food and drinks, and make sure you are out front, smartly dressed, talking to

everyone. Be enthusiastic and excited about what you are doing, and what you hope to achieve. And, it sounds obvious but even if it's chaos behind the scenes put on a brave face and calm front for your public.

> **TIP**
> Don't launch before you are ready. It can be tempting if you are running behind schedule to just open the doors and hope for the best. However, customers don't want to see a wall that's in need of one more layer of paint, or be waiting 20 minutes for their coffee because you ran out of time to train your staff.

PR

PR, which stands for public relations, is the coverage and reputation you have with the public, which is usually achieved through press articles, reviews and features and word of mouth. It differs from advertising because you don't pay for it. While paying for advertising buys you the right to put whatever you want about yourself and your coffee or tea shop on the page, advertisement, listing or banner you paid for, PR is more of a way for you to get your name out there, with some 'good news' stories about your coffee or tea shop, the new opening, a new menu, or a review.

Effective initial and ongoing PR can be fantastic for securing good quality coverage for your coffee shop, both in its early stages and throughout its existence, and this is something you should think hard about before opening.

> **TIP**
> PR is very important, but you can do a lot of it yourself and don't necessarily need the expense of hiring a PR agency.

Generally speaking, your best bet when you open your coffee or tea shop is to go for your local paper. It is much more likely to take a keen interest in what's going on in its 'patch'. The national press isn't going to take an interest in you unless you set yourself up as a type of independent coffee or tea shop spokesperson. Interestingly, this is exactly where a PR company could be useful, but we'll cover more on that later.

DIY PR

For independent coffee or tea shops, the best PR is community based. You can think about:

- Tastings outside your shop
- Sponsoring local events
- Getting involved with local or regional organisations/charities
- Offering weekly deals or low prices on certain foods

Back to the local press. To generate interest you will need to send out a press release about your opening, and as time goes on keep the press informed with releases about new promotions, changes in your offering or a second venue opening.

Press releases

The key is to send out a press release that makes your coffee or tea shop newsworthy. Have something interesting and relevant to say. Remember, journalists get a *lot* of stuff sent to them every day. If you want to make sure your release doesn't end up lining the waste paper basket, get some help putting it together. If you decide to go down the PR agency route, they will take care of everything from writing press releases and liaising with newspaper editors to organising a launch party. However, if this is beyond your budget, we've included some useful ideas for writing a press release.

TIP

Avoid sending your press release cold. Phone up first and find out who the best person to send it to is and follow up a day or two later to pursue the story.

The words you use

- Make sure the wording is correct. The message should be clear and direct so that a journalist will be able to use it even if they do not contact a member of your coffee or tea shop team or PR team.
- Your release should convey a sense of importance but not seem over-hyped. You want to provide information about your coffee shop in a newsy format,

not a marketing letter. Besides, if your announcement is worth sending a release out about, it can probably stand on its own without marketing hype.

- The first sentence should be direct, relate what is going on, convey a level of importance of the news and start off with the name of your coffee shop.
- Provide your contact details for journalists who want to find out more and speak to you; these usually go at the bottom of a press release.
- Keep the release to one page. Any longer is just waffle.
- Spell-check and then proofread it again! Nothing will make your efforts look more amateurish than an incorrectly worded release.

Catching the journalist's attention

- Get the name of the journalist you are targeting right the first time. There is no point in asking for a writer who left five years ago to work in Dubai.
- All press releases should answer the journalist's five basic questions of: Who, What, Where, Why and How. This will require you to put yourself in the shoes of a journalist and chances are, answering those questions will give you a clearer idea of what you want to write.
- Make the journalist's job easier by finding the 'angle' for them. New coffee and tea shops and restaurants open all the time: why is yours different? Have you quit working in the city to live the country life and start your own business? Are you going to grow all your own produce for the coffee or tea shop organically? Will you be using your Mexican roots to serve unique and different coffees and make traditional Mexican cakes? Are you taking over the lease of a long abandoned building to bring a fresh look to the high street?
- A punchy headline should be included that matches the release's first sentence, or lead, as those in the trade call them. The headline should be factual. It shouldn't try to make a joke or be smart.

The personal touch

- Include a quote from you. It can personalise the press release and give the journalist an idea of who to speak to.
- Most journalists will seek their own quotes by following up releases with interviews, but having a quote gives journalists the option to use it.

IN MY EXPERIENCE:
Raymond Voce, Royal Teas

Added boosts have come when we have been included in *Time Out*, in newspaper articles and on various 'best of' websites. We have been lucky that these things have just happened without any coercing from us. There is no reason though not to get your new café written about. Contact the newspapers. They need something to write about.

Finally, before you send it off . . .

Include a brief cover letter, especially if you are emailing it, to introduce yourself and to say you have attached a release about a great new coffee or tea shop. Mention your angle and say you look forward to hearing from them.

Staying ahead of the game

If you are passionate about the independent coffee and tea shop industry, have superior knowledge of coffee or tea, and want to position yourself as a spokesperson, keep an eye on, for example:

- Any relevant news
- Trends in coffee and tea prices
- Independents versus chains
- Chain shop closures

When such news breaks, be ready with a comment on anything affecting your industry. Contact local and national papers, and local and national radio stations; they are always in need of experts to comment on recent events.

Keeping the interest high

You may have had coverage in a local paper or free magazine when you launched, but how do you keep the PR momentum going once you have been open a few months? There are plenty of ways to get free coverage but do make sure you don't rub journalists up the wrong way. One way is to build a story around yourself or your coffee or tea shop. If you source all your ingredients ethically and want to publicise the fact that you run a green/fairtrade establishment, send out a press release to relevant publications and tell them about it. You could also offer journalists from your local newspaper a barista training day as an incentive to write about it after the experience.

TIP

Make sure every staff member has been trained in the art of PR for your coffee or tea shop. They should be prepared in case they are the ones who answer the phone to a journalist or critic.

How to get the media on your side

- Invite some journalists round for a complimentary hot drink and pastry. If you have met and spoken to them face to face, they are far more likely to give you the time of day later on.
- But don't contact them too often. If you start to become too familiar, they will avoid you.
- Don't contact them with irrelevant stories. It's important you tailor any press releases, stories or promotions to fit in with their publications and what their readers want to see.
- Find out when deadline day is. If you contact a journalist when they are about to go to press they are unlikely to have time for you. Find out when their publication goes out and contact them straight afterwards as this will be the time they are most likely to listen to you.
- Write a good press release. Journalists receive endless quantities of them so you will need to make yours stand out if you want a chance of it being read and covered.
- Take a look at the Marketing and PR channel of Startups.co.uk for more detail on how to write a winning press release.

Hiring a PR company

Think carefully before committing to this. Of course, it's an option if your budget is a big one. But most effective PR is achievable on your own without hiring a third party which is going to be a drain on your financial resources.

Saying that, there is no average price for taking on a PR company. It's entirely dependent on the level of service you want and the reputation of the company you choose. For more guidance on what it's likely to cost to promote your coffee or tea shop contact the Public Relations Consultants Association (www.prca.org.uk). You can fill out an online application detailing your requirements and they'll send you a list of recommended companies that can then come up with a tailored plan and quotation for you. You can also check out the industry 'bible', *PR Week* to see for yourself the type of PR companies working in the retail/leisure sector and the campaigns they've done recently.

IN MY EXPERIENCE:

Raymond Voce, Royal Teas

When we were in *The Times* this attracted a lot of out-of-towners to us and our regular customers were having difficulty getting in. It can be a difficult balancing act. The effects of such an article are immediate but will last only for a short time and one's regular customers are your bread and butter for the rest.

Online presence

There are several websites out there dedicated to promoting independent coffee or tea shops. Get in touch and invite the editor to your establishment. Give them a fantastic coffee or tea drinking experience – and get listed. Some good examples include www.cosycoffeeshops.co.uk, which reviews as many independent coffee shops as it can and http://delocator.co.uk, another vociferous champion of independent coffee and tea establishments.

If you are entrepreneurial enough to start your own coffee or tea shop, why not create a website to accompany it? Even if it's just one page with your establishment's name, address, opening hours and contact details, it's a great and simple way to get yourself out in the public domain. Nearly half of small businesses still have no online presence despite the fact that there is a whole generation of people out there who find almost all their information online. A basic site can often be free, or cost as little as £1.99 to set up, take a matter of hours to go live, and you don't have to have any knowledge of computer programming to design your site.

> **TIP**
> There are a number of free services out there such as Microsoft's Office Live, or BT's Tradespace, which give you a free site that you can create and update yourself as often as you want. Visit www.smallbusiness.officelive.com or www.bttradespace.com and get yourself an instant web presence for free.

Of course, if you want something a bit more impressive, there are programs available online that allow you to buy a website address for very little, and then provide a template for you to design your site from. Alternatively, you can approach a professional web designer to do it for you. Again, shop around, listen to personal recommendations and word of mouth on who is doing good work at a reasonable price, and you should be able to get something fairly decent from around £400 upwards. Shop around for the best deal – if you find a design agency struggling to find work, you can get companies to tender for the job based on a list of your requirements.

What to include on your website

- Obvious details, such as contact details, where you are located and how to find you
- A sample menu of coffees and/or food
- Any current promotions, special offers or membership
- Photographs of the outside and inside of the coffee shop – this is great for new customers who want to scope you out before they visit for the first time
- Personalise the site by telling your customers about you and your staff
- Think about how the theme and tone of what you say on your website helps to establish your coffee or tea shop's identity
- Check out other independent websites to see what works and doesn't
- Writing a regular blog can also do wonders to build a regular following and can get your coffee shop higher up in search engine rankings

More online marketing ideas

Another way of marketing your business online is to keep your customers informed with email or e-newsletter updates. You could always start a Facebook group for your most loyal customers, encouraging them to be part of your 'coffee' or 'tea' community. You can also have a sign-up form on your website where they can opt in to any updates.

Promotional ideas

One way of attracting new customers is to run special offers or promotions on various days, times or for certain periods. Here are a few promotional ideas you can try in your coffee or tea shop.

TIP

Use email marketing sparingly. Customers don't like being inundated with junk mail.

Loyalty card

This is something that can be stamped or signed so that each time a customer visits they build up to something for free. It could be a free hot drink of their choice, or piece of cake for every six visits. The main point is it gets your customers to come back regularly.

Buy one, get one free

Ah. My mother's *Mastermind* topic of choice. You have seen them in the supermarkets, especially during the current economic climate, but why not offer two coffees or teas for the price of one on a particular day? If a certain phone provider can do 'Orange Wednesdays', then why can't your establishment do 'Coffee/Tea Fridays'? This is just a suggestion and it's important that your business can afford to do it, but it should give you some inspiration.

Early bird discounts

In much the same way as a lunchtime offer can attract customers during the quieter hours, a discounted rate for customers who order their cuppa before 9am could provide the extra few cappuccinos you need to get your profit margins up.

Promotional pastries

Again, this depends entirely on whether you incorporate food into your menu, and what type you decide on. But if, for example, you are offering cakes with coffee or tea, why not offer a 'flavour of the month' and create a mouth-watering sugar sensation for customers to try? Adding a special indulgent dessert to the menu can also generate a fair amount of interest. Or adding a healthy alternative too.

Local newspaper promotion

This can be a great way to create local awareness of your coffee shop and increase footfall. Think about doing a giveaway with your local newspaper. Or sponsoring a competition or charity.

Seasonal promotions

Make the most of months of the year, seasons and public holidays. Have fun with Halloween and provide scary cakes and treats for children; serve cock-a-leekie soup as a special on St Andrew's day; offer turkey and stuffing sandwiches around Christmas and make an indulgent chocolate cake for Mother's day.

LISTINGS AND GUIDES

Getting yourself listed in a local directory doesn't have to cost much time or effort. Most directories such as *Thomson* or the *Yellow Pages* allow you to have a basic entry with the name of the coffee or tea shop, the address and phone number for free. However, if you want a bigger advert with more prominence you will have to pay.

Have a think about other places where your coffee or tea shop can be easily and locally advertised, such as the booklets and directories left in doctors' surgeries, dentists, information centres or local authority properties. These come in both printed and online formats. The printed guides or directories will have details on how to get your coffee or tea shop listed within them. Online versions will also have details of how to list for free or how to pay for greater prominence, for example: thebestof.co.uk, Welovelocal.com and Toplocallistings.co.uk. Don't forget to speak to your tourist office to get yourself listed in free town guides, or try your local council to see if they produce a newsletter or magazine about the local area.

However, a spot or thumbs up in a travel or tour guide is likely to generate much more custom. So why not submit your details to the likes of *Time Out*? Let them know who you are and where you can be found, and you may just find one of the guide writers pays you a visit. If they like what they see, you could land yourself in the guide, and bag a whole load of new customers to boot. You could also contact bigger guides to the UK: Rough Guides, Lonely Planet, Berlitz etc. While there aren't as many up-to-date books devoted to independent coffee and tea shops out there, there are plenty of websites, so get surfing!

Here's a list of publications, guides and websites you may want to get in touch with to let them know you are open for business:

- *Time Out* eating and drinking: www.timeout.com/london/restaurants/
- Yahoo! Travel Guide: www.travel.yahoo.com
- London *Evening Standard*: www.thisislondon.co.uk

- Cosy Coffee Shops blog: www.cosycoffeeshops.co.uk (for independents)
- caterersearch.com: www.caterersearch.com/Home/
- trusted places: www.trustedplaces.com
- QYPE: find it, share it: www.qype.co.uk

TIP

Don't forget www.toptable.co.uk; while it's primarily focused on restaurant reviews, it does offer up some details on where to find steaming espresso coffee, hot chocolates and the perfect desserts, so it's definitely worth getting in touch. The website has over a million users per month, all looking for somewhere to eat and drink.

How to stand out from the crowd

We introduced Tom Hiskey, who runs the non-profit Cosy Coffee Shops blog, www.cosycoffeeshops.co.uk in Chapter 1.2. Here he tells us how a blog can help draw attention to what you do:

'I started my blog after my gap year travels. I had developed a taste for lazy afternoons sitting on comfy sofas, sipping cappuccinos and watching the world go by. On my return, I discovered a lack of guides to these sorts of places in Britain. So, almost by accident, I set up the website. I take a few photos, write a little description, and hopefully point people in the direction of great coffee houses.'

Also take a look at *Boughton's Coffee House*, the magazine for the retail coffee and tea trades. Its website www.coffee-house.org is a fantastic source of coffee-related information with everything from finding new suppliers and entry forms for the latest UK barista championships to training, trade reports and good old coffee industry gossip.

Advertising

You can of course take out paid-for advertisements, but do your research and plan carefully; otherwise you are at risk of being out of pocket as well as out of the public eye, instead of in it.

IN MY EXPERIENCE:

Simon Robertson, Leoni

The only advertising I do is to support local charities. We have not advertised in local papers since the opening 12 years ago.

Print advertising

A few forms of print advertising that could be useful are trade directories, telephone directories and local websites. Get in touch and see what costs are involved and what type of return you can expect. Ask about the readership, who reads it, and how many of them, and make sure this is your target market before handing over some money. A good way to track an advertisement is to offer a free cookie or something similar on a coupon, keep a note of these coupons and see if the response you had to the advertisement tallied with what the sales guy promised you.

IN MY EXPERIENCE:

Raymond Voce, Royal Teas

If it's just numbers you are after, advertise away. If it is return custom you are after, perfect your product.

Things to remember:

- Have a clear and defined marketing strategy before you start spending your money.
- Use PR effectively, it's some of the best free advertising around – but be sparing as well. Don't become a nuisance to journalists.
- Get online! At the very least, have your own website or blog promoting your coffee or tea shop.
- Use promotions and special offers to encourage more customers and repeat business.
- Send your details to guide books/websites. They might pay you a visit.
- Be careful with advertising and spend your money wisely. Ask other coffee and tea shop owner-managers where they've had success advertising.

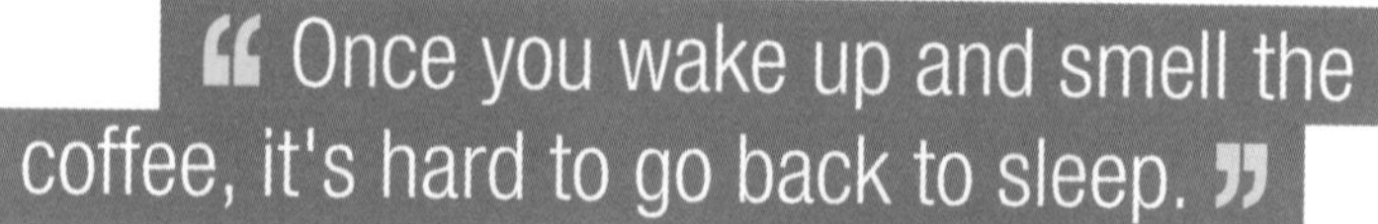
“Once you wake up and smell the coffee, it's hard to go back to sleep.”
Fran Drescher

“Harry found the tea seemed to burn away a little of the fear fluttering in his chest.”
JK Rowling

7

Up and running

7.1 Surviving the first six months

The launch party is over. You have had the first few customers through the door. You have hired your staff. You have cleared your schedule for the foreseeable future. The coffee machines are bubbling away, and there is a cake in the oven. This, however, is just the start. You don't want to be a five-minute wonder. So now comes the task of actually making your coffee or tea shop work, long-term, and earning a proper living from it.

In this chapter we'll cover:

- Preparing for a slow start
- Difficult customers
- The critics
- Assessing your idea
- Updating your menu
- Contingency budgets
- Price changes and pricing
- Seasonal variations
- Opening hours
- Dealing with suppliers

BUILDING UP YOUR CUSTOMER BASE

Preparing for a slow start

Don't be disappointed if customers aren't rushing through the doors and forming a disorderly queue round the corner for your cappuccino or Nilgiri tea. It's likely that, even with the help of any preliminary marketing, your first few weeks will be slow. Be prepared for it and accept it. It's actually quite positive because it will give you some time to settle in and really hone your operation; perfect things, test your ideas and assess what works – and fix what doesn't.

TIP

Your days, especially at the beginning, will be long and tiring. Be prepared. You will be called in on a day off to sort something out, staff will go sick, equipment will need replacing. It's all par for the course.

While your reputation in the area grows, so too should your customer base, and you can get to know them by name and foster that sense of community you feel so strongly about. If you have done your business plan properly, slower trade should have been built into your initial forecasting, but once you have opened and you start to get a rough idea of average trade, you can make gradual adjustments to your figures. This should help you when it comes to ordering stock (and any ingredients if you have incorporated food into your menu) as you won't have an accurate idea of the amount and frequency at which to order things until you have opened.

Enjoy the quiet time and make the most of it. If things go your way, you won't have a lull like it for a long while. Now's the time to think about your marketing and PR skills. Consider the different kinds of special offers you can introduce to try to boost trade. Part 8 (*Business development*) gives you far more detail on this but it's something to consider during your early stages of trading. It can be difficult to get a lot of press coverage before you have opened, but now is the time to get yourself out there. Talk to the local press, offer them a coffee

TIP

Invite local journalists for a cup of coffee so they can get to know you and your establishment.

or tea and cake in return for a review, and if necessary, advertise in the local papers. At the opposite end of the spectrum, you should also be prepared for a massive influx of curious passers by when you open. Welcome them with open arms!

IN MY EXPERIENCE:

Tim Hume, Redroaster Coffee House

It was quite hard in the early days. Our customers took a while to come. When we opened it was just at the beginning of autumn 2000 when it proceeded to rain every day for about two months. During poor weather people won't venture further than their usual haunts so there wasn't much of the 'look see' factor. It wasn't until the next spring that things began to pick up. During that winter I tried not to think about failure but, if I'm honest the thought was in the back of my mind. Fortunately, working 16-hour days seven days a week left me too knackered to worry.

Difficult customers

Don't be surprised or even disappointed in yourself if mistakes occur at the beginning. It would be incredible if it didn't happen. Messing up somebody's order, making them wait 20 minutes for a cappuccino, running out of clean cups or tallying their bill wrong: these things happen, and while you can work quickly to sort them out, remember that first impressions are lasting. If people aren't impressed with your coffee or tea shop, they'll vote with their feet, and tell all their friends about their poor experience. Word of mouth is a powerful thing.

IN MY EXPERIENCE:

Raymond Voce, Royal Teas

We very rarely have any complaints but if we do we most definitely acknowledge them. Our goal is for everyone to leave the café happy and so we will do up to a degree anything to achieve this. We regularly adapt items on the menu for people, have gotten in particular items for others, and made specific dishes asked for by our customers. I just want to do everything in my power within reason to ensure every customer leaves with a positive view of the café.

Get customer savvy and start to recognise the signs that someone is not having a good time in your coffee or tea shop. If there is a queue, look out for customers who are getting impatient. Reassure them that you will serve them as soon as you can and thank them for their patience. If they've been waiting a while, offer them free biscotti as a goodwill gesture. It costs very little to you but will reap its own rewards in customer satisfaction and hopefully, future loyalty!

> **TIP**
> Remember what your regulars like to drink and always introduce yourself and your staff to new customers.

Whether it's a muffin or a bowl of soup with ciabatta, keep an eye out for any customers who have barely touched their plate. Be friendly and casually ask if they were unhappy with the food. It may be that they simply weren't hungry enough to finish it, but if there was a problem with it, offer something as compensation – a free coffee and Danish pastry perhaps. They will remember it and may well give you a second chance. If there is a serious issue with any item, be smart and take it off the bill completely. The lost revenue from the bowl of soup is much easier to swallow than the lost customer.

> **TIP**
> If you feel a customer is unjustified in their complaint, stay calm when talking to them. Raising your voice or completely dismissing their claim won't do you any favours and may attract unwanted attention from other customers. You don't want a reputation as a coffee shop diva.

The customer may not always be right, but you will still end up looking bad if you don't do all you can to try to sort it out to their satisfaction. Check out Chapter 2.4 (*Getting legal*) for more information on a customer's right to refuse to pay. Ultimately it's best to use your initiative if someone wants a refund or refuses to pay, rather than having a set policy. Each situation is different and your ability to keep their business will have a lot to do with how you manage their complaint, and whether you treat them as an individual and not like lost revenue.

Critics

The idea of a critic in your coffee or tea shop may seem terrifying but you won't make a name for yourself unless the people talk about you. (Hopefully in a positive way!) Local papers and magazines, guides and dedicated coffee or tea shop websites can also decide to send a reviewer round to your new place. First of all, view this as some assurance that your marketing is working. People know that you are open and find the concept of your coffee or tea shop interesting enough to check it out.

If you truly believe in the quality of your coffee or tea shop and everything it stands for, whether proud independent or brand-loyal franchisee, you should have enough confidence to welcome a critic on any day of the week. Bear in mind too that a critic is there not only to check you can make a decent cup of brew, but the quality of your service and type of ambience.

> **TIP**
> If you feel you aren't ready for the critics then you need to ask yourself why, and start making the appropriate changes immediately.

Some critics may do a James Bond and go 'undercover' so you might never actually know you have been critiqued until you read the review. Although if they are from a website promoting independent sites, they may be more open and friendly towards you. Be aware, however, that it's not just local papers that'll be checking you out. Online user-generated content means anyone can publish their views on your establishment, from blogs to dedicated coffee and tea websites.

> **TIP**
> If you want a thorough review of your own coffee or tea shop so that you can really judge where its weaknesses lie, why not enlist your own anonymous inspectors? Get a friend or family member that none of your staff know to come along to the shop and pretend to be a customer. They'll be able to report back on service and food quality from the point of view of a regular customer and may pick up areas of concern that you weren't aware of.

ADAPTING YOUR IDEA

Assessing what works

Your first six months should be a constant process of assessing and reviewing your forecasting, service, stock and staffing requirements. You may even have to review your business plan and ask yourself some tough questions, such as:

- Is your concept working?
- Are you spending more than you are earning?
- Are you selling the right products?
- Are customers asking for something you don't have?
- What do you need to change or adapt?

You may have to do this on a weekly basis initially – it helps you keep a track on what's happening, and you will start to know your business inside out. Don't be disheartened if you aren't yet showing a profit. It may take months or even years to get back in the black after you launch, but that doesn't mean your coffee or tea shop isn't successful. It just takes time to recoup your investment.

Early days: how to interpret the figures

Your initial figures may not be a true reflection of how successful your concept has been as they may not show how satisfied your customers are. Even a coffee or tea shop that serves poor beverages can have a busy first few months, riding solely off the back of the curiosity of the locals at seeing a new place to try. The real measure is whether your customers are returning three, four or six months after opening. There are certain situations where most of your customers will be one-offs, such as in tourist hotspots. However, in a residential area away from the centre of town, you will go out of business very quickly if you can't get people to come back. So even if your coffee or tea shop is jam-packed every day for the first two months, have a look at who's filling it. Are you seeing the same faces again and again? If you are, then you have obviously been successful. If not, then you need to ask yourself why, and start thinking of ways to adapt your idea to get people to come back.

New ideas/trends

It's important to keep up with the latest coffee or tea trends, so where and when it's possible, go out and take a look at your competitors. What are they doing that's new and working? What promotions are they running throughout the year? Gingerbread lattes during the Christmas season for example. Or cold summer drinks during the warmer months (of course, being in the UK means this may not be a prolonged period of time, but still). We've also come across pumpkin spiced coffee (Halloween) and eggnog crème brûlée. So spice it up. Get creative.

If your coffee or tea shop is in a predominately multi-cultural area, find out what the major festivals are and support them with your own range of special coffees and teas. It will certainly build a loyal following.

Check out any relevant coffee/tea/food shows and exhibitions. Keep up to date with your trade press, such as *The Caterer*, and websites such as www.talkaboutcoffee.com and the British Coffee Association. Look at dedicated independent coffee or tea shop websites, such as www.cosycoffeshops.co.uk or www. tea.co.uk to see how you compare against the competition.

CASHFLOW

Contingency budgets

Your first few months of trading are all about learning the ropes. There is only one certainty during this period – you will come across unexpected costs. Not until you have had at least two years of trading will you be able to accurately map out peaks and troughs. There may also be equipment you didn't realise you needed before opening and therefore hadn't budgeted for. Things can go wrong with your premises at any time, requiring the call out of plumbers, electricians and builders. You may have completely underestimated the amount of coffee or tea or milk you need. A particular brand may prove unpopular and sit unused. These occurrences cost money, and if you don't have spare cash in the bank to cover it, you can get the business and yourself into some serious debt.

Prepare for the unexpected. Build room in your ongoing budgeting for unexpected costs. As the saying goes, 'think of a number, then double it' for your contingency. The bigger the percentage of your turnover you can realistically put aside, the better. This can be difficult in the early stages of trading when every last penny already seems accounted for. However, constantly trying to survive by living dangerously close to your overdraft limit leaves you vulnerable, something you can ill afford as a fledgling business.

Price changes

Coffee is the second most valuable commodity in the world. Oil is the first and you probably have first-hand experience of how fluctuations in petrol prices have affected how much it costs to fill up your tank. So you can imagine that the same factors, weather, politics, unexpected natural disasters, transportation, storage and handling costs, could have a potential effect on your business.

However, most of the expenses involved in bringing coffee into the UK are fixed, which means the level of your outgoings shouldn't change too drastically. Should a price increase be passed on to a coffee shop the price per cup is barely affected. Take this example: a bag of beans costing £10 is increased by 5% (so now £10.50); based on an average of 130 espresso shots per bag the cost per espresso shot is 7.5p. With the 5% increase per bag that cost is now only 8p per espresso shot. It would be very rare for a coffee shop to immediately increase the coffee menu prices just to recover the half a pence extra cost of the cup.

IN MY EXPERIENCE:

Simon Robertson, Leoni

From my experience menu prices are changed annually and reflect several cost increases, i.e. wages, utilities, other raw materials and sundries or the fact that I need to pay for a new car! Price increases in other areas have been much more dramatic, e.g. dairy prices have risen considerably in the past 18 months; the effect of this on the cost of a cappuccino or café latte (drinks based on 80% milk) is more considerable than an increase in the cost of coffee beans.

Although you won't need to hike up prices immediately following a change in cost from your supplier, you may still need to adjust your pricing early on, to ensure you have pitched your costs accurately.

Ask yourself the following:

- Is your pricing right?
- Are customers buying?
- Are they staying away in droves because you have priced yourself out of the market or are you selling yourself short by leaving your prices too low?

Again, the only way to know is to research the market, see what's out there and get customer feedback.

TIP

If you think prices are too high, try some price cuts to see the difference it makes, or offer some 'economy drive' deals – coffee or tea and cake for £3.50 between 10am and 12pm on weekdays, or buy one, get one free on cappuccinos every Thursday lunchtime.

Spending a little time and effort in asking your regulars what they think will be enormously helpful. You may not always hear what you want to, but then again you may also be pleasantly surprised.

Can you try offering more for the prices you are charging, including a free biscotti or chunk of shortbread with all your 'drink-in' coffees? The key thing is to use this opening period to try new things, and find what works best for you and your customers. There will be a solution, so just stick with it.

IN MY EXPERIENCE:

Tim Hume, Redroaster Coffee House

I worked out price rises by comparison with competitors initially, and subsequently in line with rising costs to keep my profit margin. It's pointless trying to test what the customers will bear. Price rises are usually far less traumatic than you can ever expect.

IN MY EXPERIENCE:

Raymond Voce, Royal Teas

I find it extremely difficult to increase prices. I have in the past always associated a price increase with some form of improvement to the café.

SEASONAL VARIATIONS AND OPENING HOURS

Seasonal variations

There are obvious peaks and troughs which you can predict such as Fridays and Saturdays being busier than an average Tuesday. Bear in mind though, that if you base yourself in a financial centre, such as the City in London, the weekend is likely to be extremely

TIP

If you are a family-oriented coffee shop, be aware of the school calendar and prepare accordingly! Half term and summer holidays could have a real impact on your trading.

quiet – most of your clientele will be at home as the City and its shops don't open for business on the weekends. And if you are in a family-oriented area you may find mornings are busiest as mums pop in after the school-run drop off and local businesses pop in for their pre-work cappuccino fix. However, seasonal variations are a bit trickier. A great coffee or tea shop in a key location will be busy all year round but others rely on specific seasons for more trade. For example, if you have got outside seating, you can expect a larger turnover during the summer months. Not only will more customers be attracted because they can relax outside, but you will also increase the capacity of your coffee or tea shop.

Seasonal themes

There are a few periods throughout the year that you should be aware of as they can give you the opportunity to tailor your menu (beverages and/or food) and offer more of a themed customer experience. If you go down this route, make sure you are prepared for a sudden influx of customers, by having extra staff on call and by preparing your suppliers for additional, larger or more frequent orders. These events can include days such as Mother's Day and Valentine's Day.

Opening hours

Your opening hours should be a balance between what your customers are looking for and when you and your staff can realistically work. Once you have been open a while you will have a better understanding of the days or periods that are most cost-effective to open on. Are you going to be open during the evenings, for example? Is it cost-effective to do so?

It's all about trial and error. See what works and what doesn't.

TIP

Many coffee and tea shops keep the standard business hours of 9am to 5.30pm but if you want to take advantage of the pre-work rush, you are better off opening around 7.30am. If you go down this route, you will need to factor in some early starts for your staff, who'll need to be at the shop in good time to set up.

DEALING WITH SUPPLIERS

Once you have established a network of suppliers you are happy with and can rely on, it's important you maintain a good working relationship with them. And this is not just about paying your bills on time.

Building relationships with your suppliers

- Try to deal with the same sales representative or agent whenever you order. Building a relationship with one person is more likely to inspire trust and the odd favour when you need it.
- Keep a check on prices and review your bills against what other suppliers are offering. Even if you don't want to change suppliers you may be able to negotiate more competitive prices.
- Check the quality of all food and drink when it arrives at the coffee or tea shop. If something's wrong with it, politely but firmly ask for replacements. Don't let quality slide. Your suppliers need to keep up their end of the bargain.
- Try to keep on top of your orders so you aren't constantly on the phone to your supplier in panic, asking for an emergency delivery. And when they do help you out, remember to say thank you.
- Ask them about new products and suggestions, and listen to their answers – they might be able to let you know what other local coffee and tea shops are doing, as well as give you ideas for a new coffee or tea you could pilot.

Building good credit

The relationship between you and your suppliers is an important one. Regardless of whether they are a cash and carry, a farmer, a grower or a wholesaler, you have the right to expect a quality product, delivered on time for a reasonable price. In return, your supplier will expect to be paid on time, and in a manner that suits them.

It's best to lay your cards on the table when agreeing to payment terms with suppliers. Agree dates and stick to them, but ask for payment terms that are reasonable and achievable for you to manage. And discuss what would happen if you were late with a payment, or they were late with a delivery. If you have worked out a contingency *before* things go wrong it can help immeasurably when there is a problem as you already have an agreed way of dealing with it.

If you start missing payment dates your suppliers will soon get tired and may drop you from their client base. Once you get into a spiral of debt and bad credit it can be hard to climb out of it. You will soon find that the network of decent suppliers available to you is smaller than originally imagined and the last thing you want to do is sacrifice the quality of your ingredients because of a couple of late cheques.

It might be a good idea to set up a direct debit for any deliveries you have regularly, which avoids all the issues of forgetting to pay; you could even have a separate account for these bills so you could ensure there was always money for stock and supplies.

Things to remember:

- Don't expect a stampede of customers when you first open. Use a slower build up of trade as an opportunity to hone your operation.
- Always try to hold a little cash in the bank back for emergencies.
- Make sure you are prepared for busy periods such as Christmas, Valentine's Day and Mother's Day and have something a little bit different up your sleeve to surprise your customers.
- Try to gain a good understanding of the opening hours which work for you and your customers.
- Keep a healthy balance between affordable ingredients and noticeable quality.
- Don't feel obliged to order everything from the same few suppliers. Constantly reassess to check if you are getting the best deal.

7.2 Managing the books

Ah, yes – the financial side. You will (hopefully!) already have familiarised yourself with projections, forecasts and basic costings during the planning stage, but the reality of running any business is you need a firm grip on the numbers at all times. Although you will have looked at most of this before opening there will be things that you will have to learn as you go along. Don't berate yourself if you get things wrong initially; the trick is to look at the figures and accounts on a daily basis until you are more confident about running and understanding them.

In this chapter we'll cover:

- Accounts
- Balance sheets
- Profit and loss sheets
- Cashflow forecasting
- Value-added tax (VAT)
- Managing payments
- Hiring an accountant
- Paying your staff

ACCOUNTS

Running a business involves meticulous record-keeping, some of which you are obliged to do, and some of which simply helps you run your business more efficiently. Even if you are determined to outsource this part to a qualified accountant, make sure you at least have the basic grasp of what is going on. Your accounts can be separated into two main categories: financial and management.

Financial

If your business is incorporated, i.e. a limited company, you are required by law to put together a set of financial records every year and file them with Companies House. Unincorporated businesses are not required to do this but they must still keep thorough accounting records to be used alongside their annual tax returns. You are obligated to keep a minimum of the past six years' worth of accounts for HMRC to call upon at any time.

There are detailed guidelines for how to prepare financial accounts on the Companies House website (www.companieshouse.gov.uk). However, you will generally have to include the following:

- Balance sheet
- Profit and loss account
- Cashflow statement

IN MY EXPERIENCE:

Simon Robertson, Leoni

The weekly figures are transferred to a spreadsheet on my PC; from this I calculate quarterly VAT. This spread sheet is then passed on to an accountant who completes my company and personal annual tax returns. The spreadsheet I use is very, very simple (it has to be, I wrote it). I am sure if I asked my accountant he would suggest I use an accounts software package, as this would doubtless make his life much easier. I have never been comfortable with PAYE – it has always seemed like a minefield to me so my accountant takes care of the PAYE for me too.

Management

Your management accounts are the records you must keep in order to run your business well. Here's where you will cover everything from how many cups of coffee or tea you served to how much your staff are due to be paid. You simply won't be able to run your coffee or tea shop efficiently without up-to-date records.

What records do you need to keep when running a coffee shop business? Your accounting records will be split into daily, weekly, monthly and annual figures, all of which are important. Efficient records will allow you to identify the strong and weak areas of your business and therefore take appropriate action in your day-to-day management and long-term planning.

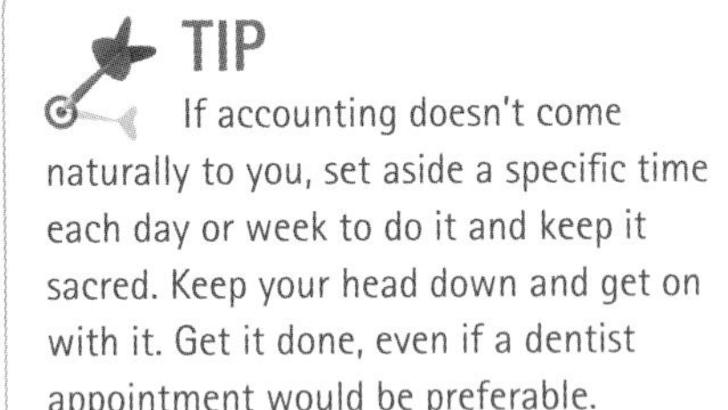

TIP

If accounting doesn't come naturally to you, set aside a specific time each day or week to do it and keep it sacred. Keep your head down and get on with it. Get it done, even if a dentist appointment would be preferable.

Boring but essential

The records you should keep to have an accurate reflection of your coffee or tea shop's financial health include:

- Customer transactions – including how may drinks and dishes/snacks were ordered
- Stock levels – daily, weekly and monthly
- Receipts both for cash and credit card transactions
- Invoices from suppliers and service providers
- Staff shifts and wages
- Cost of other overheads including premises and utilities

BALANCE SHEETS

Essentially, reading a balance sheet is like checking your bank balance on a monthly basis – it simply tells you what the business owes or owns at any particular time. But unlike your bank balance it doesn't just give you a number, it also tells you what makes up that number. In essence it is everything your business owns – its assets. The second part is everything you owe – the liabilities.

The first part of the balance sheet should give you a figure that shows you the net worth of your business. That figure should also show in the second part of the business – also the net worth but working back from what capital you started with, any profits you have made and kept in the business or any money that you have taken out.

IN MY EXPERIENCE:

Shelagh Ryan, Lantana

We have an accountant who calculates the payroll and helps balance the books. I deal with all the invoices and expenses.

An example balance sheet is shown at the back of this book in the appendices (page 335). Here we've given a more detailed explanation of all of the sections of a balance sheet.

- **Fixed assets** – this is typically anything that you count as an asset of the business – anything that you own that has an actual commercial value. So this includes any premises, equipment or furniture that you use for the business. It does not include something that you are likely to sell as part of your daily business.
- **Current assets** – anything that you sell or serve.
- **Stocks** – it's probably worth separating your assets into raw ingredients such as coffee beans and tea leaves and ready-to-sell items such as pre-bottled water and soft drinks.
- **Debtors** – anyone who owes you money should be included in here, whether they are your regular customers or local business people who visit at lunchtime.
- **Current liabilities** – anything that you owe that is payable within one year. In our list we have included creditors – which might include your suppliers as you will typically pay them in around 30 days – and the overdraft as this is probably repayable on demand.
- **Net current assets** – this is simply the sum of your current assets and liabilities both of which are likely to be under one year in lifespan. It is quite a useful figure to calculate as it will show whether you could pay all your debts if you collected all the sums due to you.

- **Total assets less current liabilities** – unlike the last number you can include all the long-term assets like property in this number.
- **Equity** – any money that is invested in the business, for example your savings if you used those to set up the business initially.

PROFIT AND LOSS (P&L) SHEETS

Put simply, a P&L sheet details your business's transactions, subtracting the total outgoings from the total income to give you a reading of how much, if any, profit you have made.

If your company is incorporated, you are required by law to produce a P&L sheet for each financial year. If your coffee or tea shop is not trading as a limited company you don't have to produce one, but the information you give to HMRC to work out your tax bill will amount to the same thing anyway. Even if you aren't required to produce one, the P&L sheet is useful to shop owners, investors and shareholders to see how the business is doing at a glance.

> **TIP**
>
> A P&L sheet, unlike a balance sheet, displays the financial health of your company for a period of time – a month, a quarter or a year. A balance sheet only represents your finances at a particular moment in time.

You can find an example coffee and tea shop P&L sheet on page 337.

CASHFLOW STATEMENTS

A cashflow statement shows your coffee or tea shop's incoming and outgoing money, enabling you to assess how much money you have at your disposal at any one time. Poor cashflow is one of the main causes why businesses such as yours can fail. Some businesses can be profitable on paper, earning more than their outgoings, but if the cash isn't in the bank to buy stock and pay the staff you will soon find yourself in trouble. It's an issue coffee and tea shops are less at risk of getting into trouble with however, because of the nature of how they are paid by their customers, i.e. instantly after receiving service.

Having said that however, don't panic in your first few months which are the time you are most likely to run into difficulties with cashflow. A lot more money will have been spent by you – on premises, initial stock, equipment, staff – than the first few customers will pay you for their cappuccinos. Try to keep calm and follow these tips to improve your cashflow as quickly as possible:

- Lease rather than buy the really expensive equipment, such as coffee machines, even if it's just for the first few months. You will then pay a monthly or annual charge rather than having to splash out all at once.
- Order less stock – don't order at once too many of the items that will sit in your stockroom. Some short-life ingredients, such as milk, can be bought weekly, instead of a bulk monthly buy through your local dairy.
- Make sure you forecast your cashflow as accurately as you can. That way you can plan ahead for slower revenue periods and make sure you still have enough cash in the bank to cover your outgoings.

Cashflow forecasting

Good cashflow forecasting isn't just important for your own business management. You may be required to provide this kind of detail if you need a loan from the bank during your first few months of trading. The forecast will allow you to identify the amount and origin of cash coming into your business and the amount and destination of cash being paid out during any given period of time.

Generally you will produce a forecast for a quarter or year in advance, but during the early stages of trading you might want to do this more frequently, such as a month in advance. When compiling a cashflow forecast it's important that you don't overestimate your incoming cash.

> **TIP**
>
> It's much easier to get an accurate reflection of your outgoings as you will know what these are at this stage. However, you won't yet have a really accurate estimate of how many customers you will have each month, so err on the side of caution to be safe and keep your incoming cash estimates low.

There is an example of a cashflow forecast sheet on page 338..

VAT

VAT applies to the majority of transactions involving the sale of goods or services. Once your business reaches a certain level of turnover, £67,000 per year at the time of writing, you are legally obliged to register for VAT. You will then have to apply VAT to what you sell and keep records of your income and outgoings in order to pay the correct amount of VAT to HMRC.

TIP

To register for VAT, use the VAT Online Registration Service on the HMRC website (www.hmrc.gov.uk).

There are three rates of VAT:

1. The standard rate: 17.5%*
2. The reduced rate: 5%
3. The zero rate: 0%

Most of the items bought in, i.e. coffee beans, tea and food items, are free of VAT so, apart from the VAT charged on some of the sundries and utilities there is very little VAT to claim back in a coffee or tea shop business.

It's very important to register for VAT in good time because you will be liable for all VAT due from the time that you should have been registered. In other words you have to pay HMRC the right amount of VAT even if you didn't charge your customers for it. You could also be liable to pay a fine for delaying your registration. How much you will be fined is dependent on how late you registered but fines start at £50.

TIP

If you find the prospect of dealing with VAT daunting, don't worry. You can appoint an agent – accountant, bookkeeper or tax adviser – to deal with it on your behalf by registering them on HMRC's VAT Online Registration Service.

The average time for processing VAT applications is about one month. However, it can take up to six months if HMRC feels it needs to carry out extra checks on the application. You must account for and pay VAT between applying for your registration and receiving your actual VAT

**In 2009 the VAT rate was dropped to 15% but it reverted to 17.5% in January 2010. If you are operating during a time when the VAT rate changes, you will have to make a decision as to whether you change prices at the till when people are paying, or adjust all your labelling, price boards and menus.*

number, but you are also allowed to reclaim any VAT you have paid suppliers on your purchases during this point. To do this you need to keep accurate records of any invoices where your suppliers have charged you VAT. Keep all your receipts!

MANAGING PAYMENTS

Stashing the cash

Although some customers will pay with plastic, credit or debit cards (which we've already covered in more detail in Chapter 2.4, *Getting legal*) most are likely to pay for coffees or teas in cash. Make sure you have a float with plenty of change. We'd suggest that you keep at least £100 in various notes, including as many £5 notes as possible. You may find you need to get some from the bank if you don't have a large enough supply. You will also need plenty of pound coins and smaller denominations as you are likely to give some change back with nearly every cash payment. An incentive to keep prices simple – less fiddly change and fewer sums to do!

TIP

If you don't have a safe on your premises, don't keep loads of cash around. Make sure you have somewhere you can stash your cash before you can deposit it at the bank. It's common sense, but rooms where cash is stored should be as far away as possible from coffee and tea shop exits. If you do have a safe it's a good idea to have it fitted to the floor or within a wall.

Cheque and credit card payments

Unless you have your local businesses paying for a large order they've agreed in advance for a meeting, it's highly unlikely that a customer would pay for a coffee and Danish with a cheque. Think about it. Have you ever done it?

TIP

Try not to go more than a day without taking cash to the bank, but avoid making deposits at the same time each day – it's important to vary your route so that you don't become an easy target for thieves who are watching you walking to the bank regularly.

Credit and debit card payments will probably be the most popular way your customers pay for their food and drink but you need to be meticulous about your record keeping and storing of receipts. For more information on setting up credit card payments for your restaurant, see Chapter 2.4 (*Getting legal*).

ACCOUNTANTS

If you can afford it, get one! If it saves you working into the early hours on your invoices, PAYE slips and tax returns, it's got to be worth it. It makes sense to hand that responsibility over to an accountant so that your time is free to spend on planning, development and running your coffee or tea shop.

Choosing an accountant

They are going to be handling your livelihood, so get one you can trust. Recommendations are a good way to find one so why not ask friends and other business contacts if they would recommend their accountant.

TIP

Your solicitor or bank manager may be able to recommend someone, or if not a particular person they should be able to point you in the right direction for an accountancy firm that specialises in coffee and tea shops.

When seeking recommendations, make sure you ask people what they used their accountant for, as you might not need the same kind of service. Ask what in particular they recommend about them and what their weak points are if they have any. Most importantly, choose someone who is a member of one of the main professional accounting bodies. There is no legislation to stop anyone setting up as an accountant so asking for member accountants in your area will ensure you are getting someone fully qualified.

Main accounting organisations in the UK

Association of Chartered Certified Accountants
Tel: 020 7059 5000
www.acca.org.uk

Institute of Chartered Accountants, Scotland
Tel: 0131 347 0100
www.icas.org.uk

Institute of Chartered Accountants, England and Wales
Tel: 020 7920 8100
www.icaew.co.uk

Where possible, choose an accountant familiar with your coffee or tea shop, or at least the service industry, as they will be more familiar with the specific legislation that applies to you. And if you are going to be spending a lot of time with your number cruncher, try to choose someone who you can actually get on with. If you find someone you think you like, ask if you can speak to their other clients. This is like asking for references and will be a real test of the calibre of the firm or individual accountant. If they are confident that their service has impressed, they shouldn't have a problem referring you to a few people.

Accounting software

If you decide you are going to manage the books yourself, using an accountancy software package to manage your finances will save you a massive amount of time and effort. From reminders for chasing payment to generating invoices, a good package is like a virtual accounts department. It can tell you how much you are owed and by whom; how long it takes you to pay your bills; what you have in stock and what you have in the bank at any moment in time. More importantly, it could also give you those vital breakdowns of how much you are making on each service, day or month. Of course, there is nothing stopping you or your accountant working that out from a basic Excel spreadsheet, but bear in mind that a good accountancy software package can drastically reduce your accounting bill every year.

There are plenty of packages out there, each tailored to the size and type of business being run. You can also choose a package that links up to your EPoS system if you have one, which we have already covered in Part 5 (see page 236).

Choosing an accounting software package

Consider the following before you buy one:

- Value for money – what services do you get for your hard earned cash?
- Level of support – does the package include a free helpline you can call for technical or set-up support?
- Is the software industry-specific?
- Does it integrate easily with HMRC's online filing system? This can save you a lot of time when it comes to filing your returns.

PAYING YOUR STAFF

Coffee shops and cafés often have a lot of casual and temporary staff, and it can be tempting to just pay them cash at the end of each week or shift. However, it's your responsibility as an employer to make sure all payments are above board and both your staff and your business are making the appropriate tax and National Insurance contributions.

PAYE

PAYE (pay as you earn) is HMRC's system for collecting income tax and National Insurance at the source of payment, i.e. before the employee receives it. It's your responsibility to make sure you know how much to deduct from your staff's payment in terms of their personal tax requirements. You must send the deducted amounts to HMRC by the 19th of every month (or the 22nd if you make electronic payments). However, if monthly payments are under £1,500, you can do this on a quarterly basis.

You have three choices when it comes to organising PAYE. You can keep written accounts and calculate tax and National Insurance deductions yourself, buy specialised software to calculate it for you, or outsource the whole operation. PAYE is applied to all payments your employees receive when working for you. This includes:

- Wages
- Overtime
- Tips
- Bonuses
- Statutory sick pay
- Statutory maternity/paternity/adoption pay
- Some lump sums including redundancy payments

TIP

Once again, a quick visit to the HMRC website will allow you to register your business for PAYE. You should have already done this before employing your first member of staff, but if you haven't done so, give the HMRC's New Employer Hotline a call on 0845 60 70 143 and request a New Employer Starter Pack. This will guide you through the basics of registering.

Staff records

There are three main types of documentation you need to give your staff so they have a record of what they've earned and how much income tax and National Insurance they've paid. These are:

- Wage slips – this shows how much they've earned and how it has been calculated.
- P60 form – this shows the tax deducted during the whole tax year. You can order this from HMRC by calling the Employers Orderline on 0845 7646 646.
- P45 – you give this form to an employee when they stop working for you. It will contain their individual tax code which they need to pass on to their new employer.

Outsourcing payroll

Many small businesses decide to outsource their payroll duties so they don't have to calculate tax and National Insurance deductions themselves. This will obviously be an added expense for your coffee shop, but it can save you a lot of hassle in the long run. By outsourcing your payroll you get rid of one of the biggest administrative headaches of running a small business. Your accountant, if you choose to have one, should be able to advise you – and may even be able to do it for you themselves. As with any type of outsourced service, shop around for the best deal.

Thinking of outsourcing your payroll?

Make sure you consider the following:

- Are they used to dealing with coffee and tea shop businesses?
- Do they supply monthly or weekly pay slips? (You may find weekly slips are more suited for casual staff.)
- How much will they charge for setting up your payroll system?
- What are the ongoing fees?
- How easy is it to add extra members of staff to the account?
- Is the software they use approved by HMRC?

Things to remember:

- Be thorough in your record keeping. The better organised your figures are, the better organised your coffee or tea shop will be.
- Be cautious in your forecasting. It's better to underestimate trade and be pleasantly surprised.
- Make sure you register for VAT in good time to avoid HMRC delays.
- Acknowledge your own skills and time limits. Hire an accountant if you need one.
- Consider outsourcing your payroll but carry out the appropriate checks before handing the process over to a third party.

7.3 Managing yourself and your staff

Your coffee or tea shop is only going to be as good as the team you have around you to run it. You will need to be a confident and effective manager as well as ensuring your staff are well supervised and motivated. Getting good staff doesn't end with recruitment, it's an ongoing process – so you have to take active steps to reduce staff turnover and keep up to date with human resources (HR) legislation.

In this chapter we'll cover:

- How to manage yourself
- When to take advice
- Time management and holidays
- Employing a manager
- Managing staff
- Dealing with staff problems
- Staff incentives

 MANAGING YOURSELF

The minute the doors of your new coffee or tea shop open, you will change. You will suddenly become the boss and the manager. The buck stops with you.

Advice, mentors and role models

We covered the value of taking advice from others in Part 1, but it's important to remember this is not something you should forget about once you are up and running. Just as your business will grow and develop, so should you as a manager and entrepreneur. Mentors and more established entrepreneurs can have something to offer your business. It's always good to have an outsider's perspective – they may be able to tell you where your strengths lie, and which areas of the business or management you are neglecting. It's also great to have someone you can trust as a sounding board.

TIP

Try networking at events such as industry trade shows and exhibitions (for more information, see page 281).

IN MY EXPERIENCE:

Simon Robertson, Leoni

Initially the Business Enterprise appointed a mentor who I met with monthly to look at things like the cashflow. To be honest the business was doing very well so I didn't need to call on them for much assistance; however getting the books in order before our monthly meeting proved to be a good discipline.

Identifying your strengths and weaknesses

Every day will be different and each day will offer you opportunities to develop and hone your skills as a business owner and manager. Bear in mind though, that it's important to invest time in yourself as well as your coffee or tea shop, especially if you plan to expand the business.

Even if you are running a successful coffee or tea shop business, it doesn't necessarily mean you are a successful business manager. That's where the focused and planned development of your knowledge and skills through training can benefit you. Running a coffee or tea shop, much like running any other kind of small business, requires you to be multi-skilled. The role of manager can involve everything from brewing coffee, dishing out Danish, re-stocking the toilet with loo paper and serving, to marketing, business planning and taking care of the accounts. Regardless of whether you have a hands-on position in all of these roles you need to at least be familiar with what they all entail.

Create a personalised MBA by learning as much as you can about your own business. Ask questions of your accountant. Make sure you can understand the basics of a tax form. If you can't afford an army of experts to staff your restaurant with, then take advantage of the help available to you. Contact your local regional development agency (www.englandsrdas.com) or contact a Business Link (www.businesslink.gov.uk) adviser. They can point you in the right direction to what's on offer in terms of training. Many courses are free for small business owners, so you can't even use lack of funds as an excuse.

The industry moves fast. You need to keep up to date with the latest trends and fashions and be inspired with new ideas, new contacts, possible suppliers and even customers.

Motivating yourself

The fact that you have even chosen to start a coffee shop shows that you have entrepreneurial flair, but once the doors have opened and the regular customers start to flock, how can you make sure you maintain that level of 'oomph'? The start-up process is incredibly demanding both physically and psychologically. After all that hard work you clearly need to slow down the pace slightly, but you can't sit back and hope the coffee or tea shop will run itself.

Set yourself achievable goals, weekly and longer term. You will find your confidence and self-esteem will rocket once you start ticking off boxes of goals achieved.

IN MY EXPERIENCE:

Tim Hume, Redroaster Coffee House

Although there are now schools that can show you the basics, it takes quite a lot of practice in the working environment to become good at running a business. After about three to six months you won't improve *a lot* unless you have been doing something very wrong. On the other hand, if you are trying to be the best you will always be improving.

Time management

Managing your time effectively could mean the difference between life and death for your business. The most important aspect of time management is to prioritise everything you need to do. This will allow you to recognise the difference between what's important and what's urgent. Running a coffee or tea shop will involve various 'to do' lists. There are your long-term goals, such as growing turnover and improving your margins, nurturing and expanding your customer base and developing your own skills as a business owner.

Then there are your monthly goals, which could involve researching new types of coffee, recruiting new baristas, and getting your accounts in order. And of course there'll be daily and weekly objectives, such as testing out a deal or promotion, getting customers to try sample coffees.

Whatever your role within the actual coffee or tea shop opening times, you need to set aside enough time to get on with these tasks as they are just as important as serving customers when it comes to running a successful establishment.

Here are some ideas for prioritising workloads and making sure you don't neglect important aspects of running your business:

TIP

Work out how much 'face' time you want to have in the coffee shop and how much time you can afford to be sitting out of sight in the back office. Do you have enough confidence in your manager's people skills while you are AWOL?

- List all the tasks you need to do, and then prioritise them in order of what is most urgent and important.
- Don't underestimate the amount of time interruptions can steal from your schedule. When allocating time for a particular task, build in room for disruptions.
- Don't be afraid to turn off your phone or email when you really need to concentrate. If having no distractions helps you get a task done more quickly, you may end up with extra time to deal with clients, customers or staff.
- Break large tasks up into manageable chunks. It's tempting to run lots of little errands instead of getting stuck in to a big important job. However, completing it one stage at a time will make it seem less daunting.

- Build room in your schedule for unexpected problems or events. If nothing unforeseen crops up, you will end up ahead of schedule.
- Make sure no more than half your time is allocated to top priority work. All those little jobs that aren't as time sensitive will start to mount up if you don't crack on with them.
- If possible, delegate. You may think the business will fall apart if you don't oversee everything, but perhaps your time can be more valuably spent on other tasks. And you will be inspiring confidence in your team by letting them get on with it themselves.

Holidays and work–life balance

It's a good point to consider. When the buck stops with you, is there a right time to take a holiday? Your family may be pestering you for some quality time, especially if they feel they've hardly seen you during the set-up and launch phase of the coffee shop.

At such an early stage in your coffee or tea shop's life you may feel you simply can't afford to leave it in someone else's hands, even if you are desperate to get away. The main thing to remember is that you need a balance between working hard to make sure your coffee or tea shop thrives during its early days and not burning out. Working too hard without a break won't do you any favours, and it's always best to take a breather before you get to the point where you collapse from exhaustion.

> **TIP**
>
> Why not factor in your holiday in a new promotion on your return? Buy some local coffee from your holiday destination and theme your coffee shop accordingly.

If you do decide to take a break, test the waters first. Don't book two weeks in the sun without knowing for sure you have got a solid team in place to run things in your absence. Try handing over the reins for a weekend while you are still around. That way you can test whether things are capable of running smoothly in your absence while still being nearby if any real problems arise. Once you are confident the whole operation won't collapse as soon as you have closed the door behind you, you will find you have a far more rewarding break and can come back refreshed, raring to go, perhaps even inspired by the coffee or tea shops you have visited during your time away.

FROM THE EXPERTS:
Sahar Hashemi, Coffee Republic

When I started, the word 'entrepreneur' didn't exist. Now there is a lot of support for entrepreneurs. A lot has changed. We live in a world where technology has enabled us to break barriers between work and home. You can work from home and that makes a lot of difference to women entrepreneurs. The whole idea that you can be connected wherever you are gives you flexibility to be a mum and have a family.

Handing over the reins

Bringing someone in to run your coffee or tea shop for you is a big deal. It's gut-wrenching. Whether or not you do this from the outset will probably depend on how big your business is and how involved in the day-to-day running you decided to be from the beginning. Before you even think about hiring a manager, you must be sure it's what you really want. You will have to delegate a lot of responsibility and you will run into problems if you aren't willing to relinquish some control and allow the manager to have a degree of autonomy.

TIP

Take time to employ the right people and don't be afraid to delegate and let go. You can't physically or mentally be there 24/7 and the only way to be successful is to develop a good and trusted team. If you try to do everything yourself, you will be running on empty very quickly.

Think about *why* you have decided to take someone on in this role. Are you just looking for someone to watch over your coffee or tea shop when you aren't there, or are you handing over more responsibility so that you can have time with your family? How much input will they have? What role do you still want to play, if any, in the day-to-day running of the business? Are you wanting to take more of a step back and be a silent partner, leaving the day-to-day running to their expertise? Will they be completely in charge of hiring and firing other staff? How much time do you want to be splitting between your business and personal lives? Can you be honest with yourself and say with confidence you will be able to let go?

Think it through carefully *before* you start recruiting as it will determine the type of person you are looking for, how much you are willing to pay them and what kind of relationship they'll have with both you and the other members of staff.

TIP

Get an assistant manager as soon as you can afford it if you want to get out at all. Even then you are in danger of spending most of your time in your coffee or tea shop.

MANAGING STAFF

Obviously this will depend on how big your coffee or tea shop is. If it's a small, intimate family-run business, you will have just yourself and a couple of key staff to look after. If, however, you have launched something a lot bigger, then you have got to let people know you are in charge and they answer to you. It's a difficult balance to get right. You want to create a sense of community and family with your staff, but you can't afford to get too familiar as you run the risk of being taken advantage of.

It's a good idea to have regular team meetings, not just to assess how the business is going, but to boost morale and tell staff if they are doing a good job (or if they are not!). It's important to make your staff feel part of the business; they'll be more loyal to a company they have a vested interest in. Is there any particular training you or your staff would benefit from? Do they have ideas they would like to test out? Put yourself in their position – how would you like to be managed?

IN MY EXPERIENCE:

Tim Hume, Redroaster Coffee House

In general, our staff members are in tune with the business and motivated to do the best possible job because they like the café. For most of them it's where they would and often do come in their leisure time. We pay higher than average wages but expect high standards in return. Staff retention levels are good.

Staff training and courses

If you are truly serious about the coffee you are serving up, there are barista training courses you can send your staff on. We've covered some of these on page 249, but remember you should speak to the company you bought or hired your coffee machines from; such companies are usually in a good position to offer you advice.

FROM THE EXPERTS:
June, Bettys Café Tea Rooms

Internal training covers everything from a thorough 'Induction', through to basic craft skills, master craft workshops and team leadership training. We encourage and support our staff to achieve NVQ standards (in some areas we even have our own in-house NVQ assessors) and professional qualifications. And we also run a wide range of non-vocational training schemes in house, from key skills in literacy and numeracy – through to sign language and even salsa dancing!

Dealing with staffing problems

Most employers will have problems with certain members of staff at various points in their career. It's a given in any business, large or small. The coffee and tea shop and general food trade has high levels of staff turnover so keeping hold of staff that you trust and who are dedicated and loyal to your business isn't easy. Unless you are extremely lucky, or as we've mentioned earlier, only hire friends and family to work in your coffee or tea shop, it's likely you will have to confront some of the following problems.

Theft

It's not nice but it happens. Develop a thick skin and deal with any problems firmly and quickly. Theft can occur anywhere from the stock to the tills. Any business that deals largely in cash transactions could fall victim to staff theft. And it's your profit that's walking out of the door, not turnover. If somebody is taking £10 a day on a turnover of £1,000 that's only 1% and you might think you can live with that. But if you are pulling in 6% profit (£60) on that £1,000, then thieves are taking one sixth of your profits.

TIP

Losses through theft need to be seen as a percentage of your net profit and not of your gross turnover.

There are steps you can take to reduce the risks and temptations of staff theft. The best place to start is with recruitment. Even if you are only employing part-timers, check their references. Sadly it's the casual staff that you need to pay the most attention to. The next step is to explain to all members of staff the security controls operating in your business. Everybody should know what will happen to them if they are caught stealing, then at the very least they can evaluate the risks involved before they pinch anything from you. You should also ensure the lines of authority and responsibility are clearly defined – staff need to know who they are responsible to and for. That way you stand a much better chance of a member of your team confiding in you if somebody is stealing.

We'd also strongly advise you to put in place systems that will alert you to possible staff theft problems. For example, you should be able to average out cashflow and sales over a week and over a month. This allows you to build up a picture of how much you should be taking on a Monday in September, so that if the till is suspiciously low on a day when it should be quite full, there should be a very good reason for it.

Don't tempt fate by leaving loads of cash in your till. You only really need to carry enough cash to give change from £100; anything extra should be removed regularly and banked.

What to do if you catch staff stealing

Once you are absolutely convinced you know a member of staff is stealing from you, confront them. The simplest approach is to take them to one side and explain that you have discovered their theft and show them your proof. Unfortunately it's unlikely you will even be able to trust someone again if you catch them stealing and the best option for your own peace of mind may be to let them go. If the stealing is more serious than a few small items, you may wish to call the police – at the very least you can ask for some advice from them. If you do decide to give the member of staff another chance, however, make sure you give them a formal written warning which will make it easier to justify dismissal, should the problem happen again.

IN MY EXPERIENCE:
Tim Hume, Redroaster Coffee House

As far as staff dishonesty is concerned, my view is if you think they might be stealing from you, you are probably either paranoid, or no good at hiring, or both of these (and right). What are you going to do? If you start trying to catch them out, 'just in case', you really are in the wrong job.

Bad service, laziness and body language

There is no excuse for bad service from your staff. This isn't a game; it's your business and your livelihood. And just as importantly, it's a place for your customers to relax, enjoy themselves and have a break. For those reasons alone, you and your staff need to provide them with a pleasant experience. Again, put yourself in your customers' shoes. What sort of experience would you want from your ideal coffee or tea shop?

If you are permanently positioned front-of-house, you will be able to pretty quickly spot if your team aren't bothering to give customers their full attention or if customers are unhappy with the level of service they are receiving. Bad service can close a business – the customers will vote with their feet and won't come back. You can't afford for that to happen. Encourage your staff to be enthusiastic but not too imposing. There is a fine line between being friendly and spending 10 minutes chatting to a customer while a queue develops behind them. Body language should reflect enthusiasm and a willingness to attend to customers as and when they need service.

Appearances are also important. Do you want your staff to wear a uniform? Or do you want a more relaxed atmosphere? Start as you mean to go on; even if you have stipulated that your team can wear what they want, make sure there is some basic dress code in place so that your establishment looks respectable.

Discrimination

We've already touched on the issue of discrimination in Chapter 5.4 (*Recruiting and training staff*) but it's important to note this is something you must always have in mind. There is plenty more detail on how to comply with discrimination laws on Startups.co.uk but to summarise, you must consider the following in the day-to-day running of your coffee or tea shop or you could find yourself in trouble.

Legislation outlawing age discrimination came into force in 2006. It includes every member of staff that works for you, both young and old. Employers must have age-positive practices. This means you can't recruit, train, promote or retire people on the basis of age unless it can be objectively justified. Many people over 50 want to work but are prevented from doing so by ageist practices. But remember, the recent legislation doesn't just concern older people; it covers young and old alike throughout their working lives.

Skills, experience and the ability to do the job are what you should be looking at, not someone's age. However, the legislation doesn't just have advantages for employees. Stamping out age discrimination can have a positive effect on staff turnover, higher morale, lower recruitment costs, better productivity and increased profits. You want your staff to feel part of a family. And families look after each other.

The same applies when it comes to discriminating on the grounds of race, sex or disability. It's your responsibility to make sure that not only do you treat all your staff equally, but that discrimination does not take place between other members of the team. Discrimination can take many forms, and it's not just a case of refusing to hire someone for being a woman/gay/65 years old/having body piercings. There is also indirect discrimination, where certain members are denied opportunities within employment, harassment such as unwanted advances or comments of a sexual nature, or bullying. If somebody working for you is a victim of any of these kinds of discrimination you could find yourself fighting in an employment tribunal, which is costly in terms of time, reputation and turnover.

Staff handbook

In an industry with such a high rate of staff turnover, you may have staff that only stay a few months or even weeks. You can make an official record of standard employee policy in a staff handbook. Here you can list your expectations of all staff and your policy on issues such as theft, absence, dress code and general working attitude. That way if there is ever a problem you can refer back to the handbook as an explanation of why you may be taking disciplinary action.

However, you should also use the handbook as a way of flagging up staff benefits and the elements of your coffee or tea shop that you think are the advantages of working there.

What goes in a staff handbook?

Your staff handbook should cover your policy on:

- Company morals or ethos
- Dress code
- Dealing with customers
- Absence and lateness procedure
- What day of the week or month salaries are paid
- Holiday entitlement
- Any bonus or reward schemes
- Health and safety procedures

Staff benefits

Staff loyalty is key. And one of the ways in which you can keep your staff is to let them know what you offer them, and how it differs from other establishments your staff may have experienced. Here are a few examples of the kind of things you can do for staff to encourage loyalty and hard work:

- Provide them with coffee or tea and snacks either at the start or end of their shift.
- Offer bonuses or gifts for staff who never miss a shift or never turn up late, or just generally as a reward for hard work and enthusiasm.
- Celebrate birthdays or special occasions – this could be something as simple as a card signed by all the other members of the team or a small chocolate cake with a single candle – simple, cheap yet effective in creating bonhomie.
- Offer extra benefits for long-term service. Offering an extra day's holiday per year of service can be far more cost-effective then going through a recruitment process for a new barista every couple of months.
- Offer regular appraisals and give staff the opportunity to discuss any issues they want to raise. There may not be time during normal shifts to talk about problems or ask questions. Make sure you are approachable when staff need you to listen.

FROM THE EXPERTS:
June, Bettys Café Tea Rooms

We offer a competitive salary, and believe in sharing our financial success with everyone via our profit sharing bonus. We also provide our staff with free meals, drinks and snacks during working hours, additional long service holiday entitlements, Christmas bonus and birthday vouchers and staff discounts as well as providing subsidised private healthcare, a childcare voucher scheme and a Bike to Work Initiative. We're committed to sharing our success not just with our staff but all our stakeholders – the farmers we rely on for our tea and coffee, the local communities we work alongside and the environment, both local and global.

Things to remember:

- Take advice as and when you need it, whatever stage in your coffee or tea shop career you're at.
- Set goals for effective time management, taking breaks when you need them.
- Learn to delegate. Accept that you can't do everything on your own.
- Be firm but fair with staff to ensure they feel a part of your coffee or tea shop.
- Reward good work wherever possible. An atmosphere where staff are only singled out when they do something wrong is bad for team morale.

“All true tea lovers not only like their tea strong, but like it a little stronger with each year that passes.”

George Orwell, A Nice Cup of Tea

“Everybody should believe in something. I believe I'll have another coffee.”

Author Unknown

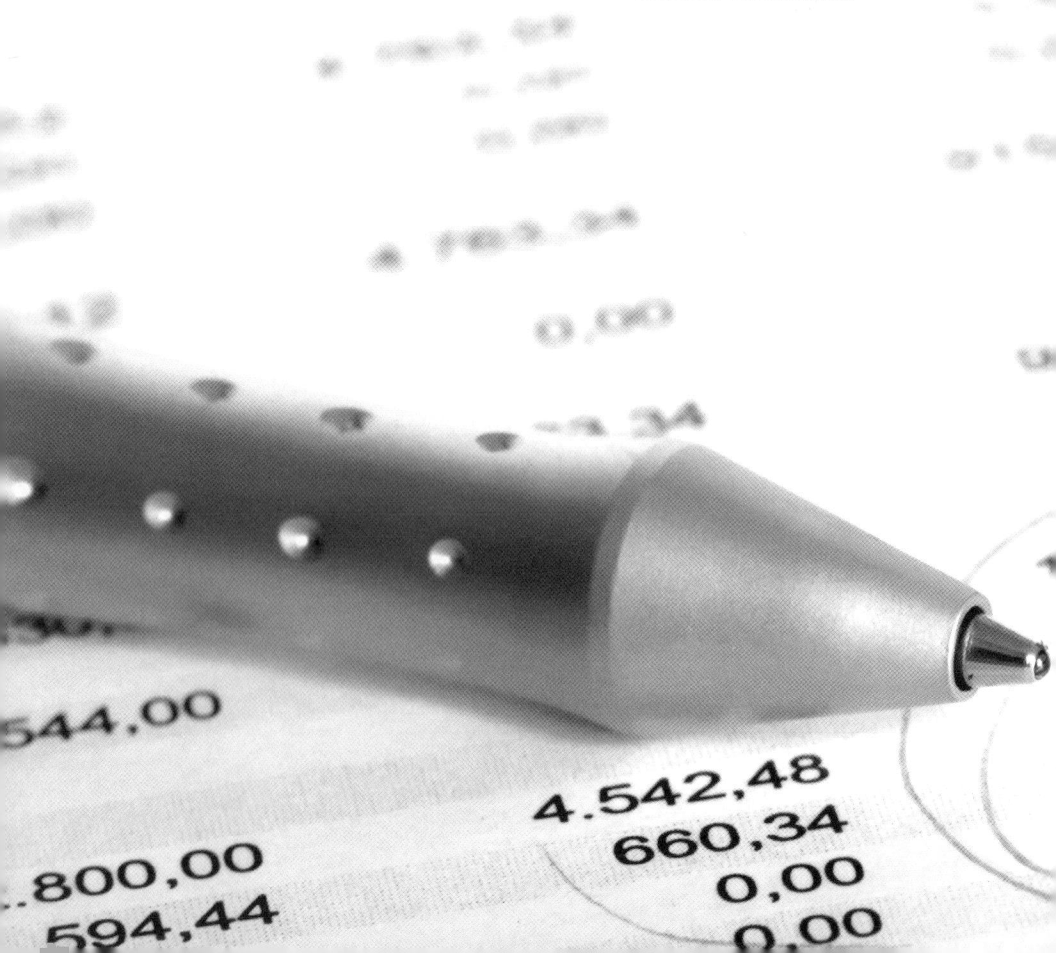

8

Business development

Business development

Perhaps one coffee or tea shop is quite enough for you, although you have big plans for developing what you currently offer. Or you may have always harboured an ambition to have several, or have been inundated with requests to open another one in a nearby town or village. If you choose the 'growth' route, there are several options worth considering.

In this chapter we'll cover:

- Diversifying
- Opening a second coffee or tea shop
- Franchising
- Selling
- Passing the business on

DIVERSIFYING

This is an exciting alternative route for expansion and can enable you to develop your knowledge and expertise of the coffee industry as a whole. Diversifying can be anything from introducing some unique and rare coffee and teas for customers to try to developing the coffee or tea shop into a music venue, mini cinema, internet centre or successful deli. Some of these things will affect your licensing, the prices you charge, your opening times and your staffing costs, so there is a lot to think about, but if you have a solid, successful coffee shop and are ready to take the next step it can be an exciting development.

Beverages

You may have perfected the art of espresso making and want to start offering a more diverse range of coffees and teas, either by developing your own blend of coffee, making some unique and delicious teas, or branching into some more adventurous drinks. Think about perhaps featuring a new unique tea or coffee each week or month – look back to Part 3 for inspiration. You could even sell particular teas and coffees for a limited time.

Food

Another way to develop your offering, and you might want to start serving breakfasts and lunches, or even offer food in the early evenings. Perhaps you have been buying in most of your sandwiches and cakes and now want to try your hand at providing everything homemade? As with beverages you could also try new things on a temporary basis, perhaps theming each week or month with cuisine and drinks from a certain country or region? Or you could develop links with a local restaurant, deli or bakery and showcase some of their food – a mutually beneficial arrangement that allows you to offer some great food without having to employ a chef.

Outside catering

Another option, if you are confident you can manage the extra work, is to branch into catering for parties and formal events – such as anniversaries, meetings, launch parties, christenings, funerals. You will often need to provide the staff, serving dishes and crockery as well as the food, but it can be quite lucrative and offer some extra money in the evenings when you are closed. It also works in reverse as good advertising for your coffee or tea shop. The best way to start doing this is to practise with friends and families, and then move on to smaller groups, growing the numbers as your confidence grows. Let customers know you offer this service with a sign by the till or a note in the menu.

Entertainment and culture

A popular option if you have got the space is to put on a range of performances and readings, either throughout the day or as a way to draw in an evening crowd. You could even show films, especially if you have got a separate room where this wouldn't disrupt the rest of your customers but check licensing laws before you do this. Contact local bands and singers, who will appreciate the chance to showcase their music, and invite local literary figures to discuss their latest book, or read from their most recent work. If you decide to do anything like this, you will need a premises licence, which will enable you to use your coffee or tea shop for evening events such as music, cultural events and parties. You would need to confirm that your staff would be happy to be rotated on day/evening shifts but this could open up a whole new customer segment for your business.

Deli

If you have a passion for gourmet food as well as superior coffee or tea, this could be an option for you. You will need to think carefully about the balance between your beverage and food offerings and how you combine the two. Is one going to take precedence over another? Will you market yourself as a coffee or tea shop with deli, or deli and coffee or tea shop? If you choose to sell speciality products, effectively they'll need to be premium or luxury offerings. That way you can expand your customer base by offering hard-to-find delicacies your customers won't find in the supermarkets.

Retail

You could start to sell bags of your teas and coffees to customers, along with cups and saucers, tea pots and coffee mugs. You could even sell branded crockery, a great way for customers to show their loyalty and for you to get some free advertising! You don't even need to keep your products coffee-centric – books, art, music, films, magazines and newspapers also sell well in coffee or tea shops and could bring in some extra custom as people browse while enjoying their coffee. Start by stocking a few small products to see if there is a market before turning a corner of your café into a shop.

FROM THE EXPERTS:
Robin Arkle, Costa franchisee

Our store in Southampton High Street has a meeting room upstairs which we hire out to local businesses by the hour, half day and full day. This is proving very popular with local solicitors and banks. Of course in addition to the room hire we have a captive audience for food and drink for the duration of the day.

Space

You will also need to consider how much space is given over to each part of your shop and whether your premises have enough room to do your concepts justice. If this idea is one you have had from the beginning, then space and appropriate locations are points you would have considered before choosing your site. If, however, you decide to go down the deli or entertainment route after you have opened, then you need to start small. Don't invest a fortune in expensive items if they won't sell. Don't sign up 10 new bands if they'll be playing to an empty room. Speak to your regulars. What do they think of the idea? What would they buy and how much would they be prepared to spend on more luxury deli items? Would they welcome some live music while they sip their cuppa? If you jump straight in and cut off a large section of your coffee or tea shop for retail or entertainment then find your customers aren't willing to buy, you will end up losing money on coffee drinking space.

OPENING YOUR SECOND COFFEE OR TEA SHOP

The effort involved in opening your first coffee or tea shop may be a little like childbirth – you are absolutely positive you aren't going to do it again! However, if you are ambitious about having your own coffee or tea shop empire, you will need to plan just as carefully second time around. Getting the model right in one location is challenging enough; balancing two or more is a juggling act. Are you ready?

TIP

If you are thinking about expanding, speak to your family first. They should have an input in your decision. How is it going to affect your personal life, especially if you have a young family? And if you are planning on two or more establishments, what will it mean for your vision of an independent coffee or tea shop? How will you ensure continuity, standards, quality and the same customer experience?

Although difficult in many respects, such as splitting your time even further, managing more staff and having more to juggle, starting a second coffee or tea shop can be easier for a number of reasons. You won't be making the same mistakes that you had to learn from with the first venture. All the issues that may have held up or hindered your first opening should be avoidable this time round. You will already have made contacts in terms of suppliers, who should be happy to negotiate deals if you 'up' your orders with them to cater for both shops. Talk to them *before* you start your planning for the second venue, and ask what kind of deals they can offer you if you double your purchases.

FROM THE EXPERTS: Bettys Café Tea Rooms

While we may have now opened six Café Tea Rooms, they are all based in Yorkshire and by keeping the branches close together we are able to control every last detail. Everything we serve is made by hand at our craft bakery or freshly to order in our café tea rooms. The bakery vans can get around the circuit of branches every morning with fresh goods for the day ahead.

In terms of funding the second coffee or tea shop, you may have made enough profit from the first site to expand with either your own funds or a loan. If you go with investors they'll want to see evidence of success with the first venture, so your records should be in pristine order. See page 325 on preparing your business for a sale to get a feel for the kind of record-keeping investors will want to see.

Now for the potential downsides. As well as the possible implications on the 'soul' of your independent business, can you handle the responsibility of a second coffee or tea shop? Think long and hard about whether you are really up to it. Spreading yourself too thin can not only mean your second outlet suffers, but it could have a knock-on effect on your original business. You will need to make sure both shops have a solid team in place, with people you can trust to look after each site when you aren't there. It's when you are confident that either shop can survive without you there all the time to watch over things that you are ready to branch out and open a second business. In addition, are you prepared for the administrative and financial reality of running two coffee or tea shops? You may end up spending more time in the office than with your customers.

IN MY EXPERIENCE:

Tim Hume, Redroaster Coffee House

A modest growth to two or three outlets in the locality may be sustainable without damaging quality but the premises would have to be carefully selected. We would not be interested in 'rolling out the concept' as they say. The only potential pro of running a chain would be wealth, but this would be gained on the back of employees and at the expense of the soul of the business. The cons would hit at the heart of what our business is. Quality cannot be maintained when hundreds or thousands rather than tens of employees are concerned as there is an unavoidable tendency for standards to fall close to the level achievable by the weakest.

FRANCHISING

What is it?

One option for growing your coffee or tea shop into a chain without running each site yourself is to turn the concept into a franchise. A franchise is a successful business blueprint which you can then sell to other people. Franchisees finance and manage their own business, but use the brand, identity and concept that you have created.

How does it work?

If you want to franchise your coffee or tea shop you will need a complete business package or manual. Your franchisee buys this from you, but must agree to trade under your company name and abide by whatever trading methods you specify. You can stipulate that all stock or ingredients must be bought from you, or a particular supplier. You can also request additional items to be purchased from you including staff uniforms, furniture and menus, etc. How much of this is included in your initial fee and package is down to you and the contract you draw up with your franchisees.

This contract stipulates what ongoing financial obligations a franchisee owes to you, and specifies exactly how much influence or control you have over the way they run their coffee or tea shop. However, the franchisee will also require some assurances too. They'll want to know how much support they'll get from you in setting up the business and its ongoing management. They'll probably also expect a degree of marketing by you on the overall brand.

Costs

You need to decide how much you want to charge for the initial licensing of your coffee or tea shop. Most franchise companies charge somewhere in the region of a couple of thousand pounds to buy the franchise so that franchisees can afford the start-up capital to get their coffee or tea shop up and running. You will then receive ongoing revenue from a share of the turnover of each business. You can also make money from a mark-up on anything you sell to your franchisees.

How to do it

If you decide to franchise your business the first thing you need to do is go back to the drawing board in terms of research. You need to think long and hard about whether or not your coffee shop concept is suited to franchising. If you are meticulous about quality control then a franchise may not be the best option for you. However, if you have created a concept that you feel can be successfully managed by others then it's definitely an option to consider.

Guidance on franchising

The British Franchise Association (www.thebfa.org; 01865 379892) can give you help and advice in getting your concept off the ground. It's a good idea to contact the organisation early on in your planning stage.

There is also a whole section dedicated to franchising information on startups.co.uk. You can find useful information on franchising as well as list your own coffee or tea shop on the website so potential franchisees can contact you.

Attracting franchisees

To make a substantial amount from a franchise concept you need to have enough franchisees. Remember, it's only a *share* of the profits you will be getting from each business. Your franchisees will need to be able to keep the majority of the revenue, otherwise what's in it for them? To gain enough franchisees you need to have an attractive package and market it well. Here are a few tips:

- Your initial fee and ongoing royalties need to be low enough to be affordable and attractive to potential franchisees. However, you need to strike a balance between affordable for them, and profitable for you.
- Your coffee or tea shop should also be well established, secure and have an excellent reputation before you even think about franchising. You need to be able to prove to your potential franchisees that it's a business concept worth investing in. The only way to do that is to hone your own operation into a finely tuned concept.
- You need to offer enough management support. It's no good just throwing in the rights to the coffee or tea shop name and a few uniforms. You need a thorough business manual with instructions on everything from recipes for the beverages you serve and customer service to counter layouts and prices.
- You need to show a willingness to market and develop the business from central office. Franchisees are buying into a brand name, with all the security and customer recognition that offers.
- You need to prove you are willing to protect the brand which means choosing your franchisees carefully. You can't just hand out the licence to anyone willing to stump up the cash. One bad franchise brings down the reputation of all of them, and your hard-working franchisees will want reassurance that their business isn't being undermined by unsuccessful branches.

➡ SELLING OR EXITING THE BUSINESS

Should you sell?

It may seem a little premature to talk about selling when you are still considering launching, but building up a successful business that can be sold on may have been your intention from the very beginning. There are many other reasons why you may feel like selling your establishment. You may want to cash in on the financial success of what you have built by accepting an offer from another coffee or tea shop owner. Or perhaps you want to move on, either to a different location or because of family or personal commitments. Or maybe you just want to retire.

> **TIP**
> Whatever your reasons for wanting to sell, there are plenty of things to consider before you do so.

If your coffee or tea shop is in financial difficulty a sale could prove tricky. However, it may be a way of recouping some of your investment without closing it down altogether. If this is the case, you should prepare yourself for price offers that don't reflect the amount of time, effort and money you have put into the business.

Preparing to sell

Selling your business takes a lot of planning. It's not as simple as handing over the keys in exchange for a cheque. It needs to be in a sale-ready state which means making sure all your finances are in immaculate order. The same goes for the whole business operation. All tax and official records must be completely up-to-date. You will need evidence of cashflow, turnover and profits. This will apply to the financial history of the business as well as how it's currently performing and what your projections for the future are.

Finally, end as you began – with some professional help in the form of an accountant and a solicitor. Your accountant should be able to prepare the business accounts for a sale and if they don't have the relevant business sales experience, get someone else who does. Your solicitor will be the one responsible for drafting sale agreements and will negotiate with your buyer and their legal advisers if necessary.

Valuing your business

There are so many different factors that affect the value of your business and your current turnover and profit is just one part of that. Essentially your business is only worth what buyers are willing to pay. This can be affected by things that are beyond your control such as the current state of the economy, the value of property in the area and what similar businesses are going on the market for.

However, there are plenty more elements of your business that will have been shaped and controlled by you. These include:

- Financial history
- Current financial health
- The coffee or tea shop's reputation
- The coffee or tea shop's position within the community
- The business's potential for growth
- The quality of your team
- The contents and physical appearance of your coffee or tea shop

Part of presenting a valuation of your coffee shop to potential buyers will involve preparing a sales memorandum. This will generally be produced in conjunction with your sales advisers – your accountant and solicitor. The sales memorandum is a kind of marketing pitch that includes information in your company and presents it in a favourable light in order to attract buyers. Information in the memorandum includes trading history, key financial figures and how these have fared during previous years. The memorandum will also have details on your premises and your employees.

Finding buyers

Potential buyers are everywhere. You may have been one yourself when you discovered a coffee or tea shop to take over. Is there a competitor in your area who is keen to take over your business and expand their own? You can even look within your own team for a buyer. If you don't know someone personally who's in a position to buy your business you will have to advertise that it's for sale. There are several trade magazines and business directories you can use to list your coffee or tea shop in, for example Daltons (www.daltonsbusiness.com) and Businesses For Sale (www.businessesforsale.com).

TIP

It's a good idea to draw up a non-disclosure agreement for all prospective buyers to sign. This way, even if you have to reveal confidential company information to them, you can be confident they won't reveal it to anyone else.

Once you have some interested buyers that you feel are realistically in a position to take over your coffee or tea shop, you can have your advisers send them your sales memorandum. You don't have to meet all of your potential buyers at this stage, but it's likely they'll want to view it before making any kind of initial offer. If you have several interested buyers, the next stage will be to start holding meetings with them.

Choosing a buyer should never just be a question of accepting the highest bid. You should also consider how your buyer is willing to structure the sale, to what extent they are planning to change or build on what you have already developed and what you both agree is an acceptable timetable for finalising the sale.

IN MY EXPERIENCE:

Tim Hume, Redroaster Coffee House

There may come a day when we need to sell or pass on the business through old age. But we are happy and fulfilled and only a silly money offer would take it away during our normal working life.

Once you have agreed a sale with your buyer it will then be subject to the process of 'due diligence'. This is where the buyer engages in a thorough inspection of the business, covering things such as financial records, staff agreements, customer and supplier relationships, premises, legal and tax obligations and intellectual property.

Your responsibility

If you are selling your coffee or tea shop you need to be aware of the Transfer of Undertakings (Protection of Employment) Regulations 2006, also known as TUPE; it's not just a case of washing your hands of your business. You will be familiar with these regulations if you bought your business from someone else. The basis of these regulations is that when a business changes hands, the new employer is not allowed to change the terms of employment the existing members of staff currently have. All your employees, or at least a representative of them, should also be consulted and informed regarding the sale of your business.

When you sell a business you also have a responsibility to the taxman to consider. Entrepreneurs are subject to capital gains tax (CGT) when they sell off business assets. In 2008 changes to CGT came into force, including the abolition of

Taper Relief, which allowed assets held for more than two years to enjoy a reduced rate of 10%. Gains made on the disposal of business assets are now charged at a flat rate of 18%. There are a few exceptions, however, and other allowances and exemptions to CGT which is why it is advisable to seek professional advice from a specialised accountant or solicitor before you sell your business.

TIP

If your gains are equal to, or less than, the annual exempt amount, you may not have to pay CGT. The annual exempt amount for 2008/09 was £9,600. Another exemption applies where your lifetime gains do not exceed £1m. This is called entrepreneurs' relief, and it charges gains at a reduced rate of 10%. Any gains after your first £1m are charged at 18%.

PASSING THE BUSINESS ON

If you decide you want to sell the business to a friend or relative, the process above will still apply. However, you may want to pass the business on, perhaps to a son or daughter, without receiving payment for it. The first thing you need to consider is whether the person you have earmarked for taking over your coffee or tea shop is suited to doing so. Be guided as much by business acumen and intuition as family ties. They might make a fantastic cappuccino but can they run the whole business? If not, all your work and effort will disappear very quickly, together with any profits you may have made with the business. This decision needs to be taken as seriously and with as much thought as everything else involved with the initial establishment of your business.

You also need to think with your head as well as your heart. You may feel that handing your beloved coffee or tea shop over to your partner/sibling/children/other loved ones is the right thing to do, but is it the right thing for the business? Another possible problem, particularly when passing a business on to offspring is making a decision about who has overall control and responsibility. If you have more than one child, you may want them both to share in the financial success of the business, but conflict could arise if you haven't established from the outset who has overall control when it comes to management decisions. Take a look at the children of media magnate Rupert Murdoch, who have all been given varying degrees of responsibility within his huge empire. There is nothing like money and business to drive a family apart if it's not done with a great deal of thought and consideration.

Then there is you. How much day-to-day involvement do you still want, and will whoever you have passed the business on to be comfortable with that? It's no good handing over the responsibility and hard work of the coffee shop management to somebody, only to enforce your own decisions on the business. If you are really letting go of the business, then let go. Don't be a back seat driver when someone else has taken the wheel.

TIP

There may also be CGT implications involved in passing the business on to a family member even if you aren't selling it, so it's important you take sound advice from a specialist accountant and solicitor before you hand the business over.

Things to remember:

- Business development isn't just about increasing your profits. It's also about maintaining quality and improving what you have already built.
- Don't take on extra responsibility, such as retail commitments, if it puts the health of your coffee or tea shop at risk.
- Don't consider a second establishment until you are confident you can be away from your first one without it collapsing.
- Franchising demands a flawless original business model. Don't consider this route until you have achieved one.
- Make sure you take professional advice before beginning a transfer or sale of your coffee or tea shop.

Appendices

Tea and coffee in Britain: a history

1610: Dutch and Portuguese traders begin regularly selling tea to the UK as a luxury medicinal drink.

1615: Queen Elizabeth I presents a royal charter to the Dutch East India Company giving it a monopoly over all British trade with the Indies.

1652: Refined Arabica coffee arrives in Britain. The first coffee house is opened in Oxford, serving coffee black and without sugar.

1657: Thomas Garway, a coffee merchant in London, begins to serve tea in his coffee house.

1660: Coffee houses in Britain become a social phenomenon, used by artists, intellectuals, merchants, bankers and were a hive of political activities and developments. They were dubbed 'penny universities' – a single penny bought you a coffee and exposure to this world.

1665: London diarist Samuel Pepys records nearly 100 visits he made to coffee houses.

1669: Coffee houses continue to become a hub for business deals and exchanges. Edward Lloyd's coffee house – frequented by merchants and maritime insurance agents – eventually became the world renowned insurance market, Lloyd's of London. Jonathan's Coffee House in Change Alley – always full of stockbrokers – eventually became the London Stock Exchange.

1670: English East India Company monopolises British tea imports after British government bans Dutch tea imports.

1676: The growing popularity of tea causes Charles II to put a tax on it, requiring coffee house owners to buy a licence to serve it.

1680: Social critic Marie de Rabutin-Chantal, the Marquise de Sévigné, makes the first mention of adding milk to tea.

1700: Tea is sold in over 500 coffee houses, and there are 3,000 coffee houses in London alone.

1717: Thomas Twining opens the first tea house in Britain called The Golden Lyon. Annual tea importation to England tops 800,000 pounds.

1732: Bach composes a *Coffee Cantata*, with the aria 'Ah! How sweet coffee tastes! Lovelier than a thousand kisses, sweeter far than muscatel wine! I must have coffee...'

1750: Tea becomes the favoured drink of the working classes.

1822: Frenchman Louis Bernard Rabaut invents the espresso machine, which forced hot water through the coffee grounds using steam.

1835: The East India Company starts the first tea plantations in Assam, India.

1840: Anna, seventh Duchess of Bedford, launches the idea of having tea in the late afternoon to bridge the gap between lunch and dinner, and invited friends to join her. The afternoon tea party was born, and this trend quickly spread within the upper classes, remaining a British institution to this day.

1841: Englishwoman Elizabeth Dakin invents the first coffee plunger, or cafetière.

1904: In America, Richard Blechynden, a tea plantation owner, invents ice tea to keep up business during a heatwave.

1908: Thomas Sullivan a tea merchant in New York invents teabags.

1930s-40s: A migrant influx caused by two world wars and a social revolution revives café society in the UK.

1938: Nescafé instant coffee is invented by the Nestlé company.

1953: Tetley drives the introduction of teabags into the UK – now 96% of the tea drunk in Britain is made with teabags.

1971: Starbucks opens its first outlet in Seattle, named after a character in *Moby Dick*.

1995: Coffee is the world's most popular beverage, more than 400 billion cups are consumed each year. It is a world commodity that is second only to oil.

1998: King's Road in Chelsea becomes the first location for Starbucks in the UK, selling cappuccino or mocha latte at £2.

2000: The UK coffee shop market rockets with daily sales of 4.4 million cups. Coffee-selling becomes a billion-pound industry, with UK-owned chains such as Caffé Nero and Costa offering stiff competition.

2006: The Starbucks empire grows to 12,500 outlets and £4bn in revenue.

Sample questionnaire for customer surveys

Customer Satisfaction Survey

At the Cosy Teapot, we really value your opinions and suggestions, and it's our aim to make drinking here the best experience we can.
Please rate each question from 1 to 5, by circling your choice.

1= very dissatisfied
2= dissatisfied
3= neutral
4= satisfied
5= very satisfied

Are you a first time visitor to Cosy Teapot? Yes / No

The prices at the tea shop are reasonable 1 2 3 4 5
The products offered by the tea shop meet my needs 1 2 3 4 5
If not, what other products would you like to see us offering?

....

The products offered by the tea shop are good quality 1 2 3 4 5
The serving staff were friendly and knowledgeable 1 2 3 4 5
I would recommend the Cosy Teapot to a friend 1 2 3 4 5
I was aware that the tea shop provides catering services for meetings and other events 1 2 3 4 5
I am aware of the free wireless access in the tea shop 1 2 3 4 5
The Cosy Teapot is a good place to meet someone for a conversation or meeting 1 2 3 4 5
Overall, I am satisfied with my experience at the Cosy Teapot 1 2 3 4 5
Do you plan on returning? Yes / No
Do you have any other comments?

....

Balance sheet

ASSETS	**Beginning** as of mm/dd/yyyy
Current Assets	£
Cash in bank	2500
Accounts receivable	4000
Inventory	7000
Prepaid expenses	1500
Other current assets	1000
Total Current Assets	**£16,000**
Fixed Assets	£
Machinery & equipment	10000
Furniture & fixtures	5000
Leasehold improvements	4000
Land & buildings	
Other fixed assets	1000
(LESS accumulated depreciation on all fixed Total Fixed Assets (net of depreciation)	**£20,000**
Other Assets	£
Intangibles	1500
Deposits	500
Goodwill	500
Other	
Total Other Assets	**£2,500**
TOTAL Assets	**£38,500**
LIABILITIES AND EQUITY	
Current Liabilities	£
Accounts payable	8000
Interest payable	500
Taxes/Social Security payable	1000
Other current liabilities	
Total Current Liabilities	**£9,500**

Long-term Debt	£
Bank loans payable	1500
Other long term debt	500
Total Long-term Debt	**£2,000**
Total Liabilities	**£11,500**
Owners' Equity	£
Invested capital	20000
Retained earnings – beginning	3000
Retained earnings – current	2000
Total Owners' Equity	**£25,000**
Total Liabilities & Equity	**£36,500**

Example profit and loss sheet

Coffee Shop Profit & Loss Account

For month ended ....

	£		£
Sales/Turnover			**60,894**
Opening Stock (1st of Month)	3,000		24,253
Add Purchases	24,253		
		27,253	
Less Closing Stock (30/31st of month)		4,278	
Cost of Goods Sold		31,531	
Direct labour costs		7,364	
			38,895
Gross Profit			**29,363**
Overheads			
Rent & rates		3,294	
Heat, light & power		783	
Insurance		106	
Indirect wages & salaries		7,296	
Marketing costs		571	
Printing, stationery and consumables		2,951	
Computer costs		1,758	
Telephone		1,239	
Depreciation of assets		3,697	
Legal & professional fees		750	
Bank & finance charges		264	
		22,709	
Net profit before tax		**6,654**	

Example cashflow sheet

Cash Flow Forecast

	Month 1	Month 2	Month 3	Month 4	Month 5	Month 6	Month 7	Month 8	Month 9	Month 10	Month11	Month 12	YTD
Receipts													
Debtors	8,297	8,572	6,798	7,569	7,719	8,071	7,765	7,175	6,179	7,637	5,978	7,173	88,933
Cash	276	421	1,403	1,386	874	835	1,142	1,607	1,946	818	2,036	918	13,662
TOTAL RECEIPTS	**8,573**	**8,993**	**8,201**	**8,955**	**8,593**	**8,906**	**8,907**	**8,782**	**8,125**	**8,455**	**8,014**	**8,091**	**102,595**
Payments													
Purchases	1,687	1,967	2,173	2,469	2,284	2,982	2,642	2,381	2,974	3,129	2,367	2,894	29,949
Rent	2,160	-	-	2,160	-	-	2,160	-	-	2,160	-	-	8,640
Rates & utilities	528	528	528	528	528	528	528	528	528	528	528	528	6,336
Telephone	-	-	509	-	-	521	-	-	539	-	-	517	2,086
Wages & salaries	2,750	2,750	2,750	2,750	2,750	2,750	2,750	2,750	2,750	2,750	2,750	2,750	33,000
PAYE	1,018	1,018	1,018	1,018	1,018	1,018	1,018	1,018	1,018	1,018	1,018	1,018	12,216
VAT	102	-	-	47	-	-	156	-	-	174	-	-	479
TOTAL Payments	**8,245**	**6,263**	**6,978**	**8,972**	**6,580**	**7,799**	**9,254**	**6,677**	**7,809**	**9,759**	**6,663**	**7,707**	**92,706**
NET OPERATING CASH FLOW	**328**	**2,730**	**1,223**	**(17)**	**2,013**	**1,107**	**(347)**	**2,105**	**316**	**(1,304)**	**1,351**	**384**	**9,889**
Fixed asset purchases	539				1,299				3,675				5,513
Loan repayments													-
													-
Net cash inflow/(outflow)	**(211)**	**2,730**	**1,223**	**(17)**	**714**	**1,107**	**(347)**	**2,105**	**(3,359)**	**(1,304)**	**1,351**	**384**	**4,376**
OPENING BANK BALANCE	1,628	1,417	4,147	5,370	5,353	6,067	7,174	6,827	8,932	5,573	4,269	5,620	1,628
CLOSING BANK BALANCE	1,417	4,147	5,370	5,353	6,067	7,174	6,827	8,932	5,573	4,269	5,620	6,004	6,004

Index